1 MONTH OF
FREE
READING

at
www.ForgottenBooks.com

By purchasing this book you are eligible for one month membership to ForgottenBooks.com, giving you unlimited access to our entire collection of over 1,000,000 titles via our web site and mobile apps.

To claim your free month visit:

www.forgottenbooks.com/free1375415

ISBN 978-1-397-30612-8
PIBN 11375415

NINETEENTH

ANNUAL REPORT

OF THE

Alumni Association,

WITH THE EXERCISES OF THE

SIXTY-SECOND COMMENCEMENT

OF THE

Philadelphia College of Pharmacy,

FOR THE YEAR 1882-83.

ORGANIZED JULY 15, 1864.

PHILADELPHIA:
1883.

Officers of the Association

For 1883 and 1884.

PRESIDENT,
LUCIUS E. SAYRE, Ph. G., S. W. Cor. 18th and Market Sts.
(Class of 1866)

FIRST VICE-PRESIDENT,
DR. CHAS. A. WEIDEMANN, Ph. G., 543 N. 22d St.
(Class of 1867.)

SECOND VICE-PRESIDENT,
JACOB S. BEETEM, Ph G., 941 Spruce St.
(Class of 1878.)

RECORDING SECRETARY,
WM. E. KREWSON, Ph. G., N. E Cor. 8th and Montgomery Ave.
or 145 N. 10th Street.
(Class of 1869.)

CORRESPONDING SECRETARY,
JOHN A. WITMER, Ph. G.
(Class of 1876.)

TREASURER,
EDWARD C. JONES, Ph. G., S. E. Cor. 15th and Market Sts.
(Class of 1864.)

EXECUTIVE BOARD,
LOUIS GENOIS, Ph. G., (1 year), 1412 Walnut St.
(Class of 1881.)

DAVID W. ROSS, Ph. G., (1 year), 580 E. Cumberland St.
(Class of 1877.)

HENRY TRIMBLE, Ph. G., (2 years), N.W. Cor. 5th and Callowhill.
(Class of 1876.)

WALLACE PROCTER, Ph. G., (2 years), 900 Lombard St.
(Class of 1872.)

THOMAS H. POTTS, Ph. G., (3 years), S. E. Cor. Broad and Parrish.
(Class of 1871.)

C. CARROLL MEYER, Ph. G., (3 years), 1802 Callowhill St.
(Class of 1873)

TRUSTEE OF SINKING FUND,
THOS. S. WIEGAND, Ph G., 145 N. 10th St.
(Class of 1844.)

ORATOR FOR 1884,
ROBERT HAYS VANSANT, Trenton, New Jersey.
(Class of 1879.)

PROCEEDINGS

OF THE

Nineteenth Annual Meeting.

The Nineteenth Annual Meeting of the Alumni Association of the Philadelphia College of Pharmacy was held in the Alumni Room, at the College, 145 North Tenth Street, on Wednesday afternoon, March 14, 1883.

The meeting was called to order by the President, Thos. H. Potts, at ten minutes of 3 o'clock, P. M., the following members being in attendance:

Wm. C. Bakes,	Class, 1855,	Ocean Grove, N. J.
Chas. W. Hancock,	" 1857,	West Philadelphia, Pa.
Edward C. Jones,	" 1864,	Philadelphia.
H. Edward Wendel,	" 1865,	"
Prof. Jos. P. Remington,	" 1866,	"
Lucius E. Sayre,	" 1866,	"
Chas. A. Weidemann, M. D.,	" 1867,	"
Wm. E. Krewson,	" 1869,	"
Henry D. Schell,	" 1870,	"
Thos. H. Potts,	" 1871,	"
Howard B. French,	" 1871,	"
Wallace Procter,	" 1872,	"
C. Carroll Meyer,	" 1873,	"
Wm. I. Lerch,	" 1873,	"
Frederick P. Power, Ph.D.,	" 1874,	"
John A. Witmer,	" 1876,	"
Henry Trimble,	" 1876,	"
David W. Ross,	" 1877,	"
Jacob S. Beetem,	" 1878,	"
Robert H. Vansant,	" 1879,	Trenton, N. J.
Samuel W. Strunk,	" 1880,	Quakertown, Pa.
Wm. C. McClintock,	" 1881,	Ardmore, Pa.
Wm. F. Jungkunz,	" 1883,	Freeport, Ill.
Harold B. Miller,	" 1883,	Carlisle, Pa.
Chas. B. Baumgardner,	" 1883,	Altoona, Pa.
Lawrence A. Neuhart,	" 1883,	Caldwell, Ohio.
Harry G. Kalmbach,	" 1883,	Philadelphia, Pa.
Whitmel H. Mac Nair,	" 1883,	Tarboro, N. C.

Harry H. Deakyne,	Class, 1883, Smyrna, Del.
Wm. H. Walter,	" 1883, Philadelphia, Pa.
Chas. W. Ott,	" 1883, " "
Mimms W. Coleman,	" 1883, Selma, Ala.
Chas. Harry Baker,	" 1883, Trenton, N. J.
Robt. C. Browning,	" 1883, Indianapolis, Ind.
Henry H. Gregg, Jr.,	" 1883, New Lisbon, Ohio.
Chas. F. Rickey,	" 1883, Mt. Sterling, Ill.

And I. Spencer Phillips, Class, 1883, Philadelphia, Pa., Henry M. Jones, Class, 1883, Winchester, Ky., as visitors.

The minutes of the last Annual Meeting were read. Mr. Chas. W. Hancock moved that they be adopted as read. Agreed to.

The Secretary moved that the reading of the minutes of the Executive Board and Social Meetings be omitted as they were to be published in the next Annual Report. So ordered.

The President, Thos. H. Potts, then read his Annual Address, which is as follows:

PHILADELPHIA, March 14, 1883.

To the Officers and Members of the Alumni Association
of the Philadelphia College of Pharmacy.

FELLOW MEMBERS:

In presenting this, as my address to the Nineteenth Annual Meeting of the Alumni Association, I do so without any misgiving in regard to the complete success of its many undertakings during the past year, which has been an exceptionally prosperous one for the Association.

The Executive Board has held its regular meetings during the interim which were well attended by its respective members, and much important business was transacted, which will inure to the benefit of the Alumni.

The social meetings, of which there were five held, were an unprecedented success; not only were they largely attended by members of the Senior and Junior Classes respectively, but also by members of the Alumni at large. The subjects presented were unusually interesting, and met with unqualified approval, and gentlemen, permit me to say right here that the successful issue of these social meetings of the Alumni is due mainly to the indefatigable efforts of the Committee on Social Meetings, and I think that this Association is under a debt of gratitude to those gentlemen for their labor in its behalf.

The Alumni Quizzes, I am pleased to say, have met, as far as those for the Senior Class are concerned, with success beyond our expectations, but I regret to report those for the Junior Class somewhat below those of the preceding year in point of attendance, and consequently not as successful as we might wish for.

The Class in Microscopy, of which you are all fully aware was originated by our Alumni, although not largely attended, has met with that success which justifies us in anticipating for it a prosperous future, and thereby adding revenue to our treasury, as well as conferring lasting benefits on those who receive its instructions.

In regard to our Secretaryship, I would suggest, that inasmuch as it has become a very laborious position, not only in regard to the multifarious duties to be performed at our regular stated and special meetings, but mainly in the preparation of the Annual Report, that it be a salaried one in the future, and I would also suggest for the present, the appropriation of a sum of money as a slight recompense to the Secretary for his arduous duties during the present year ; and, gentlemen, while on the subject of the duties of the Secretary, I would congratulate the Association on the success of our last Annual Report. It is without exception the most complete and interesting ever disseminated by the Alumni ; it was in demand from all quarters, and was highly prized by the recipients, and it seems to me that this Association is under lasting obligations to our present very efficient Secretary, for the able manner in which he has fulfilled his duties and also for his great interest in the Alumni.

I also would wish to convey to you, through my modest address, the debt of gratitude I feel we are under to our able Quiz Masters, Mr. Lucius E. Sayre, of the Class of 1866, and Mr. Louis Genois, of the Class of 1881, to whom the great success of our Quizzes may be attached, and I also wish to include another very worthy gentleman to whom we are indebted to—I refer to Mr. Albert P. Brown, of the class of 1862, who had charge of the Class in Microscopy, and who by his ability contributed so largely to its success, and gentlemen, I would feel that I was remiss in my duties did I fail to mention one well known to you all, who has served this Association faithfully and well for a long term of years, and I know I only repeat the sentiments of every individual one of you, when I express the hope that he may live to still serve us in the future as in the past—I refer to our worthy Treasurer, Mr. Edward C. Jones.

And now, in conclusion, fellow members and officers, I am deeply sensible of the great honor conferred on me as your presiding officer, and thank you heartily for your consideration, and trust for a happy future for our grand old Alumni.   THOS. H. POTTS,
President.

Mr. C. Carroll Meyer moved that the President's address be received and spread upon the minutes, and published in our Annual Report. So ordered.

Mr. Henry Trimble moved that a committee of three be appointed to take into consideration the suggestions contained in the President's address. So ordered.

The President appointed Henry Trimble, Chas. W. Hancock and Jacob S. Beetem as the Committee.

The Secretary stated that a member present had an important matter to bring before the Association, and was unable to remain at the meeting the entire afternoon as he was desirous of taking a train at 4 o'clock. He would therefore move that the order of business be transposed and that new business be taken up. So ordered.

Mr. Wm. C. Bakes then arose and said it was an unfortunate fact, yet nevertheless it was true, that many Pharmacists were in the habit of selling intoxicating liquors over their counters as a beverage ; this practice was to be deprecated and he thought that the time had arrived that the Alumni Association should take some action upon the subJect.

He then offered the following resolutions :

WHEREAS, The sale of intoxicating liquors as a beverage in Pharmaceutical stores is a growing evil tending to degrade the profession of Pharmacy, and damaging to the morals of the community ; therefore, be it

Resolved, That the Alumni Association of the Philadelphia College of Pharmacy place on record its abhorrence of this practice, and its purpose to suppress the growth of this traffic by druggists.

Resolved, That if any member of this Association shall be legally convicted of selling intoxicating liquors, he shall be expelled from membership in this body, and published in the Annual Report.

Mr. Chas. W. Hancock moved that the above resolutions be adopted, which was unanimously agreed to.

The Secretary then read the following Annual Report for the years 1882 and 1883.

PHILADELPHIA, PA., March 14, 1883.

To the President, Officers and Members of the Alumni Association,
Philadelphia College of Pharmacy.

GENTLEMEN :

Your Secretary would respectfully report that during the year the Executive Board have held 4 regular and 1 special meeting. The attendance of the members has been as follows :

Thos. H. Potts, attended 3 meetings ; Lucius E. Sayre, 3 ; Chas. A. Weidemann, 4 ; Wm. E. Krewson, 5 ; Wm. A. Ball, 1 ; Edward C. Jones, 3 ; Jacob S. Beetem, 5 ; David W. Ross, 3 ; Henry Trimble, 4 ; Thomas S. Wiegand, 2 ; and the following were absent from *every* meeting : John E. Cook, Louis Genois and Wallace Procter.

During the winter 5 social meetings were held with an average attendance of 63 students and members present. Papers were read and discussed by Dr. A. W. Miller, L. E. Sayre, John E. Cook, Dr. Lawrence Turnbull, Dr. Louis J. Lautenbach, Dr. C. C. Vanderbeck and Prof. J. P. Remington ; Miss F. Lizzie Pierce and Prof. Adams were also present at several of the meetings, and entertained those present with numerous recitations.

The Senior and Junior Quiz Classes were formed at the commencement of the course of lecture. The Executive Board appointed 2 Quiz Masters this year for the Senior Class, Mr. L. E. Sayre and Mr. Louis Genois, who gave those students who availed themselves of the opportunity, 2 hours Quizzing every Wednesday afternoon ; sixty-seven of the members of the Senior Class took the Quizzes, and sixty-five of the number came up for final examination, and the other two took the modified or partial examination. Sixty-three of the members passed the examinations of the College successfully, and were recommended by the Board of Trustees of the College for the degree of Graduate in Pharmacy (Ph. G.) Two were unsuccessful and failed to pass. Three other members of the Graduating Class who passed successfully were members of the Quiz Classes of 1880-81 and 1881-82, and are also entitled to membership in the Association according to our rules, making a total of sixty-six new members from the Quiz Classes. Four out of the seven who got honorable mention, and six out of eight who got meritorious mention, are members of the Quiz Class.

Mr. Henry Trimble was appointed Quiz Master for the Juniors, but fifteen of the latter students availed themselves of the Quizzes, and all but two passed the Junior Examination successfully.

The Senior students receiving the Alumni prizes this year are as follows:

Gold Medal, Wm. Frederick Jungkunz, of Freeport, Ill.

Certificate on *Materia Medica*, to Gustave Charles Frederick Helm, Jr., Philadelphia, Pa.

Certificate on Pharmacy, to Wm. Edwin Saunders, of London, Ontario, Canada.

Certificate on Chemistry, Wm. W. Light, of Oregon, Ill.

Certificate on General Pharmacy, to Louis Chas. Leonhard, Dayton, Ohio.

Certificate on Pharmaceutical Manipulations, to Chas. Fitz Randolph, of Altoona, Pa.

The Junior Testimonial is awarded to William Frederick Dohmen, of Milwaukee, Wis., he having received the highest general average of the Junior Class.

The total amount received from the Quiz Classes this year is $745.00. The salary of the Quiz Masters and the expenses for printing, etc., amounted to $435.00, netting the Association $310.00 clear of all expenses.

At the commencement of the Course of Lectures a class in Microscopy was formed under the instruction of Mr. Albert P. Brown, of Camden, N. J., and an active member of the Association.

The Class was composed of 12 members, as follows: 2 graduates of the College, 2 Junior students and 8 Senior students. The amount realized from this Class was $77.50, and after deducting the salary of the Instructor ($60.00), leaves a balance of $17.50 to the Association.

The Committee intend to open a Spring Course in Microscopy, about April 1st, in this room. Each member of the Association received a circular with their notice of the Annual Meeting, giving full particulars. It is earnestly hoped that as many of our members as possible will avail themselves of this opportunity of studying this important branch.

During the year 41 of the graduates of the College have become active members of the Association by taking out certificates of membership; making, together with the 66 members of the Quiz Class, a total of 107 added to our number since the last annual meeting. Six of our number have died during the year, as far as known, as follows:

Dr. Hiram Gold, Class of 1864, and first Secretary of the Association.
Benj. F. Shugard,   "   1868.
Pratt R. Hoagland,   "   1868.
Jas. A. Maston,   "   1875.
Chas. Wm. Elkins,   "   1880.
Simon E. Wolf.   "   1882.

Also the death of 3 other members, who died two or three years ago, were reported to the Secretary during the year, viz: Geo. W. Patrick, Class of 1846; Wm. J. Watson, Class of 1853; Mortimer H. Eayre, Class of 1868, of which the Committee on Deceased Members will report more fully.

Our roll now numbers 750, after deducting those who are known to have died.

Arrangements are being made by the Committee on Publication to have the Nineteenth Annual Report published as usual. The contract has not been awarded as yet, but will be in a few days. The Committee desire to make the Report as full and complete as possible, and will publish the names and addresses of all the active members.

The Secretary desires, in closing, to congratulate the Association for the advance it has made in the past year, and for its bright prospects for the future, and hopes it may long continue to be a useful help to our Alma Mater.

In retiring from the Secretaryship of the Association, I desire to express my thanks to the officers and members of the Executive Board, and to the membership at large, who have aided me in the performance of my duties as Secretary, and hope that my successor may receive a like assistance from your hands. I also would like to return my thanks to the Professors and members of the Board of Trustees of our College, for the aid in various ways that they have given me in the performance of my duties.

Respectfully submitted,

WM. E. KREWSON, *Secretary*.

Mr. C. Carroll Meyer moved that the Report of the Secretary be accepted, spread upon the minutes and published in the Annual Report. Agreed to.

The Report of the Treasurer was then called for, but his Report not being quite ready, it was deferred until later.

The Report of the Committee on Deceased Members was then called for, and Frederick B. Power, a member of the Committee, read the Report. (See Obituaries.)

On motion of the Secretary, the Report was accepted, and ordered printed in the Annual Report, and whatever material that may be received by the Committee upon those not fully reported be added to the Report prior to going to press.

The following bills were presented and read, after being approved by the President and Secretary:

Craig, Finley & Co., bills for printing notices of Annual Meeting, circulars to students, stamped envelopes, programmes, etc., amounting to,	$44 35
Public Ledger, for notices of Annual Meeting,	4 00
C. R. Morgan, reporting 5th Social Meeting,	5 00
Wm. Mann, record book, ink, seals, blotters, etc.,	1 86
Thos. H. McCool, filling up 3 certificates,	90
J. G. Ditman & Co., for envelopes,	1 20
E. C. Jones, Treasurer, for postage and incidentals,	1 65
Wm. E. Krewson, Secretary, " "	2 30
L. E. Sayre, for Quizzing, Senior Class (67 students),	167 50
Louis Genois, " " " "	167 50
Henry Trimble, " Junior Class (15 students),	75 00
Total,	$471 26

The Committee appointed to take into consideration the suggestions contained in the President's address, reported as follows:

To the President and Officers of the Alumni Association.

GENTLEMEN:

Your Committee appointed to take into consideration the suggestions contained in the President's address, would recommend that the sum of $50.00 be given the Secretary, Wm. E. Krewson, for services during the past year, and that the sum of $100.00 be annually allotted the Secretary in the future. · Respectfully,

HENRY TRIMBLE,
CHAS. W. HANCOCK,
JACOB S. BEETEM,
Committee.

On motion, the report was received, ordered, spread on the minutes, and the Committee discharged.

The Treasurer then submitted his Annual Report as follows :

TREASURER'S REPORT.

Edward C. Jones, Treasurer, in account with the

ALUMNI ASSOCIATION, PHILADELPHIA COLLEGE OF PHARMACY.

DR.

1882, 3d mo., 13th, To Balance on hand per last Report, . .		$582 07
" 9th " 15th, " Advertisements in 18th Annual Report,		325 00
" 3d " 9th, " Amts. received from Senior Quiz Class, .		670 00
" " " " Junior " " .		75 00
" " " " Class in Microscopy,		77 50
" " " " Sale of Slides and Covers, . .		9 72
" " " " Sale of Reports,		5 80
" " " for 41 Certificates of Membership @ $5.00,		205 00

Total, $1,950 09

CR.

1882, 3d mo., 1, By Burk & McFetridge, for Printing 18th Annual Report, ...		$410 38
2, " Donation to Secretary for 1881-82, . .		50 00
3, " Lehman & Bolton, Engraving Certificates,		16 50
4, " A. Gentzsch, Rollers, ...		1 50
5, " Wrappers and Stamps for 18th Annual Report, ...		41 20
6, " C. R. Morgan, for Reporting 18th Annual and 5 Social Meetings, . . .		30 50
7, " J. Shonert, for Frames for Prize and Sample Certificates, ...		11 55
8, " Craig, Finley & Co., for Printing during the year, ...		123 34
9, " Edwin Morgan, Printing, . . .		1 50
10, " R. T. Wilson, Picture Wire and Nails, .		42
11, " Wm. Mann, Roll Book and Quiz Tickets,		3 95
12, " Wm. Mann, Record Book, Ink, &c., &c.,		1 86
13, " Jos. Zentmayer, Microscopes, etc., .		267 32
14, " Philip C. Shaffer, 6 Tables, . .		12 00
15, " P. J. Baral & Bro., 3 Brass Keys, .		60
16, " L. B. McClees & Co., Blackboard & Pads,		12 25
17, " Jas. W. Queen & Co., Microscopic Accessories, ...		15 75
18, " Thos. H. McCool, filling up 67 Membership Certificates, (1881-82-83), . .		20 10

1882, 3d mo., 19,	"	Thos. H. McCool, filling up 6 Prize Certificates, 1882, ...	7 60
20,	"	Thos. H. McCool, filling up Sample Prize and Membership Certificates, and Lettering Blackboard, . . .	10 60
21,	"	Aschenbach & Miller, Pharmacopœia, .	4 00
22,	By	J. G. Ditman & Co., Envelopes, . .	1 20
23,	"	Secretary's expenses for sending out 18th Annual Report, . . .	6 73
24,	"	Secretary's expenses Postage and Incidentals for year, ...	11 88
25,	"	Senior Quiz Masters' Salaries, . . .	335 00
26,	"	Junior " " " . .	75 00
27,	"	Instructor in Microscopy, . . .	60 00
28,	"	Ledger Advertising 19th Annual Meeting,	4 00
29,	"	Treasurer's Expenses, ...	1 65

$1,538 38

Balance in Treasurer's Hands,   411 71

$1,950 09

On motion of John A. Witmer a committee of three was appointed to audit the Treasurer's account.

The President appointed John A. Witmer, Jacob S. Beetem and Dr. Chas. A. Weidemann to audit the account, and they retired to perform that duty.

Mr. Edward C. Jones spoke about the museum being opened for the benefit of the students during the Winter and asked if there was not a committee appointed at the last meeting of the Association to request the Board of Trustees to grant the Association permission to have it open. The Secretary stated that he had brought the matter to the attention of the Board and that they gave permission to the Association to allow the students in the Museum, provided, a member was present with them, but as the assistant Professors had also been granted the same privilege, and as they were all active members of the Association he thought that was sufficient, and did not think it worth while for the Association to take any further action in the matter.

The Secretary then stated that the following gentlemen had made application for membership since the last meeting of the Executive Board :

Emile Ott, '79, Philadelphia, Pa.; Wm. M. G. Corrie, '82, Philadelphia, Pa.; Chas. Wm. De Frehn, '82, Philadelphia, Pa.; Wm. F. Jungkunz, '83, Freeport, Ill.; Wm. W. Light, '83, Oregon, Ill.; Chas. Benj. Baumgardener, '83, Altoona, Pa.; Byron Edwin Bruenchenhein, '83, Milwaukee, Wis.; John Henry Balmer, '83, Elizabethtown, Pa.; John Peter Frey, '83,

Union City, Indiana; William Charles Franciscus, '83' Lock Haven, Pa.; Fredk. Chas. Lehman, '83' Philadelphia, Pa.; Daniel Schramm, Jr., '83' Philadelphia, Pa.; Jacques V. Quick, '83' Flemington, N. J.; Stephen C. Bolton, '83' Watertown, N. Y.; Louis C. Leonhard, '83' Dayton, Ohio; Frank B. Fleming, '83' Shippensburg, Pa.; Alfred B. Norcross, '83' Trenton, N. J.; Andrew Jackson Seeler, '83' Philadelphia, Pa.; Harry Irvin Davis, '83' Hollidaysburg, Pa.; M. V. Cheatham, '83' Clarksville, Texas; Clark Rankin Craig, '83' Chambersburg, Pa.

The Secretary stated that he had received communications from the following members of the Association who resided out of the city and regretted their inability to be present at this meeting:

Albert P. Brown, Class of '62' Camden, N. J.; Benjamin Lillard, Class of '68' 56 Lafayette Place, N. Y. City; Samuel D. Kay, Class of '68, Jersey City, N. J.; Louis Emanuel, Class of '76' Pittsburgh, Pa.; Geo. H. Knowlton, Class of '81' Manchester, N. H.; B. Frank Moise, Jr., Class of '81' Charleston, S. C.; Geo. A. Gorgas, Class of '81' Washington, D. C.; Frank A. Matthes, Class of 1882, Lebanon, Pa.

The President appointed the usual committee to nominate officers for the ensuing year, one from each of the Classes present at this meeting as follows:

Chas. W. Hancock,	Class	1857.	Wm. I. Lerch,	Class	1873.
Edward C. Jones,	"	1864.	Henry Trimble,	"	1876.
H. Edward Wendel,	"	1865.	David W. Ross,	"	1877.
Prof. Jos. P. Remington,	"	1866.	Jacob S. Beetem,	'	1878.
Dr. Chas. A .Weidemann,	"	1867.	Robt. H. Vansant,	"	1879.
Wm. E. Krewson,	"	1869.	Saml. W. Strunk,	'	1880.
Harry D. Schell,	"	1870.	Wm. C. McClintock,	"	1881.
Howard B. French,	"	1871.	Wm. F. Jungkunz,		1883.
Wallace Procter,	"	1872.			

The Secretary requested to be excused from serving on the Nominating Committee, as his duties would keep him in the meeting. The President excused him.

The Committee then retired to the Zeta Phi Room to make the nominations.

Mr. C. Carroll Meyer moved that the meeting take a recess while the Committee are out. Agreed to.

After a recess of a few minutes, the President called the meeting to order, and the Committee on Nominations filed in the room, and through their Chairman, Mr. Chas. W. Hancock, made their report, recommending the following gentlemen as the officers of the Alumni Association for the year 1883-84.

President, Lucius E. Sayre, Class 1866; 1st Vice-President, Dr. Chas. A. Weidemann, Class 1867; 2d Vice-President, Jacob S. Beetem, Class 1878; Recording Secretary, Wm. E. Krewson, Class 1869; Corresponding Secretary, John A. Witmer, Class 1876; Treasurer Edward C. Jones, Class 1864.

To fill vacancies in the Executive Board for three years:

C. Carroll Meyer, Class 1873; Thos. H. Potts, Class 1871; Trustee of Sinking Fund, Thos. S. Wiegand, Class 1844; Orator for 1884, Robert H. Vansant, Class 1879.

On motion, the report of the Committee was received and the Committee discharged.

Mr. Henry Trimble moved that as there was but one nominee for each of the offices named, that Mr. Chas. W. Hancock be directed to cast the ballot in favor of the above nominees. Agreed to.

Mr. Hancock then deposited the ballot, and the President declared the above-named gentlemen duly elected as the officers of the Alumni Association for the year ending March, 1884.

The Committee appointed to audit the Treasurer's book announced through their Chairman, John A. Witmer, that they had examined the Treasurer's accounts and that they found them correct, there being a balance in his hands as Treasurer of $411.71. On motion, the report was accepted and the Committee discharged.

The Secretary said that there were two members of the Faculty of the College who were not graduates of our College, and, consequently, were not members of the Alumni Association, but were warm friends of the Association, and he would like to see them made honorary members, if it could be done. After some discussion it was suggested that it would be best to have a By-Law made to cover such cases.

The Secretary moved that a committee of three be appointed to revise the By-Laws, and that they report at the next Annual Meeting. The motion was duly seconded and carried.

The President appointed Wm. E. Krewson, Lucius E. Sayre and Henry Trimble as the Committee.

Prof. Jos. P. Remington then offered the following:

Resolved, That the Committee on By-Laws be requested to take into consideration the propriety of electing honorary members to this Association, and that they report at the next Annual Meeting.

The resolution was duly seconded and carried.

Mr. Thos. S. Wiegand reported through Mr. E. C. Jones that all the money in the Sinking Fund had been expended, and he had expected to have had a final report for this meeting, but for the want of time he was unable to do so.

On motion, the report was accepted, and he was requested to have his report ready for the next meeting of the Executive Board.

Mr. Sayre spoke of the coming year which we were just entering, and of the necessity of the Alumni Association procuring a full line of specimens for the use of the Quiz Classes.

The Secretary then read the list of those who have Joined the Alumni Association since our last Annual Meeting, and had received their Certificates of Membership as follows:

Albert D. Wike,	Class	1867.	Wm. M. G. Corrie,	Class	1882.
Eugene Herbert,	"	1870.	Chas. Wm. De Frehn,	"	1882.
Geo. I. McKelway,	"	1871.	Wm. F. Jungkunz,	"	1883.
Robt. Aug. Koempel,	"	1876.	Wm. W. Light,	"	1883.
Frank Moore,	"	1877.	Fredk. Chas. Lehman,	"	1883.
Benjamin C. Waterman,	"	1878.	Chas. Benj. Baumgardner,	"	1883.
Emile Ott,	"	1879.	John Peter Frey,	"	1883.
E. L. E. Castleton,	"	1879.	Byron E. Bruenchenhein,	"	1883.
John Wilson Hoffa,	"	1880.	Wm. C. Franciscus,	"	1883.
Wm. C. Dockstader,	"	1880.	Daniel Schramm, Jr.,	"	1883.
Thos. R. Gossling,	"	1881.	Jacques V. Quick,	'	1883.
Wm. E. Speakman,	"	1881.	John Henry Balmer,	"	1883.
Chas. N. Acker,	"	1882.	Stephen C. Bolton,	'	1883.
John A. Lambert,	"	1882.	Louis C. Leonhard,	'	1883.
Wm. Ernest Roeschel,	"	1882.	Frank B. Fleming,	'	1883.
Chas. M. Forney,	"	1882.	Alfred B. Norcross,	'	1883.
J. Hamilton Knouse,	"	1882.	Andrew Jackson Seeler,	"	1883.
Benjamin Franklin Sholl,	"	1882.	Harry Irvin Davis,	"	1883.
Chas. Wm. Dare,	"	1882.	Mathew V. Cheatham,	"	1883.
Chas. N. Riggs,	"	1882.	Clark R. Craig,	'	1883.
Chambers B. Clapp,	"	1882.			

The following are entitled to certificates and active membership in the Association by being members of the Senior Quiz Class, they having passed, successfully, the recent examination of the College, and are members of the Graduating Class of 1883, viz:

Milton Shimer Apple,
Chas. Fredk. Arnold,
Wm. C. Armbrecht,
Allen D. Ballentine,
Chas. Harry Baker,
Wm. Henry Barr, Jr.,
Robert Craighead Browning,
Geo. White Butler,
Joseph H. Brown,
Fredk. Smith Booth,
Henry Augustus Boorse,
Milton Campbell,
Albert D. Cuskaden.
John Henry Dare,
Wm. Henson Davis,
Harry Harttup Deakyne,
Milton J. Dundore,
Howard D. Dietrich,
Jos. W. England,
Harry Buckley Fasig,
Edgar Burnside Fell,
John Fredk. Frangkisier,

Chas. Jos. V. Fries,
Henry Hamilton Gregg, Jr.,
Whitmel Horne MacNair,
Robt. McCreight,
Wm. Worrell Maddock,
Harold Baughman Miller,
Turner Ashby Miller,
Lawrence Augustus Neuhart,
Christopher O'Brien,
Charles Wm. Ott,
Chas. Fitz Randolph,
Chas. Frank Rickey,
Wm. Ruthrauff Roedel,
Geo. Fredk. Roehrig,
Wm. A. Ruth,
John W. Reeser,
Geo. Washington Salot,
Gustav Scherling,
Albert Tobias Sellers,
Flor. Joseph Schmidt,
Jas. Samuel Scheffler,
Chas. Michael Smith,

Stephen Douglas Smith,
Chas. Lawrence Trusler,
Gustav, Hahn,
Owen Burdette Hannon,
Frank Pierce Harris,
Jas. Oliver Harrison,
J. Marshall Horsey,
Theodore Milton Johnson,
Daniel R. Jones,
Henry Geo. Kalmbach,
Emil H. Kempfer,
Frank G. Kerr,

Rudolph Kindig,
Jas. Delaplaine Krider,
Wm. Henry Walter,
Geo. Washington Weber,
Reinhard Julius Weber,
Allen Leidig Werst,
Theophilus Newton Willard.
    Quiz Class of 1880-81:
James Miles Jones.
    Quiz Class of 1881-82:
Edward Everett Baggé,
Frank H. Steacy.

On motion, the above applicants were duly elected as active members of the Alumni Association.

The following communication was received:

PHILADELPHIA, March 14th, 1883.

Mr. WM. E. KREWSON.

DEAR SIR:—I regret my inability to be present at the reception this evening, but assure you I appreciate very much the honor done me by the Alumni of the College by the presentation of the Pharmacy Certificate.

Yours very truly,
WM. E. SAUNDERS.

The President requested Mr. Henry Morford Jones, of Kentucky, a member of the Graduating Class, to receive the Prize Certificate on Pharmacy for Mr. Saunders, and he accepted the position.

As there was no further business, on motion of the Secretary, the Annual Meeting of 1882 adJourned. Attest,

WM. E. KREWSON, *Secretary.*

The following gentlemen have made application for Certificates of Membership since the Annual Meeting:

Edward T. Dobbins,	Class 1862.	Mimms Wm. Coleman,	Class 1883.
Robert H. Walch,	" 1875.	Evan G. Boyd,	" 1883.
Peter Graybill,	" 1878.	Samuel N. Benjamin,	" 1883.
August Drescher,	" 1879.	Samuel Stratton Guest,	" 1883.
Cyrus Maxwell Boger, Jr.,	" 1882.	Susan Hayhurst, M. D.,	" 1883.

Any graduate of the Philadelphia College of Pharmacy is eligible for membership in the Alumni Association, and can procure blank applications from any officer of the Association, which should be properly filled up, enclosed with the required fee of $5.00, and forwarded to the Secretary, when the certificate of membership will be expressed to the applicant. The above fee is paid but once, and no yearly dues.

ANNUAL RECEPTION

TO THE GRADUATING CLASS,

By the Alumni Association of the Philadelphia College of Pharmacy,

WAS HELD WEDNESDAY EVENING, MARCH 14th, 1883,

At the College Hall, No. 145 N. Tenth Street.

PHILADELPHIA, March 14th, 1883.

The Nineteenth Annual Reception to the Sixty-second Graduating Class of the Philadelphia College of Pharmacy was held this evening in the second story lecture room of the College. The hall was well filled with the members of the Graduating Class and their lady friends and the friends of our College.

The President, Thos. H. Potts, called the meeting to order at 8.05, P. M., with the following introductory remarks:

LADIES AND GENTLEMEN:

It is with sincere pleasure that I have the honor of welcoming you to the Alumni's Nineteenth Annual Reception to the Sixty-second Graduating Class of the Philadelphia College of Pharmacy, and to congratulate them on their successful issue. It is needless for me to remind you that this is one of the events long looked forward to by members of the Graduating Class with the most lively interest, for it is to them one of the crowning points of many years of study and labor, and to be a participant in these festivities requires no mean effort, as any one of the Graduating Class assembled here this evening can readily assure you. We, therefore, sensibly appreciate your attendance, as not only flattering to ourselves, but as proving the deep interest taken in the career of our fellow-graduates and members-elect of the Alumni Association.

The President then directed the Secretary to announce the names of the Graduating Class, which numbered 153 members; and, as the names of well-known or meritorious students were called, the Secretary was interrupted by cheers from the members of the Class, especially when the name of Miss Susan Hayhurst, M. D., was announced, she being the first lady graduate of our

College. The President then announced that the Secretary would call the roll of those who had joined the Alumni and taken out its certificate and become active members of the Association; and, as the names of the 107 who had become members during the year were called, they came forward and occupied positions in front of the President, when he presented them with the certificate of membership, with the following remarks:

GENTLEMEN:

It becomes my pleasant duty, by virtue of the office of President of the Alumni Association, to welcome you as fellow-members of the Alumni.

After the certificates had been passed to each individual member of the two detachments of the members called, they were directed to resume their seats, and the President further addressed them, saying:

In thus welcoming you to our ranks, I would remind you that it is the object and ambition of our Alumni Association to so aid and foster those pertainments so requisite for the advancement of our Alma Mater, that she may not only keep apace with her sister colleges, but that she may in the future, as in the past, have that excellence of standing as will cause one to say, with proud honor, "I am a graduate of the Philadelphia College of Pharmacy." Therefore, accept this certificate, properly signed by the respective officers of the Association, and may it always remind you that you are a component part of our membership, and that your fellow-members expect further attainments from you in the cause of our profession. In bidding adieu to you, I would congratulate you upon your successful graduation, some of you with high honors, and sincerely trust that this evening may be a starting-point for each and every one of you in a very successful career.

The President, after addressing the new members just received, as above, continuing, said:

From time immemorial, in all contests, some one came in best, and this perfection was recognized by the presentation of suitable prizes. So, too, the Alumni Association recognizes that, in the contest for a diploma from the Philadelphia College of Pharmacy, some one of the graduates must have attained a greater general average than his fellow-classmates, so as heretofore, and as pertinent to the occasion, it presents this evening to the successful competitor, Mr. Wm. Frederick Jungkunz, of Freeport, Ill., a gold medal.

Mr. Jungkunz came forward and presented himself before the President, who addressed him as follows:

Mr. Jungkunz: As you have the distinguished honor of having attained the highest general average out of a class numbering one hundred and seventy-five (175), it becomes my pleasant duty, on behalf of the Alumni Association, to present you with this gold medal, as indicative of the high appreciation placed upon excellency of merit by the Alumni; and that you may long enjoy your honors is the earnest wish of your fellow-members.

Mr. Jungkunz accepted the medal and replied as follows:

MR. PRESIDENT:

" I tender my heartfelt thanks for this high honor that you have just conferred upon me, and I truly hope that I may continue in this noble life-work with the same zeal and earnest devotion with which I have just begun it, thereby doing credit to my membership of the Alumni and my Alma Mater."

The President then introduced the orator of the evening as follows:

LADIES AND GENTLEMEN:

I have both the pleasure and honor of introducing to you this evening, as orator for the occasion, a gentleman well known to most of you as one of rare attainments, and an active member of the Alumni Association, and one who had the distinguished honor of receiving the gold medal in 1881, Mr. Louis Genois, of Philadelphia.

Mr. Genois then arose amidst the applause of the audience and delivered the following oration:

FELLOW GRADUATES, LADIES AND GENTLEMEN:

The Alumni Association of the Philadelphia College of Pharmacy extends to you its hearty congratulations on the success that you have just achieved, and invites you to active fellowship within its ranks, a privilege to enter which you are now justly entitled.

The conferring of the degree of Graduate of Pharmacy that you are to receive shortly, will mark an epoch in your lives which no lapse of time will ever obliterate from your memories.

You are about to become members of a profession, from whose ranks have risen some of the most eminent men of science, in ancient and modern times, men whose eminence has in each individual case been due to their own exertions, patient and assiduous labor and untiring perseverance.

Thanks to the zeal of your noble professors and to your own diligence, you are now fully equipped to encounter those trials and vexations that are sure to beset your paths in your professional lives, and it remains for you to decide whether you will strive to overcome and conquer them, and thus achieve triumph and make yourselves names, or allow yourselves to be vanquished.

Everywhere the pharmacist is distinguished as a useful and enlightened member of society, remarkable for his zeal, disinterestedness, and devotion to his profession, and the public, ever ready to profit by whatever is to its advantage, is so accustomed to resort to him for information, advice or accommodation, and usually with such satisfactory results, that it has come to use the privilege as a right.

The pharmacist is, in point of fact, a constant and faithful worker; with him it is a pleasure as well as a duty to study; even when his commercial interests suffer from business depression, he turns to his books for solace and compensation.

To pharmacists is due the credit of those great discoveries, without which, industries and practical arts now in such a flourishing condition, and that have contributed so materially to the development of civilization, would not exist.

The claims of pharmacy to an important share of the glory of scientific and material progress are indisputable, and can easily be substantiated.

2

Chemistry! that noble and beautiful science, so deep in its researches and investigations; that science, which enables man to make the most sublime discoveries in the study of nature; that science, that affords him the means of explaining facts which a comparatively short time since were considered impenetrable mysteries; that science, the sole one that descends from the sphere of high speculation to carry out in a practical form its theories and hypotheses for our material good; chemistry, to which so large a part of this progress is due, first saw the light in the laboratory of a pharmacist; without pharmaceutical experiments and investigations, without the numberless medicinal compounds employed in ancient times, and without the various operations to which they were subjected, it would not have come into existence.

The great work of the alchemists of old was originally directed to the production of a medicine possessed of miraculous powers—in other words, a universal panacea; the idea of the transmutation of vile metals into gold, which came to them subsequently, did not cause them to desist in their search for the wonderful remedy; on the contrary, it stimulated them to still greater efforts. If, however, they did not succeed in finding neither the philosophers' stone nor the panacea, their labors were certainly not fruitless. Their discoveries, among which may be mentioned arsenic, bismuth, phosphorus, antimony, alcohol, ether, gunpowder, nitric and sulphuric acids, several metallic salts, ammonium, etc., would prove the reverse.

After the time of the incomparable and enthusiastic Paracelsus, who, from admiration for his own genius, and his detestation of the labors of his predecessors, destroyed all of their works that he could find, in order that *his* science might prevail, alchemy continued to reign, but towards the beginning of the eighteenth century alchemical mist showed signs of dissipation, and the light of true science began to dawn.

From that time on rapid strides were made, and among the foremost scientific workers we find the names of several pharmacists, including such men as Beguin, who discovered calomel; Glauber, whose name has ever since been associated with the sulphate of sodium, and who first made hydrochloric acid and the oxysulphuret of antimony; Glazer, the discoverer of the sulphate of potassium; the great Lemery, whose lectures on chemistry were attended by audiences comprising visitors from all parts of Europe; Homburg, to whom we owe boracic acid; Klaproth, who first recognized the nature of precious stones and created the art of imitating them; Diesbach, the discoverer of Prussian blue.

A few words now about one, the greatest of them all—Scheele, of Sweden. Born of poor, but industrious parents, without more education than the village school afforded, he was apprenticed when about twelve years of age to an apothecary in Gothenburg; at twenty years he was already an accomplished chemist, and had submitted to the Stockholm Academy of Sciences the results of his original investigations, but the members were too narrow-sighted to appreciate his talents, and it remained for the celebrated Bergmann, of Upsala, also in Sweden, to discover in him the genius which was destined later to render him famous.

He was too modest to seek official employment, but accepted the charge of a pharmacy belonging to a widow in Kœping, and there spent the remainder of his life, and there he died.

Whilst he was known and admired throughout Europe, he was almost unheard of in his own country; it is related of the then King of Sweden that on one occasion, while travelling beyond the limits of his kingdom, he heard continued reference and high tribute paid to the greatness of the illustrious Scheele, of Sweden. He then felt chagrined that he had not done anything for him, and thought it due to his own glory thenceforth to bestow a mark of esteem on one who was so celebrated away from his home; he thereupon hastened to inscribe his name in the list of knights of his orders. The minister to whom was intrusted the duty of conferring that title upon Scheele was amazed. "Scheele! Scheele!" said he, "that is very singular," and he hesitated; but the order from the king was urgent and positive, and Scheele was made a knight. But Oh, Genius, where was thy lustre! It was not the peerless Scheele, it was not Scheele, the glory of Sweden, but an obscure official employee of that name, who received that mark of royal favor.

Scheele may be said to have had the instinct for discoveries; to enumerate all those he made during his lifetime would be almost to write the history of chemistry of that period. To him are due chlorine, glycerine, manganese, tungsten, citric, hydrocyanic, oxalic, tartaric acids, etc. And how did he make those grand discoveries? A few crucibles, several phials, some beer glasses and a few bladders were all the utensils and apparatus that he used in studying and isolating chemical bodies; an iron spoon sufficed him to unveil the laws governing the radiation of heat, and yet to this day his discoveries have stood the test of time; none have proved faulty; in all his conclusions he was infallible.

The number of scientific celebrities of pharmaceutical origin is almost inexhaustible, but we can mention only a few more, beginning with Lavoisier, who has been aptly called the great legislator of chemistry; Baumè, who popularized areometry, and whose name is still applied to instruments used for measuring the density of liquids; Priestly, who discovered oxygen; Vauquelin, to whom we are indebted for chromium and many improvements in the manufacture of the alums; Courtois, better known as a saltpetre dealer; the discoverer of iodine, without which the art of photography would still be unborn, and if we include fluorine, observed by Scheele, the discovery of the entire class of halogen elements must be assigned to pharmacists. Again, we have Pelletier and his colleague Caventon, who first made known the greatest remedy in the world, sulphate of quinine; and Labarraque, of chlorinated soda fame.

The discovery of the alkaloids of pyroxylon and chloroform, are also due to pharmacy. The extraction of the soluble constituents of solid bodies by the process of displacement is of pharmaceutical origin, first studied and described by Boullay and Robiquet, and subsequently practically applied by our own late lamented Procter; it is recognized to-day as by far the best method ever devised for the exhaustion of vegetable bodies. The names of Liebig, Sertürner, and Humphrey Davis, are inseparably connected with scientific progress, and they were also pharmacists.

To recall all the work of general utility accomplished by pharmacists would require considerable time indeed, but enough has been said to show what a useful, and in fact, indispensable man the progressive pharmacist has been in the past and must prove himself to be in the future. Unfortunately he has never been, and is not now appreciated as he deserves to be; but it is well established in the order of moral and physical sciences that the really useful men are never sufficiently honored. In all classes of society, the names of military heroes and national statesmen are intimately known, while those of men who by close mental application in the seclusion of a study, or by work amid the dangers of the laboratory have bestowed upon mankind much more substantial and certainly more durable benefits than those resulting from victories achieved on the battlefield or in the forum, are almost unknown. Yet, this lack of appreciation of his merits has exerted but little, if any influence on the pharmacist, and let us hope that the future will witness as great, if not greater triumphs than has yet been his good fortune to achieve.

Reflect, gentlemen, upon the immense amount of work accomplished by your predecessors of the mortar and pestle; and deliberate within your own minds whether you have reached the height of your aim in life or if you have but just begun. There are just as great discoveries to be made as there ever were; the field is limitless; rivalry here is in the highest degree honorable, the more you vie to excel your neighbor, the more credit will be yours. Do not allow what is usually termed the cares of business to completely absorb your energies; reserve a small amount to the pursuit of study, scientific study; direct your investigations toward the original—a mistake too commonly made is to offer as original, that, which justly considered is merely a compilation of selected matter; remember that he who causes a blade of grass to grow where none grew before is a benefactor to the human race; to follow this precept, plant your labor in good soil, and reap the fruit that will repay you; but do not keep it all to yourselves, share it with your fellow workers in the cause of scientific progress—if all the renowned warriors of science had kept the fruits of *their* discoveries to themselves how much would *we* know to-day? What would our actual condition be? Far behind our present state of knowledge and civilization you may rest assured.

Knowledge is a power for good or evil, and the value of our lives to our fellow men, is measured by the extent of good that we disseminate among them; let not motives of self interest overbalance what credit you may deserve. "'Tis better to err against ourselves than against our neighbors."

A story is told of the great physician Velpeau that illustrates the disappointments that greed sometimes suffers. He had attended a lady of high rank and wealth and with so much skill that she recovered from what was thought would be her last illness; grateful and overjoyed she sent for the doctor to reward him, but wishing to do it generously yet delicately, she on his arrival expressed her sincere thanks for his professional services and her high appreciation of his ability, at the same time extending to him a magnificently embroidered purse which she explained had been worked with her own hands. Velpeau surveyed the present, stepped back a little and replied, "My skill madam, which you have been so good to praise, cost me money and I cannot afford to part with it for aught but money, a fee is the only payment I can accept. "You are quite right, sir," replied the lady, "and how much is your fee?" "One thousand francs," said he; "very well, sir," said his patient, and quietly emptying the purse of its contents, she took therefrom one note of one thousand francs, handed it to the stupefied physician, consigned the others left, *nine* in number, to her own pocket, cast a look of indignant scorn on him and disappeared.

I have no fear, gentlemen, that anything of the kind will soon happen to any of you, but it is just as well to be on your guard.

There remains but little more to say; the Alumni Association is proud of you, gentlemen—we feel that your success is our success, many of you will soon return to distant homes, perhaps nevermore to see faces and things that had become familiar. Wherever you go do not forget friendships formed during your stay here, and above all, *never* forget your Alma Mater, the Philadelphia College of Pharmacy.

After the conclusion of Mr. Genois' address, the President stated that special certificates would now be awarded to those graduates having respectively the highest average in Materia Medica, Pharmacy, Chemistry, Pharmaceutical Manipulations and General Pharmacy.

He then invited Mr. Gustav Charles Frederick Helm, Jr., of Philadelphia, to come forward, he having attained the highest average in Materia Medica, and requested Dr. Adolph W. Miller, of the Class of 1862, to make the award. Dr. Miller arose and presented Mr. Helm with the certificate, with the following remarks:

It affords me a great deal of pleasure to comply with the wishes of the presiding officer and present you with this certificate of proficiency, which you labored so earnestly to obtain, with the wish that the more than usual interest and progress which has been manifested in the examination just conclued will be continued.

We all know that it is the largest Class ever graduating from our institution, and we also know that the examination, in comparison with the examination of the years past, has been one of the hardest—it rises, in fact, in mathematical proportion in the ratio of the number in the Class. If there is a certain degree of honor attached to the possession of one of these certificates in a class of forty, it is double in a class of eighty and quadruple in a class of one hundred and sixty, which has been the last one. We have just listened to an account of the discoveries that have been made by those who have preceded us in our profession, beginning with Paracelsus and ending with our lamented Procter, who offered to all freely the knowledge that he possessed, and distributed it to the best of his ability amongst those who desired to share it with him.

I trust, sir, in your future career you will follow the example of Procter, and not the example of Paracelsus. Bear with you the best wishes of the Alumni Association, of the Trustees of our institution, and of all its members.

Mr. Helm replied as follows:

GENTLEMEN OF THE ALUMNI:

I sincerely thank you for the honor bestowed upon me this evening. It will be my aim in the future to assist in the progress of pharmacy as far as my ability will allow.

The President then announced that Mr. William Edwin Saunders, of London, Ont., Canada, had attained the highest average in Pharmacy, and was entitled to the certificate in that branch, and, as Mr. Saunders was unavoidably absent, he called upon Mr. Henry Morford Jones, of Winchester, Ky., and a member of the Graduating Class, to come forward and receive it on behalf of Mr. Saunders, and requested Mr. Lucius E. Sayre, Class of 1866, and President-elect of the Association, to present the certificate. Mr. Jones came forward, and Mr. Sayre addressed him as follows:

On behalf of the Alumni Association of the Philadelphia College of Pharmacy, in presenting this certificate, I can do so best probably by reading the eloquent words defined upon the certificate itself: "Mr. William Saunders, of London, Ontario, Canada, Graduate of Pharmacy of 1883, in token of our appreciation of his proficiency in Pharmacy, and who having attained the highest average in that branch of science taught in the College, March, 1883, hereunto have affixed the names of our officers and the seal of the Association, this 14th day of March, 1883." Be kind enough, sir, to bear him our congratulations.

Mr. Jones, in reply, said:

GENTLEMEN OF THE ALUMNI:

In the absence of Mr. Saunders, I accept this certificate with the most sincere regards. He will not prize it for its intrinsic value, nor for its beauty, but because, when he looks upon this, he will see the link that binds him to his old Alma Mater, of which we are all justly proud.

The President now informed the audience that Mr. Wm. W. Light, of Oregon, Ill., had attained the highest average in the Examination on Chemistry, and invited him to come forward and receive the Certificate upon that branch from the hands of Mr. Henry Trimble, of the Class of 1876, and Assistant to Prof. Saml. P. Sadtler. Mr. Trimble in presenting it spoke as follows:

MR. WM. W. LIGHT:

Of all the certificates, it gives me the greatest pleasure to present this one. It shows that the student has attained for perfection in the science which cannot be memorized, and therefore to attain that proficiency, which warrants us in presenting this certificate, it shows that he must have become thoroughly acquainted with it. Accept it therefore with our hearty congratulations.

Mr. Light bowed his acknowledgment and resumed his seat.

The President now invited Prof. Frederick B. Power, Ph. D., of the Class of 1874, to present the certificate of Proficiency in Pharmaceutical Manipulations to Mr. Charles F. Randolph, of Altoona, Pa., he being the successful competitor for that high honor. Mr. Randolph now came forward and Prof. Power addressed him as follows:

MR. RANDOLPH:

It affords me much pleasure to present you on behalf of the Alumni Association this prize as a token of their appreciation of your proficiency in pharmacy and pharmaceutical manipulation. Please accept it with the kindest wishes of the members of the Association, as a mark of appreciation of the skill and excellence that you have manifested in our pharmacy, and may your work in future years redound to the advancement of this best of our college work and tend to your professional success.

Mr. Randolph replied as follows:

GENTLEMEN OF THE ALUMNI ASSOCIATION:

In thanking you for this certificate, I would say that I feel very much gratified in receiving this especial one, all the more from the fact that I know that these benches are full of good manipulators.

The President now invited Mr. Louis Charles Leonhard, of Dayton, Ohio, to come forward, and announced that he had received the highest average in General Pharmacy from the Committee, and was entitled to this Certificate, and requested Mr. Wallace Procter, of the Class of 1872, to make the award.

Mr. Procter, in presenting the Certificate, spoke as follows:

Mr. Louis Charles Leonhard :

I take pleasure in handing you this certificate. It is an award of merit for the excellence you have displayed in your examination by the Committee of the Board of Trustees of this College. You have answered the various and difficult queries submitted to the perfect satisfaction of your critics. Being first in this branch of the curriculum, you have earned at our hands this prize, which, we hope, will, at all times, remind you of the donors, of their sincere desire for your welfare in the future, as well as their conviction that honest preparations, neat plasters, round pills, smooth ointments, exactly divided powders, must necessarily be the result of your labors at the dispensing counter in the future. With this result, and a proper use of the stores of knowledge imparted by your several Professors during the last five months, you can at least say, "I am now qualified to learn more," not that there is nothing more worth knowing. Keep this in view, and you will surely advance in your profession. I congratulate you heartily, in the name of the Alumni Association of the College of Pharmacy.

Mr. Leonhard received the Certificate from Mr. Procter, and bowed his thanks for the same, and returned to his seat.

The President then requested those who had received the prize certificates to return them to the Secretary, in order that he might have them signed by the proper officers, and also have the seal of the Association attached, and that on Friday, if they would call upon the Secretary, at the College, they could receive them, together with their Membership Certificates.

The Secretary then read the names of the Graduating Class who had received the *grade* of " Distinguished " and are worthy of Honorable Mention :

Wm. Frederick Jungkunz, Freeport, Ill.

Wm. Edwin Saunders, London, Ont. (Canada.)

Howard Dickson Dietrich, Harrisburg, Pa.

Joseph Winters England, Philadelphia, Pa.

Wm. Wirt Light, Oregon, Ill.

Chas. Fitz Randolph, Altoona, Pa.

Flor. Joseph Schmidt, Evansville, Ind.

Also the following received the grade of " Meritorious," and were worthy of mention :

Robert Craighead Browning, Indianapolis, Ind.

Milton Campbell, Easton, Md.

John Peter Frey, Union City, Iowa.

Owen Burdette Hannon, Greene, N.Y.

Daniel R. Jones, Milwaukee, Wis.

Frank Gault Kerr, Marshall, Mo.

Louis Chas. Leonhard, Dayton, Ohio.

Gustav Scherling, Dubuque, Iowa.

The President then introduced Mr. William W. Light, of Oregon, Ill., who was chosen by his fellow-students to deliver the Valedictory Address on behalf of the Graduating Class.

Mr. Light came forward, and addressed the audience as follows :

Mr. President, Gentlemen of the Alumni and Fellow-Graduates:

Celebrating as we do this evening, the event of our admission into the Alumni Association of our College ; with joyful hearts at having ended the

struggle in which success only has made us eligible to a membership herein, it is well that our joy be unalloyed; yet let us pause in our triumphant
exultations to take a last farewell of our college life.

We have come from all the surrounding vales and hills, rich in their
memorials of the daring deeds of our ancestors; from Maine's triumphant
pines, that stand as sentinels watching the treacherous tongue of the noisy
Altantic; from the home of the "Lion" (Canada) as he bathes himself in
the soft sunshine of Her Majesty's Dominions; from orange groves and
cane and cotton fields of the South, where busy hands are clothing the
world; from the banks of the million rivers in the great valley of product-
iveness, where the silvered waters wash the brows of the laboring myriads
that are silencing the hungry mouths o'er land and sea; from the granite
peaks of the noble Rockies that lift their venerable heads to heaven; from
the peaceful valley beyond wrapped in perpetual verdure, where the golden
lips of evening print their farewell kiss; from every clime of our continent
that has been blessed with the tender ties of home, we have come together
here to mingle in the common pursuit of a common object.

This city once strange to us now greets us with an expression of
"brotherly love;" the long streets thronging with their thousands of human
souls have now become a matter of indifference to us as we tread our accustomed paths; these college halls, rich in their treasures of garnered
wisdom, have now become our peaceful abiding place; the many tasks that
once confronted us by their mountainous magnitude, have been reduced in
the crucible of honest effort. the high standing of our school, once such a
terror to our endeavors, has become a cloak of protection thrown around
our naked shoulders to warm us into a more earnest devotion to a noble
lifework; earnest instructors have freely dealt their panacea upon our undeveloped resources and have enabled us to stand more firmly upon our
own foundations; our Alumni Association, of which we may well feel proud
to become members, has ever labored for our comfort and our advancement; our respected Actuary, who has long been known as the "student's
friend," has indeed shown himself so; our societies have with magic hand
transformed a stranger's voice to a brother's clasp, and have melted the
angular cubes of coldness.to the fluidity of fellow feeling; so that to-day
when we receive the messages of our emancipation, like the Prisoner of
Chillon,

> "We almost feel that they have come
> To tear us from a second home."

To these circumstances that surround us, to these ties that bind us, to
these feelings that swell in our hearts, it is our mission to say farewell!
These two years in our young life history have brought their trials and their
pleasures, both of which we must cast aside and enter as freshmen in the
great pharmacy of the world with the earth's flora as our magazine of supplies, and nature as our instructor.

The parent bird watches and cares for her tender brood until their
earliest pinions have become strong enough to poise upon the airy sea.
Although the young are loth to leave the nest, the mother in her kindness
gives the stern command and casts them from their early home. One by
one the unskilled wings, trembling, struggle in the air and flutter towards the
ground, but the dear old mother makes a swift career and darts beneath the
sinking child and bears it aloft in the heavens to try its skill once more.
And o'er and o'er its efforts are renewed, and aye, the mother sits upon
the limb to watch and aid its movements until she deems her child strong
enough to battle in the world's great struggle for existence.

Can we see any analogy here?

For two years we have been trusting our unskilled wings upon the air,. while our Alma Mater, rich in her experience of sixty-one broods, has watched with anxious eye and aided with dextrous wing to give a deftly movement to our flight, and to-day, in her motherly magnificence, she tells her children that their own eyes and the world shall guide their flight.

To the many scenes that greet us with pleasure, the fleeting moments and the stern duties of life speak a last farewell. In a few days our homo-geneous life in this city will be changed to the heterogeneous conditions of our own diversified homes.

To our instructors, who have given a kindly aid to our advancement,. we return the best we can give—the gratitude of thankful hearts. The world is poor in thanks, but still we thank you for the faithful performance of duties.

Our Alma Mater, that has stood the test of criticism and time, we shall. always cherish with a tenfold devotion. She was born almost with the cen-tury, and, with the century, she has become grand in her greatness. Her fame is spread o'er land and sea. Her halls have become classic in our memories ; and, wherever we may be in future years, the phonograph of the soul will speak again the pleasant tones that were echoed by her walls..

The friendly grasp that knit us together in our society halls, the part-ing word must tear asunder: but thought, that knows no distance, will send its telephonic touch back to the old convivial board, and sound again in these old halls, our friendly voices bound together in one firm brotherhood.

Fellow-classmates, this, perhaps, is the last time we shall all meet together. We will soon be scattered over this broad land of ours, to write our pages in the history of our institution. She has given us credit, and it now remains for us to perpetuate her great name. Our work is just begun,. and, in the execution of our labors, may the venerable shades of the departed spirits of our ancestors, who taught the true doctrine in these halls, ever watch over us and guide us in our many wanderings, so that we will be an honor to ourselves, our societies and our Alma Mater.

At the conclusion of the Valedictory address, the President. announced that Mr. Chas. Bullock, of the Class of 1847, and Vice-President of the College, would present the Junior Testi-monial to that student having received the highest general aver-age at the Examination of the Junior Class, Thursday, February 15, 1883. That fortunate individual this year was Mr. William. Frederick Dohmen, of Milwaukee, Wis. He further stated that Mr. Dohmen was compelled to return to his home after the close of the examination, and therefore was unable to be present this. evening, but that his friend and fellow classmate, Paul Ernest Meissner, of Milwaukee, Wis., would accept it for Mr. Dohmen.

Mr. P. E. Meissner now advanced to the front of the audience and Mr. Bullock presented the Testimonial with the following. remarks :

I have the pleasure of handing you this Certificate of the Alumni Association for the best standing in the Junior Class; among the large num--ber who have distinguished themselves in that class, Mr. Dohmen has been. the most fortunate, and is the recipient of this mark of distinction by the Alumni Association ; and as the boy foreshadows the coming man, so.

we hope that the Junior may foreshadow the Senior in next year's Examination. Accept this with the best wishes of the Alumni Association.

Mr. Meissner in reply said:

GENTLEMEN OF THE ALUMNI ASSOCIATION:

In the name of my absent friend, I accept this with great pleasure, and I hope it will be followed in the succeeding year by a similar prize.

The President then announced that there were other members of the Junior Class who have received the grade of "Very Satisfactory" in the recent Junior Examination and therefore deserve honorable mention, and requested the Secretary to read their names.

The Secretary then read the list as follows:

Henry Warren Anderson, Bath, Maine
Harry Lee Barber, Phila., Pa.
Frank Frederick Bridgeman, Sheboygan, Wis.
Milton Smoker Falck, Lancaster, Pa.
Wm. Hubbell Gano, Jr., Wilmington, Del.
Henry Ernest Heinitsh, Phila., Pa.
Chas. Hector Hæntze, Fon Du Lac, Wis.
Wm. Matthew Koenig, Reading, Pa.
Clement Belton Lowe, Phila., Pa.
Tracy McKenzie, Mexia, Texas.
Henry Chas. Christian Maisch, Philadelphia, Pa.
Paul Ernest Meissner, Milwaukee, Wis.
Chas. Herman Oberholtzer, Phœnixville, Pa.
Wm. Ogilby, Carlisle, Pa.
Harlan Page Pettigrew, Sioux Falls, Dakota.
Frank Gibbs Ryan, Elmira, N. Y.
Luther Johnson Schroeder, Columbia, Pa.

The President now announced to the Graduating Class that there would be a special meeting of the Zeta Phi Society, tomorrow afternoon, at 4 P. M., also that Mr. W. C. Bakes desired the Class to meet him on the stage at the Academy of Music, on Friday afternoon, at 2 o'clock, for *drill*.

The President then stated that this concluded the regular order of the programme, but he would call upon Prof. Maisch for some remarks.

Prof. Maisch then came forward, and responded as follows:

You are aware, Mr. President—probably, undoubtedly so—that I received an invitation from the Board of Trustees of the Philadelphia College of Pharmacy to be the orator on Friday evening. Now, it would be unfair for you to expect me to expend my thunder this evening; but, in listening to the various speeches and the addresses that were made this evening, it occurred to me it would be a very proper occasion to call the attention of the Alumni Association to at least a portion of the work their Association has been doing, by somebody who knows something of the work that has been done.

When the Philadelphia College of Pharmacy erected this building, in the year 1868, there was a little room attached to it, which the Alumni Association at that time agreed to furnish for the purpose of establishing a laboratory—a chemical laboratory—and that work was commenced and organized in 1869, and I was placed in charge of it, and it was a labor of love, because there were very few students. I kept it up, however, as I knew, and was very well satisfied with the judgment of the Alumni Association, that it was perfectly correct, and that the necessity for such a chemical laboratory would soon be felt; and such in reality was the case. We soon found that the course of pharmaceutical instruction could no longer be given there, except under the instruction of my colleague, Prof. Remington, who took entire charge of the matter. At that time he was placed under very serious disadvantages. I had the laboratory in the morning until about 1 or 2 o'clock, and he had to come there in the afternoon.

In the year, 1881 the number of students in the laboratory increased to such an extent that we actually could not provide room for them; we had to send them away. When that fact was brought to the knowledge of the Board of Trustees of the Philadelphia College of Pharmacy, it induced them to order a laboratory built just for the accommodation, as it was thought at that time, of the chemical and pharmaceutical instructors. When this was under consideration the thought occurred, "Why, we might have two laboratories, one over the other—one for pharmacy and one for chemistry." That plan was adopted. Then it occurred to the committee who had that matter in charge, "Why, we need another lecture-room, as we have three professors, so that each professor may have a lecture-room of his own;" and consequently the third story was built. Then, finally, it was thought it would be an excellent plan to have a hall for the Alumni Association and a room for the students, and the fourth story was put on—and thus we have the enlarged building adjoining this one, which gradually grew from a one-story laboratory to a four-story building, as you see it adjoining. But, moreover, the classes have increased, and the importance of the course has increased to such an extent, as you are aware, that the optional course in chemical instruction was organized last year and will be made permanent hereafter.

The Alumni Association has during the past year again commenced another course of instruction. I remember very well when my friend Edward C. Jones came to me and told me he felt rather down-hearted on account of there being so little done by the Alumni Association for the College. It was some three or four years ago, and I suggested at that time that it would be a most admirable plan for the Alumni Association to take hold of the instruction by means of the microscope. It took several years to perfect that plan, but it has been at last perfected, and during the past winter the course was commenced under the able instruction of Mr. A. P. Brown, of Camden, a graduate of this College.

It will be, Mr. President, up-hill work, I know, for a short time, but I am perfectly well convinced that in a short time—in a very few years—it will succeed. I am also convinced that the course will be appreciated, and you will have a large number of students. I hope you will have so many that you cannot buy microscopes enough in Philadelphia to supply them.

Prof. Jos. P. Remington was then called upon, and came forward and responded as follows:

GENTLEMEN:

I first of all want to say to you, one and all, that I heartily congratulate you. I mean that, every word of it. (Applause.)

I have stood behind this counter, gentlemen, during the last winter, and have observed, particularly on several occasions when wrestling was going on. I assure you the wrestling I saw going on about two weeks ago was not quite so active in its physical movement, but there were quite active movements going on inside the cranium, I know. (Applause.) I want to say to you—probably what I shall not again have the opportunity of saying to you all here—that, in going over the examination papers, I was surprised, and surprised beyond conception, at the manner in which the new United States Pharmacopœia had been digested by the Class.   To be sure, there were a great many compounds that I got from the examination papers that I never heard of before.   (Laughter.)   Some of these I have noted, and you may hear from them in the future.   I have felt that on this occasion it would be proper for me to say this much to you—in fact, I almost believe that, the United States Pharmacopœia has been cut up into pieces and swallowed by you.   This was particularly the case with regard to some of the men in the front rank of the Class, who were, I believe I can say, so thoroughly posted that they seemed to know more about it than I did. I am perfectly free to say they know more about the United States Pharmacopœia now than I do, at least they have remembered more.

Gentlemen, there is a serious duty before you now.   You have had a time of serious occupation, and now is the time to have your joy and take it in its full.   I am not one of those who believe that in a time of joy it is necessary to remember the times of sorrow and the times of trial and anxiety.   That is all over now.   Then enjoy it; it is the time for it.   But you are soon to get away from the influence of your Alma Mater, as has been so well said to you by the orator of the evening, and I wish only to add take into consideration the sound advice that he has given you, and in addition to that the eloquent and beautiful address of your Valedictorian.   I am sure that I can add nothing to this.   However, possibly, to-morrow evening, I shall have something more to say in a different vein.

Prof. Sadtler was then called upon, and spoke as follows:

GENTLEMEN OF THE GRADUATING CLASS:

I make it a point never to fight against the inevitable.   I came down at once, as I thought if I did not somebody would take me by the shoulders probably.   (Laughter.)

Gentlemen, I want to say that I hardly expected to be here to-night, because of some work which was pressing upon me, but I made a distinct and desperate effort to get here, because I like to come to Commencement occasions.   It is tiresome to go through the whole examination, as much so to me as it is to the student, but I thoroughly enjoy Commencements.   You have had five days of wrestling, and now you will have three days of enjoyment, and I hope you will thoroughly enjoy them, and that you will do more than merely enjoy it in the sense of completely giving way to the glory of the occasion ; that you will take something from the outside impulses and carry them with you.   I hope that what has been so well said this evening by the orator of the Alumni Association and your own class orator will not go in one ear and out at the other, as some of the words of the Professor did, but that you will remember some of those words ; they are extremely well chosen.   I hope that you will profit by them.

I might say one word personally in relation to one thing.   On one of the examination papers a student has written, " Professor, this is the toughest paper I have ever seen," and he then crossed it out, as if it was rather too personal a remark.   I am glad to say that the examination in chemistry surprised me.   I believe I have fewer to throw and fewer fall below the standard than last year, and the class is larger.   It is gratifying to me, and I am glad that such a high average has been maintained as I find by conversation with the Professors and Committee of examination.   There have been very few who fell below the standard.   The number is smaller in proportion than it has ever been, or has been for some years past.   I think it was a good Class to go out and to make a noise in the world, and I hope that we shall hear from this Class frequently in the future, and that when we shall hear it will be to your personal credit. We will share somewhat in the glory, as being connected with the Philadelphia College of Pharmacy.

Mr. Wiegand, the Actuary, was then called for, and responded as follows:

GENTLEMEN AND LADIES:

I said "gentlemen" first, because there are so many before me. I would say that this is the first time I have seen Professor Remington and Professor Maisch go back of their class; they have done it this evening. I must only say that I am here to enjoy the time with you. I heartily rejoice that so many of you have passed so creditable an examination, as Professor Sadtler has said. You have my sincerest wishes for your success in life, that it may be fully commensurate with your success in the commencement. I cannot say more than this, and to thank you for the words which your Valedictorian has expressed, and so I bid you good evening.

Professor Power was called upon, and responded as follows:

I am glad to see such a large audience assembled. It shows the interest which is shown in you by your friends in connection with the honors you have received and the success which you have gained. I feel confident that as this Graduating Class departs from the College—many of them perhaps never to return again to its walls—as they seek their homes in the sunny South or in the distant West, they will ever feel an abiding interest in their old Alma Mater, and will be proud to think that they are graduates of the Philadelphia College of Pharmacy.

For myself, gentlemen, I only extend the heartiest wishes to one and all for your success.

Mr. Henry Trimble was then called for, and spoke as follows:

I am very glad that so many of you have endorsed the opinion that was expressed three weeks ago, and availed yourselves of the opportunity to withdraw.

Dr. A. W. Miller, was then called upon, and responded as follows:

GENTLEMEN:

You have heard so many words of wisdom this evening that I hardly know what to add to them. A few moments ago your eloquent Valedictorian was delivering his address, and he said that your work had just begun. That was a very true remark. It occurred to me that there are many scientific questions for you to answer yet and many things to be discovered. I hope that you will honestly conduct your work, be prosperous and enjoy a large share of good health. Now, what is necessary to attain and preserve good health? I would most carefully enjoin you against being too closely confined in your stores. The best thing is for you to pursue some avocation in conjunction with your pursuit that will allow you to get the open air and exercise. For instance, pursue the botanical study which is already begun here and the study of mineralogy, remembering the moral, "*Mens sana in corpore sano.*"

Mr. Edward C. Jones, the Treasurer of the Association, being loudly called for, responded as follows:

I am glad to see that our family is increasing and that there are many who will put their shoulders to the wheel to carry on our glorious work. I hope that you will be successful in your voyage through life. (Applause.)

The President then thanked those present as follows:

LADIES AND GENTLEMEN:

Before finally closing, allow me to thank you for the large attendance this evening; and I sincerely trust that the occasion has been as pleasurable to you as it has been to ourselves.

I now declare the Nineteenth Annual Reception to the Graduating Class of 1882 and '83 closed.

When the large audience quietly wended their way from the old halls, seeming well pleased with the interesting exercises of the evening. Attest,

WM. E. KREWSON, *Secretary.*

The first Alumni Gold Medal was awarded in 1871, and has been given each year since to the student who has received the highest general average of his Class.

* The First was presented March 15, 1871, to Charles F. Bolton, of Frankford, Philadelphia, Pa. Class of 1871.

Second. Presented March 15, 1872, to Wallace Procter, of Philadelphia, Pa. Class of 1872.

Third. Presented March 18, 1873, to E. C. Batchelor, of Macon, Miss. Class of 1873.

Fourth. Presented March 10, 1874, to Edward Seymour Dawson, Jr., of New York. Class of 1874.

Fifth. Presented March 15, 1875, to Howard Grant Jones, of Philadelphia, Pa. Class of 1875.

Sixth. Presented March 13, 1876, to Joseph LeRoy Webber, of Springfield, Mass. Class of 1876.

Seventh. Presented March 15, 1877, to Olaf Martin Oleson, of Fort Dodge, Iowa. Class of 1877.

* Eighth. Presented March 13, 1878, to David Patrick Miller, of Virginia. Class of 1878.

Ninth. Presented March 12, 1879, to Joseph Brakeley, of New Jersey. Class of 1879.

Tenth. Presented March 15, 1880, to George Havens Colton, of Springfield, Mass. Class of 1880.

Eleventh. Presented March 14, 1881, to Louis Genois, of New Orleans, La. Class of 1881.

Twelfth. Presented March 13, 1882, to Virgil Coblentz, of Springfield, Ohio. Class of 1882.

Thirteenth. Presented March 14, 1883, to Frederick Wm. Jungkunz, of Freeport, Ill.

---

* Deceased.

Minutes of the Executive Board.

Hall of Philadelphia College of Pharmacy,
No. 145 N. 10th Street,
May 4th, 1882.

The First Regular Stated Meeting of the Executive Board of the Alumni Association, was held this afternoon, in the Library room of the College.

The meeting was called to order at half-past four o'clock, P. M., by the President, Thos. H. Potts.

The Secretary called the roll, and the following members were present: President, Thomas H. Potts; First Vice-President, Lucius E. Sayre: Second Vice-President, Dr. Chas. A. Weidemann; Secretary, Wm. E. Krewson; Members of Executive Board, Jacob S. Beetem, David W. Ross, Henry Trimble and Thos. S. Wiegand, Trustee of Sinking Fund.

A communication was received from Wm. A. Ball, Corresponding Secretary, stating that he was unable to be present. Messrs. Edward C. Jones, John E. Cook, Louis Genois and Wallace Procter were also absent.

This being the first meeting of the Board for this year, and there being no minutes to read, the President called for reports of Committees.

The Secretary reported that the Committee on Publishing the Eighteenth Annual Report would have to report progress. The material was all in the hands of the printers, and two of the forms were completed, and he had copies of the same here with him, and from the appearance of these forms he thought our coming report would be equal to any of the former ones. The Committee could therefore only report progress, but thought in about three weeks it would be finished. He would therefore suggest that when we adjourn it be to meet at the Call of the Committee, in order to hear the final report of the Committee.

The Chairman of the Committee on Reception, Mr. E. C. Jones, being absent, there was therefore no report.

The Secretary reported that very few of the last Class had complied with the request of the Committee on Album, only a few photographs being received.

The following bills were presented and read, after being approved by the President and Secretary:

To Craig, Finley & Co., to 100 postal cards and printing, .	$1 75	
" 100 3-cent stamped envelopes and printing, ...	4 99	
" Composition and printing 300 circulars, ...	2 25	
" 100 postal cards and composition and printing, . . .	$2 00	$10 99
" Lehman & Bolton, 200 membership certificates, . . .		$16 50
" Thos. H. McCool, filling in 51 membership certificates, @ 30 cents, ...	$15 30	
" Filling 3 prize certificates, @ 40 cents, ...	1 20	
" Filling 2 prize certificates, @ 70 cents, ...	1 40	
" Filling 1 junior certificate, ...	5 00	$22 90
Making total of		$50 39

On motion, the above bills were ordered paid,

The following applications for membership were then read, viz :

Albert D. Wike, Class of 1867, of Marietta, Pa. ; Eugene Herbert, Class of 1870, of Philadelphia, Pa. (1201 Spruce St.) ; Robert August Kœmpel, Class of 1876, of New York City ; Chas. N. Acker, Class of 1882, of Philadelphia, Pa. ; John A. Lambert, Class of 1882, of Indianapolis, Ind. ; Wm. Ernest Roeschel, Class of 1882, of Carthage, Mo. ; Chas. M. Forney, Class 1882, Trenton, N. J.

The Secretary stated he had received the necessary fee, and that they had all received their certificates, and were now active members of the Association.

The subject of the Alumni Association continuing the Quiz Classes during the next course of lectures, now came up. The Secretary stated that he thought that if the Association deemed it advisable to have the Quizzes as heretofore, that it would be well for the Executive Board to take some action in the matter at this meeting, so that he could have a notice put in the coming report.

He spoke in favor of the Alumni Association conducting Quizzes as in former years, and also of the success of the former Quiz Classes financially to the Association, as well as increasing our membership and making it popular with the students.

Mr. L. E. Sayre spoke in favor of continuing the Quizzes, and was willing to do his part towards making them a success.

Dr. Chas. A. Weidemann, Mr. Jacob S. Beetem and David W. Ross also were in favor of continuing the Alumni Quizzes.

The Secretary then made a motion that the Alumni Association form Quiz Classes, and continue the Quizzes as heretofore, which was duly seconded, and so ordered.

Mr. David W. Ross moved that a Committee of five be appointed to form Quiz Classes, and take the whole matter in charge, and that the President, Secretary and Treasurer be upon the Committee. So ordered. The President then appointed Henry Trimble and Jacob S. Beetem as the two additional members of the Committee.

The Secretary moved that a Committee of five be appointed to bring forward plans and to purchase microscopes, and, if advisable, form a Class in Microscopy and Toxicology, in connection with the Quiz Classes during the next course of lectures. The motion was duly seconded, and so ordered. The Secretary suggested that two of the Committee be from the Association at large, and named Albert P. Brown, of Camden, N. J., and Dr. A. W. Miller. Whereupon the President appointed Albert P. Brown, Dr. A. W. Miller, Dr. Chas. A. Weideman, Edward C. Jones and L. E. Sayre as the Committee.

The President appointed Wm. W. Moorhead, Alonzo Robbins and Fred'k B. Power a Committee on Deceased Members, and directed the Secretary to notify them of their appointment.

Mr. T. S. Wiegand, the Trustee of the Sinking Fund, reported that there was $30 or $40 yet in his hands of the Sinking Fund, but that there was two or three bills yet to be paid on account of the fitting up of the Pharmaceutical Laboratory, which would about exhaust that fund, and he had intended to have made a final report and presented it at this meeting, and ask to be discharged from further service, but from want of time would defer it until the next meeting of the Board, when he would make such a report.

Mr. D. W. Ross moved that when we adjourn, it be to meet at the call of the Secretary, to hear the report of the Committee on Publishing the Eighteenth Annual Report, and other business that might come before the Board. So ordered.

There being no further business, on motion of Mr. David W. Ross the Board adjourned. Attest,

WM. E. KREWSON, *Secretary.*

MINUTES OF THE SECOND REGULAR MEETING.

Alumni Room,
Philadelphia College of Pharmacy,
No. 145 N. 10th Street,
Thursday, Aug. 3d, 1882.

The Second Regular Stated Meeting of the Executive Board of the Alumni Association, was held this afternoon in the Alumni Room.

The meeting was called to order at quarter of four, P. M., by the President, Thos. H. Potts.

The roll was called, and the following members were present : President, Thos. H. Potts; First Vice-President, Lucius E. Sayre; Treasurer, Edward C. Jones; Secretary, Wm. E. Krewson; Executive Board, Jacob S. Beetem (5).

Communications were received from Dr. Chas. A. Weidemann, Wallace Procter and David W. Ross, regretting that they were unable to attend. Messrs. Wm. A. Ball, John E. Cook, Henry Trimble, Thos. S. Wiegand and Louis Genois were also noted as being absent. Mr. Sayre stated that Mr. Genois was absent from the city.

The minutes of the last meeting of the Executive Board were read and approved.

Reports of Committees being in order, the President called for the report of the Committee on Preparing and Publishing the Eighteenth Annual Report, which was read, as follows :

Philadelphia, Pa., Aug. 3, 1882.

To the President, Officers and Members of the Executive Board :

GENTLEMEN:

Your Committee appointed Feb. 9th, 1882, to prepare and publish the Eighteenth Annual Report of the Alumni Association, P. C. P., submit the following as their report :

The Committee desire to offer an apology for the long delay in issuing their report, caused by the large amount of labor and material required, together with the slowness of the foreman having charge of the printing ; we were unable to get it ready for delivery before July 1st, or two months later than usual.

The Committee solicited and procured advertisements from thirty-four firms and from the College, making 24½ pages, together with the three pages of the cover used for advertisements.

They asked for and received estimates from three well-known printers of the city.

The contract was awarded to Messrs. Burk & McFetridge, No. 304 Chestnut street, they giving the lowest estimate.

The estimate was given for the same style and size as last year's report, of 140 pages, at a cost of $340.00 for 3000 copies, but owing to the large amount of material which the Committee had referred to it for publication, including the proceedings of the social meetings and the opening of the new Alumni Room, Dec. 30th, 1881, the two occupying over fifty pages, making the report larger than last year of twenty-six pages, costing $61.38 more than the estimate called for, together with $9.00 for extra time on revising proof, making a total of $70.38 above the estimate given.

The report contains 166 pages, including the advertisements, and cost $410.38. The cost of mailing and distributing will be about $50.

The amount received for advertisements is $308.50.

The proceedings of the Zeta Phi Alpha occupy seven pages, and they agreed to pay accordingly, which will amount to $16.50, as their proportion of the expense. This will make a total of $325.00. Deducting this amount from the cost of printing and distributing the report, will leave $135.00 to be paid out of the funds of the Association.

The Committee have mailed copies to all the active members of the Association outside of the city, and have distributed to all the members in the city, together with all the graduates, and putting one or more copies in every drug store throughout the city and suburbs, in all about 900 copies, by hand.

The Committee were greatly aided in the distribution of the city by the use of a horse and carriage, furnished by our Treasurer, Edward C. Jones.

The Committee still have wrappers and stamps sufficient for sending out about 500 copies, which they propose to send to graduates of our College, who are not members of the Association, thereby hoping to stimulate them to come forward and become active members of the Association.

In conclusion, your Committee feel that although this report has cost the Association more than any of its former ones yet, that it will repay the Association in the large addition it will make to its membership by showing to the graduates of our College that we are a live Alumni Association, and are keeping pace with the advances of our Alma Mater.

Your Committee now desires to be relieved from further service.

Respectfully,

WM. E. KREWSON,
EDWARD C. JONES,
LUCIUS E. SAYRE,
Committee.

Mr. Jacob S. Beetem moved that the Report of the Committee be received and spread upon the minutes, and that the Committee be discharged, with the thanks of the Executive Board. The motion was duly seconded and carried.

Mr. E. C. Jones, the Chairman of the Committee on Reception and Bestowment of the Annual Prizes, read the following Report:

To THE EXECUTIVE BOARD:

Your Reception and Prize Committee would respectfully report that they have had the following Prize and Certificates made out and saw them distributed, viz:

The Gold Medal, Virgil Coblentz, of Springfield, Ohio.

Certificate of Materia Medica, Benjamin A. Cunningham, of Frederick City, Md.

    "   " Pharmacy, Jonas G. Clemmer, of Philadelphia, Pa.

    "   " Chemistry, Wm. Henry Mehl, of Leavenworth, Kansas.

    "   " General Pharmacy, to Charles Augustus Schoenenberger, of Ashland, Pa.

    "   " Pharmaceutical Manipulations, to Theodore W. Reuting, of Titusville, Pa.

Alumni Certificate, for the best Junior Examination, was awarded to Miss Grace Lee Babb, of Eastport, Maine.

The Annual Address was delivered by Prof. Frederick B. Power, Ph. G., Ph. D., Class of 1874, of Philadelphia, Pa., and the Valedictory Address, by Henry Webster, of Salem, Ill.

The lecture-room was well filled, unusually so, on account of many being present who afterwards attended the Triennial Banquet of the Zeta Phi Alpha Society, which was held the same evening, after the close of the reception. Very respectfully submitted,

EDWARD C. JONES.
S. E. Cor. Fifteenth and Market,
WM. E. KREWSON,
N. E. Cor. Eighth St. and Montgomery Ave.,
LUCIUS E. SAYRE,
S. W. Cor. Eighteenth and Market Sts.,
Committee.

Philadelphia, 8th mo, 3d, 1882.

The Secretary moved that the Report be accepted and spread on the minutes and the Committee discharged. So ordered.

The Secretary stated that he had notified Mr. A. P. Brown, of Camden, N. J., of his appointment as Chairman of the Committee to Purchase Microscopes, and that he had written his acceptance.

Mr. E. C. Jones, a member of the Committee, reported progress, and stated that the Committee had met, and, after visiting several well-known manufacturers of microscopes, had purchased from Jos. Zentmayer, optician and manufacturer, No. 147 S. Fourth St., the following microscopes and microscopic accessories, which were to be delivered in September, viz:

½ Dozen botanical dissecters @ $12, . . .	$72 00
1 Section cutter (for soft substances), . . .	8 00
1 " " (for hard substances), . . .	12 00
1 Turn-table, ...	6 50
1 Section knife, ...	3 25
1 Gross slips (ground edges), ...	3 00
1 Ounce No. 2 covers (circles), ...	2 75
1 Stage micrometer, ...	1 00
1 Eye-piece micrometer (disk), ...	2 00
1 Camera lucida, ...	6 00
1 Student stand, complete, ...	38 00
1 Extra eye-piece, ...	5 00
Total	$159 50

Mr. Jones stated that they would make their final Report at the next meeting.

The Committee appointed at the last meeting to form Quiz Classes stated that they had nothing at this time to report, as they had not met as a Committee since their appointment, but would like to have the views of those present in reference to the mode of conducting the Quizzes during the coming winter, and would like to bring the matter up under the head of new business, if there were no objections.

There being no objections, the matter was deferred until later in the meeting.

The Secretary reported that he had officially informed Messrs. Wm. W. Moorhead, Alonzo Robbins and Frederick B. Power of their appointment by the President as a Committee on Deceased Members, and that they had all accepted.

The following bills were presented, after being approved by the President and Secretary, and, on motion of Mr. E. C. Jones, were directed to be paid.

Burk & McFetridge, 3000 copies Eighteenth Annual Report,
        166 pp. and cover.

140 pp. and cover, as per estimate,	$340 00	
26 pp. extra, ...	61 38	
Extra time on revising proof, . .	9 00	
		$410 38

Wm. E. Krewson, Secretary, 1000 2-ct. wrappers, . . $21 20
                  1000 2-ct. stamps, . . 20 00
                                                 $41 20

A. Gentzsch, 100 rollers, @ 1½, ... 1 50
Cyrus R. Morgan, M. D., reporting Eighteenth Annual
               Meeting, ... 5 50
Wm. E. Krewson, Secretary, 1 piece blue ribbon, . . 50
                   Wrapping paper, . . . 50
                   Postage and incidentals in
                   preparing and distributing
                   Eighteenth Annual Report, 5 73
                                         $6 73

           Making a total of, ... $465 31

    The Secretary stated that Mr. Louis Genois had been informed officially by the Corresponding Secretary, Wm. A. Ball, of his election as Orator for 1883, and had accepted the position. The Secretary also stated he had received the acknowledgment from the Mercantile Library Association, of New York City, for the donation of the Eighteenth Annual Report, which they had placed in the Library.

    The following applications for membership have been received since the last meeting of the Board:

    E. L. E. Castleton, Class 1879, of Galveston, Texas.

    J. Hamilton Knouse, Class 1882, Harrisburg, Penna.

    John Wilson Hoffa, Class 1880, Harrisburg, Penna.

    Benj. C. Waterman, Class 1878, No. 3901 Aspen St., West Philadelphia, Penna.

    Benj. Franklin Sholl, Class 1882, Lancaster, Penna.

    Thos. R. Gossling, Class 1881, No. 1602 Richmond St., Philadelphia, Pa.

    The Secretary stated that the above had all paid the necessary fee, and had received their certificates, and were now active members of the Association.

    The Secretary reported that the following members had died since the last meeting of the Board:

    B. Frank Shugard, Class 1868, died Sunday, May 28th, 1882, at Georgetown, Colorado, aged 41 years.

    Simon E. Wolf, Class 1882, died Monday, May 29th, 1882, at his home. in Harrisburg, Pa., aged 21 years. Mr. Wolf was a member of the last Graduating Class, also of the Quiz Class.

    Dr. Hiram Gold, Class 1864, died suddenly on Wednesday, July 12th, 1882, at his residence, 411 Pine St., this city, aged 49 years. Dr. Gold was the first Secretary of the Alumni Association, and one of its organizers.

    The friends of the above have promised to furnish the Committee on Deceased Members with the proper obituaries.

    The following delegates to the American Pharmaceutical Association, which meets at Niagara Falls, Sept. 12th, 1882, were nominated:

    Joe Jacobs, Athens, Georgia, Chairman ; Geo. W. Kennedy, Pottsville, Pa. ; Edward S. Dawson, Jr., Syracuse, N. Y. ; Wm. Weber, Philadelphia, Pa. ; John A. Witmer, Philadelphia, Pa.

There being no other nominees, on motion of the Secretary, Mr. E. C. Jones was directed to cast the vote of the Board for the above-named gentlemen, and that they have power to appoint alternates. Mr. Jones cast the vote in favor of the candidates, and the President declared them elected delegates to represent our Association at the session of the American Pharmaceutical Association, to be held at Niagara Falls, Sept., 1882, and directed the Secretary to notify them of their election.

Mr. Jacob S. Beetem moved that a Committee of two be appointed to attend the introductory lecture at the opening of the course of 1882 and 1883. So ordered.

The President appointed Mr. Jacob S. Beetem and Edward C. Jones as the Committee.

On motion of the Secretary, a Committee of five was appointed on Social Meetings.

The President appointed the following as the Committee :

Dr. A. W. Miller, Henry Trimble, Lucius E. Sayre, Chas. F. Zeller and Wallace Procter.

The Secretary stated that Wm. Bernard Bicker, of the Class of 1875, said that he had paid the fee of membership in the Association to one of the former Secretaries, but had never received the certificate.

Mr. Jones said that there must be some mistake about the matter, as he had never received the fee, and he moved that the Secretary write to the former Secretary for information regarding the matter. So ordered.

The Secretary stated that at the annual meeting he was authorized to have the five prize certificates on Materia Medica, Pharmacy, Chemistry, Pharmaceutical Manipulations and General Pharmacy, as well as the Junior Prize and a Certificate of Membership properly filled up, with the names of our deceased professors and friends of the College, in order to have them framed and hung up in the Alumni Room, and he had prepared the following list and desired the Board to direct him to have the work done.

Membership Certificate, Dr. Hiram Gold, Ph. G.

Certificate on Chemistry, Dr. Robert Bridges.

    "   " Materia Medica, Dr. Robert P. Thomas, Ph. G.

    "   " Pharmacy, Wm. Procter, Jr., Ph. G.

    "   " Practical Pharmacy, Edward Parrish, Ph. G.

    "   " Pharmaceutical Manipulations, Ferris Bringhurst, Ph. G.

Junior Prize Certificate, Henry K. Bowman, Ph. G.

On motion, the Secretary was directed to have the above names filled in the certificates ordered.

Mr. E. C. Jones offered the following :

Resolved, That the Secretary be requested to communicate with the Trustees of the College in reference to having the Museum opened during the lecture season, so that the students can have access to the specimens for their inspection, under proper supervision, and see what means çan be devised according to the resolution passed at the Annual Meeting of the Alumni Association, held in March last.

The above resolution was seconded and carried.·

The Secretary stated that he had received a check for $20 from the Treasurer of the Zeta Phi Alpha Society, for the two cases, set apart for their use, and he had handed the same over to the Treasurer.

The subject of Quizzes now came up.

Mr. Jones spoke at some length on the subject, and thought that the Quiz tickets should be made as cheap as possible.

Mr. Sayre also spoke at some length on the subject, and agreed with Mr. Jones in regard to the cheap Quiz tickets, and thought if we could put them as cheap as the College reviews, and then give the student the privilege of joining the Alumni Association afterwards, if he so desired, at a reduced rate. He also thought it would be better to have but two Quiz masters, instead of three, as heretofore.

The Secretary thought by all means that the fee for admission into the Alumni Association should be included in the price of the Quiz tickets, thereby insuring to us members of the Association after the graduation of the members of the Quiz Class.

After a general conversation of all the members of the Board present, it was suggested that the Committee hold a meeting at an early date, to perfect the arrangements for holding and conducting the Quizzes under the auspices of the Alumni Association.

There being no further business, on motion of Mr. E. C. Jones the Board adjourned.   Attest,

WM. E. KREWSON,
Secretary.

MINUTES OF SPECIAL MEETING.

Alumni Room,
Philadelphia College of Pharmacy,
No. 145 N. 10th St.,
Sept. 25th, 1882.

A Special Meeting of the Executive Board of the Alumni Association, was held this afternoon in the Alumni Room.

The President, Thos. H. Potts, called the meeting to order at half-past two, P. M.

The roll was called, and the following members of the Board were present:

President, Thomas H. Potts; Second Vice-President, Dr. Chas. A. Weidemann; Secretary, Wm. E. Krewson; Corresponding Secretary, Wm. A. Ball, and Messrs. Henry Trimble, Jacob S. Beetem and David W. Ross, Members of the Executive Board; Messrs. John E. Cook, Louis Genois and Wallace Procter, were noted as being absent.

The President requested the Secretary to read the call for this Special Meeting, as follows:

Philadelphia, Sept. 22d, 1882.
To the President of the Alumni Association:

We, the undersigned members of the Executive Board, desire you to call a Special Meeting of the Board, on Monday afternoon, September 25th, 1882, at 2 o'clock, to hear the report from the Committee on Quizzes and Microscopy, and to attend to any business that may come before the meeting.   Respectfully,

WM E. KREWSON,
WM. A. BALL,
CHAS. A. WEIDEMANN.

Reports of Committees being called for, the Secretary read the following report from the Committee on Quizzes:

Alumni Room,
Philadelphia, Pa., September 12th, 1882.
To the Executive Board:

Your Committee appointed by the Executive Board, at its regular meeting May 4th, 1882, to take the entire charge of the Alumni Quizzes for the course of 1882 and 1883, and to select Quiz Masters, submit the following report:

After several meetings of the Committee, they agreed to recommend that there be two Quiz Masters appointed this year for the Senior Class, instead of three, as in former years, and to put the Quiz tickets at $10 to each student, and after their graduation in the College to present them with the certificate of membership, as heretofore.

The Quizzes to be held every Wednesday afternoon, from 4 to 6, P. M., in the Alumni Room, giving one hour to each Quiz Master.

They appointed Mr. Lucius E. Sayre, Ph. G., to conduct the Quiz on Materia Medica and Practical Pharmacy, and Mr. Louis Genois, Ph.G., on Chemistry and Theoretical Pharmacy.

They also agreed to recommend that there be one person appointed to take charge of the Junior Quiz Class, and to give them one hour and a half conversational quiz on Materia Medica, Chemistry and Pharmacy, the same to be held every Saturday afternoon during the course, from 2 o'clock till half-past 3, P. M., the tickets for the Junior Students to be placed at $5.00 each.

To conduct the Junior Quiz they appointed Mr. Henry Trimble, Ph. G.

The Senior Quiz Class will meet for organization on Wednesday afternoon, Oct. 4th, 1882, at 4, P. M., and the Junior Quiz Class will meet for the first Quiz on Saturday afternoon, Oct. 7th, 1882, at 2 o'clock, P. M.

The Committee further agree to guarantee to pay the Senior Quiz Masters $100.00 each for forty students or less, and for every additional student above forty, at the rate of $2.50 for each student.

The Junior Quiz Master to receive $75.00 for twenty-five students or less, and for every additional student above that number, at the rate of $3.00 for each student.

The payment of the Quiz Masters shall be due and payable at the close of the course.

The gentlemen selected need no words of recommendation from the Committee, as they are well known to the Association as among their most active members, and we feel that the Alumni Association should be congratulated upon their selection.

The Committee also ordered circulars to be printed and distributed among the students, giving them all the required information.

Respectfully submitted,
THOS. H. POTTS, President,
WM. E. KREWSON, Secretary,
EDWARD C. JONES, Treasurer,
HENRY TRIMBLE and
JACOB S. BEETEM,

Committee.

Attest,   WM. E. KREWSON, Secretary.

Mr. Wm. A. Ball moved that the Report of the Committee be accepted and filed, and that they be instructed to carry out the provisions of the Report, which was duly seconded and carried.

The Secretary then read the report of the Committee on Microscopy, as follows:

Philadelphia, Pa., Sept. 25th, 1882.

To the President, Officers and Members of the Executive Board
of Alumni Association of Philadelphia College of Pharmacy:
GENTLEMEN:

Your Committee appointed to purchase microscopes, and to form a Class in Microscopy, beg leave to present the following Report:

A meeting of the Committee was called on May 15th, 1882, and, after consultation, concluded to purchase microscopes and microscopical apparatus. They visited several dealers, and finally settled upon Jos. Zentmayer, and purchased the enclosed invoice. (See invoice in minutes of last meeting, page 35.)

At a subsequent meeting, held Sept. 12th, the Committee concluded that the dissecting microscopes would not be of much use in teaching practical microscopy, and concluded to ask Mr. Zentmayer to exchange them for the "student" stand. This would incur an additional expense of about $100.00.

The Committee concluded to form classes, and to appoint a suitable person to give instruction in the practical use of the microscope.

They also make the following recommendations : That the *tickets* be placed at $5.00 to all students in the Senior Quiz Class; other students, $7.50. Graduates of the College, $10.00.

And that the Class organize on Friday, Oct. 13th, 1882, and continue during the winter ; and on Friday afternoon, Oct. 6th, 1882, a microscopical exhibition be given in the Alumni room, and an invitation be extended to all students, in order to show them that the Alumni Association are in earnest in this undertaking.

Also, that the instructor be paid, as a compensation for his services, the sum of $5.00 for each student, and that the Committee be empowered to purchase suitable tables for the microscopes, and that the glass slips be sold to members of the class at 30 cts. per dozen, and cover glasses, 20 cts. per dozen.

All of which is respectfully submitted,

ALBERT P. BROWN, Chairman,
A. W. MILLER, M. D.,
CHAS. A. WEIDEMANN, M. D.,
EDWARD C. JONES,
LUCIUS E. SAYRE,
Committee.

The Secretary stated that the report was signed by only two members of the Committee, but if action was postponed until later in the meeting, that other members of the Committee would be present, whereupon the further action was deferred until later in the meeting.

The Secretary stated that he had some other business upon the table, and if there was no objections, or by unanimous consent of those present, it could be taken up. There being no objections, the President announced that new business would be taken up.

The Secretary stated that he had officially informed the delegates elected at the last meeting of the Board, to attend the American Pharmaceutical Association, at its session held at Niagara Falls, and that Messrs. Joe Jacobs, George W. Kennedy and Wm. Weber had accepted the position, but Messrs. Edward S. Dawson, Jr., and John A. Witmer were compelled to decline, on account of their inability to attend the meeting, thanking the Association for the honor conferred upon them.

He also stated that he had notified the gentlemen appointed by the President on Social Meetings, and Dr. A. W. Miller, Lucius E. Sayre and Henry Trimble had accepted, but Wallace Procter and Chas. F. Zeller had declined, on account of other pressing duties.

On motion of the Secretary, the President was authorized to appoint two gentlemen to fill their places.

The Secretary also reported that he had written to Clemmons Parrish, as per motion at last meeting, in reference to the application of Mr. Wm. B. Bicker, and Mr. Parrish, in reply, stated he did not remember of ever receiving it.

The Secretary stated that he had received the following acknowledgments from libraries and institutions who received our Eighteenth Annual Report:

The Mercantile Library Co., of Philadelphia, Pa.

Astor Library, New York.

Boston Public Library, Boston, Mass.

State Library of Massachusetts, Boston, Mass.

Boston Medical Library Association, Boston, Mass.

Department of the Interior, Bureau of Education, Washington, D. C., John Eaton, Com. of Ed.

Nederlandsche Maatschappij ter Beyordering der Pharmacie, Amsterdam.

Mr. Wm. A. Ball, Corresponding Secretary, also reported the following:

New Hampshire State Library, Concord, N. H.

Amherst College Library, Amherst, Mass.

Library University of Vermont, Burlington, Vt.

U. S. Marine Hospital Service, Treasury Department, Washington, D. C., John B. Hamilton, S. S. General.

Library of U. S. Congress, Washington, D. C., A. R. Spofford, L. of C.

The Secretary also stated that he had received from Mr. A. P. Brown, Secretary of New Jersey State Pharmaceutical Association, their reports for 1880 and 1881.

The Calendar of the Pharmaceutical Society of Ireland, 1882.

Transactions of the South Carolina Medical Association, 1882.

Proceedings of the Connecticut Medical Society, 1882, and

The Druggists' Circular of New York, which also contained notice of our Report.

The *Am. Journal of Pharmacy* and *The New Remedies* had also given the Report complimentary notices.

A communication was received from the Postmaster of Chicago, stating that there were six copies of the last Report remaining in that office unclaimed. The Secretary stated that he had forwarded the required postage, and they were returned to him.

The following applications for membership were received and read:

Charles Wm. Dare, Class 1882, Troy, Bradford Co., Pa.

Frank Moore, Class 1877, Cherry Hill, Cecil Co., Md.

The Secretary stated that the above gentlemen had paid the necessary fee and had received their Certificates of Membership, and were now active members of the Association.

The Secretary announced the death of Mr. James A. Maston, Class of 1875, an active member of the Association, who died on Saturday, Sept. 16th, 1882, at the Episcopal Hospital, in this city, of consumption.

The following bill was presented, and, after being approved by the President and Secretary, was ordered to be paid:

The Secretary, To postage and sundries, . . .	$2 68
To ink, mucilage and twine, . .	40
	$3 08

Mr. Henry Trimble moved that we take a recess until after the meeting of the College. Agreed to.

Mr. Jacob S. Beetem and Mr. Wm. A. Ball desired to be excused from further attendance, which was granted. The Board then took a recess.

Re-assembled quarter after 4, P. M., President Potts in the chair, and Messrs. Lucius E. Sayre, First Vice-President; Edward C. Jones, Treasurer, were present; also Mr. Wm. R. Warner. Jr., member by invitation.

The President stated that he would appoint Mr. David W. Ross and Mr. Wm. R. Warner, Jr., on the Committee on Social Meetings.

The Report of the Committee on Microscopy was again read.

On motion, the report was accepted.

The Secretary moved that Mr. A. P. Brown, of Camden, N. J., be appointed by this Board Instructor in Microscopy for the session 1882 and 1883, which was duly seconded, and so ordered.

Mr. E. C. Jones moved that the Chairman, Mr. A. P. Brown, be authorized to purchase the additional microscopes, together with suitable tables to put them upon in the Alumni room. So ordered.

The following bill, after being approved by the President and Secretary, was ordered paid:

Craig, Finley & Co.—

To composition and printing 600 letter circulars, . . $5 50		
" " " 600 1-ct. envelopes, . 8 25		

$13 75

The Secretary moved that Mr. Henry Trimble be appointed to take charge of the Junior Quiz Class, in accordance with the Report of the Committee on Quizzes. So ordered.

Mr. E. C. Jones moved that the time of holding the Junior Quiz be changed from Saturday afternoon to Thursday afternoon of each week, at half-past 4 to 6, P. M.

Several of those present thought that the change would be better, not only for the Quiz Master, but would also make it more popular with the students. The motion was duly seconded and carried.

There being no further business, on motion of Mr. Henry Trimble, the Board adjourned.   Attest,

WM. E. KREWSON, *Secretary.*

MINUTES OF THE THIRD REGULAR MEETING OF THE EXECUTIVE BOARD.

Hall of the Philadelphia College of Pharmacy,
No. 145 N. 10th Street,
Nov. 2d, 1882.

The third Regular Stated Meeting of the Executive Board of the Alumni Association, was held this afternoon in the room of the Association.

The meeting was called to order at 3.45, P.M., by Mr. L. E. Sayre, First Vice-President, in the absence of the President (who was serving on the jury).

The roll was called, and the following members were present:

First Vice-President, L. E. Sayre ; Second Vice-President, Dr. Chas. A. Weidemann ; Treasurer, Edward C. Jones ; Secretary, Wm. E. Krewson ; Members of the Executive Board, Messrs. Jacob S. Beetem, David W. Ross and Henry Trimble.—7.

Mr. A. P. Brown was also present, by invitation.

Mr. T. H. Potts, President, and Messrs. Wm. A. Ball, John E. Cook, Louis Genois, Wallace Procter and Thos. S. Wiegand, were noted as being absent.

The minutes of the last Regular Meeting and of the Special Meeting held September 25th, were read and approved.

Reports of Committees were called for.

Mr. Beetem, Chairman of the Committee to attend the introductory lecture, made a verbal report, stating that he and Mr. Jones attended the lecture, which was ably delivered by Prof. J. P. Remington, to a large audience, composed of students and friends of the College. One of the members of the Senior Class, Mr. Wm. D. Kerr, took down the short speeches that were made by the various gentlemen called up after the close of the introductory address, which were in the possession of the Secretary. Prof. Remington had sent him his address for publication in our next Annual Report, and he would hand it over to the Secretary.

On motion, the report was accepted and the Committee was discharged.

The Secretary reported that the Senior Quiz Class was duly organized, and was a success, as far as members are concerned. Sixty of the Senior students had already made application, and the most of the number had already paid for their tickets, and if all the members graduate will give us sixty new members for the Association.

The Junior Quiz Class is not so successful, but ten had made application thus far, but he thought quite a number would still join the class.

The class on Microscopy, being a new feature, numbers ten members so far. Among the number is one graduate.

He further stated that he would make the final report at the next meeting of the Board.

Mr. A. P. Brown, Chairman of the Committee on Purchasing Microscopes, was present by invitation, and reported that he had no written report, but would state that the microscopes purchased by the Committee in the spring, as per list furnished at the last meeting of the Board, were not suitable for the purpose, and at his suggestion, five of the botanical dissectors were exchanged for the American student stands, and also additional student stands were purchased, putting the Association to an extra expense, but still it was necessary, and he would recommend that a course in the spring be organized for the benefit of the students who do not now have the opportunity for taking a course, on account of the lectures and laboratory course, which take their attention.

Mr. E. C. Jones moved that the Instructor be authorized to organize a Spring Class in Microscopy, to commence about the 1st of April, and that he have circulars printed and distributed among the students, inviting those who remain in the city to avail themselves of this opportunity of acquiring this useful knowledge of microscopic instruction.

The Secretary stated that the First Social Meeting was held Oct. 10th, and was very well attended by the students and friends of the Alumni, and that the Second Meeting would be held on the 14th of this month, and Dr. Chas. L. Mitchell would deliver a lecture upon the "Germ Theory," and Miss F. Lizzie Pierce, the distinguished teacher of elocution, would give a recitation, entitled "The Swiss Good-Night," and he desired to know whether he was to notify the resident members of these meetings.

Dr. Chas. A. Weidemann moved that the Secretary be authorized to have postal cards printed and sent to the resident members of the Association, notifying them of the Social Meetings, and also have the students invited through the Professors. So ordered.

New business was now called for, and the Chairman, Mr. L. E. Sayre, invited Mr. A. P. Brown to take the chair, which he did.

Mr. L. E. Sayre then took the floor, and spoke about the Quiz Classes being a success, as we had heard through the Secretary. He spoke about the necessity of having all the helps possible, in order to give the students all the advantages of the Quizzes, and, at the same time, to assist the Quiz Master in the performance of his duties, and he would suggest that the Association purchase a set of materia medica and chemical specimens for the use of the Quiz Masters.

Dr. Weidemann also spoke upon the subject, and favored the purchase of the specimens. The Secretary inquired of Mr. Sayre about what the cost would be.

Mr. Sayre stated that he thought about $9.00 or $10.00.

The Secretary said that he had no doubt that the members of the Association would donate specimens, provided the Alumni would furnish suitable bottles.

Several of the members of the Board present signified their willingness to donate specimens, which were accepted.

Mr. Sayre moved that a contribution list be opened for the reception of specimens of materia medica and chemicals, and that the Association purchase suitable bottles for their reception. So ordered.

Mr. Henry Trimble asked to be excused, as the Junior Quiz Class was waiting for him in the next room; and Mr. Jacob S. Beetem also asked to be excused. On motion, they were excused, and they retired.

The Secretary moved that the three Quiz Masters be a Committee to have full charge of the specimens, also to purchase the necessary bottles for the reception of the specimens, and that they be authorized to purchase any specimens they may deem necessary. The motion was duly seconded, and agreed to.

Mr. A. P. Brown stated that he would donate a series of the slides of root sections, illustrating the structure of the same.

Mr. D. W. Ross moved that the donation be accepted, with the thanks of the Association. So ordered.

Mr. E. C. Jones spoke of having a social gathering of the students and members of the Alumni Association during the holidays, as there were no lectures during the intervening time of Christmas and New Year's, and suggested that it might take the form of a microscopical exhibition, together with other literary features.

Mr. A. P. Brown, and the other members present, also favored the project.

The Secretary moved that a Committee of three be appointed to devise ways and means for such an entertainment during the time specified. So ordered.

The Chair appointed Mr. A. P. Brown, Dr. A. W. Miller and Edward C. Jones as the Committee.

The following bills were then read, after being approved by the President and Secretary, viz:

Jos. Zentmayer—

To 6 American student stands, No. 38, with $\frac{8}{10}$ and $\frac{1}{5}$

a eye pieces and case, @ $38.00,	. . .	$228 00
" 6 extra eye pieces, @ $5.00, ...		30 00
" 1 stage micrometer, ...		1 00
" 1 eye piece "		2 00
" 1 camera lucida, ...		6 00
" 1 section cutter, soft substances, ...		8 00
" 1 " hard " . . .		12 00

Amount carried forward, ... $287 00

Amount brought forward, ...	$287 00	
To 1 section knife, ...	3 25	
" 1 turn table (Congress), ...	6 50	
" 1 gro. ground-edge slides, ...	3 00	
" 1 oz. No. 2 circles, ...	2 75	
" 1 botanical dissecter, No. 44, ...	12 00	
	$314 50	
Less 15 per cent., ...	47 18	
		$267 32
Philip C. Shaffer—		
To 6 pine tables, 24 x 42, @ $2.00, . . .		12 00
Wm. Mann—		
To 1 roll book and lettering, ...	$1 20	
" 2 books Quiz tickets, ...	2 75	
		3 95
C. R. Morgan—		
To reporting First Social Meeting, ...		5 00
Wm. E. Krewson, Secretary—		
To postage and sundries, ...		2 88
J. P. Baral & Bro.—		
To 3 brass keys, ...		60
L. B. McClees & Co.—		
To 1 blackboard, 3 x 4½, and stand, . . .	$12 00	
" 2 erasers, ...	25	
		12 25
Craig, Finley & Co.—		
To 100 postals and printing.	$2 00	
" comp. and printing 1000 letter circulars, . .	7 00	
" 100 postals and printing, ...	1 75	
" 500 applications for Microscopy tickets, . .	2 00	
" comp. and printing 1000 Microscopy, half-sheet		
circulars, ...	4 00	
		16 75
T. H. McCool—		
To engrossing 1 prize specimen certificate (Junior), .	$5 00	
" filling in 1 membership specimen certificate, .	30	
" " 1 Chemistry "	40	
" " 1 Materia Medica, "	40	
" " 1 Pharmacy, "	40	
" " 1 Practical Pharmacy, "	65	
" " 1 Phar. Manipulation, "	65	
" " 50 tickets (Microscopy), . . .	80	
" lettering blackboard, ...	2 00	
		10 60
R. T. Wilson—		
To 1 piece picture wire, ...	30	
" 7 nails (picture), ...	12	
		42
J. Shonert—		
To 7 oak frames, @ $1.65, ...		11 55
Total, ...		$343 32

Mr. E. C. Jones moved that the bills be paid. So ordered.

The Secretary stated that he had notified Messrs. L. E. Sayre, Louis Genois and Henry Trimble of their appointment as Quiz Masters, and that they had all accepted the positions.

Also, Mr. A. P. Brown, as Instructor in Microscopy, who had accepted. and Messrs. David W. Ross and Wm. R. Warner, Jr., as additional members of the Committee on Social Meetings, and they also accepted.

The following acknowledgments were received from libraries, &c., who had received our last Annual Report: Bowdoin College Library, Brunswick, Me.; British Museum Library, London, Eng.; Academie Royale de Medecine de Belgique, Bruxelles, France.

Also, from Mr. Jos. L. Lemberger, Treasurer of the Pennsylvania State Pharmaceutical Association, the Annual Reports of the Association for 1878, '79' '80, '81 and '82·

The following applications for membership were read:

Wm. E. Speakman, Class 1881, of Woodbury, N. J.
Geo. I. McKelway, Class 1871, of 1410 Chestnut St., Philadelphia, Pa.

The Secretary stated that he was trying to procure the correct address of all the active members of the Association.

The following deaths had been reported to him:

Geo. W. Patrick, M. D., Class 1846. Died at Terre Haute, Ind., in 1874.
Wm. Ellis, Class 1834. Died in Philadelphia, Oct., 1881.

Mr. Jones spoke about publishing our next Annual Report, and thought it advisable for the Committee to be appointed earlier than heretofore, in order that they might secure more advertisements, as those who advertise were making their contracts for next year.

He therefore would move that a Committee of three be appointed to prepare and· publish the Nineteenth Annual Report of the Association, and to solicit advertisements for the same. So ordered.

The Chair appointed the President, Treasurer and Secretary as the Committee.

There being no other business, on motion of the Secretary, the Board adjourned.   Attest,

WM. E. KREWSON, *Secretary.*

MINUTES OF THE FOURTH REGULAR MEETING OF THE EXECUTIVE BOARD.

Hall of the Philadelphia College of Pharmacy,
No. 145 N. Tenth St.,
Feb. 1st, 1883.

The fourth Regular Stated Meeting of the Executive Board of the Alumni Association was held this afternoon in the room of the Association.

In the absence of the President and First Vice-President, Charles A. Weidemann, M. D., Second Vice-President, occupied the Chair.

The meeting was called to order at 4.15, P. M.

The roll was called, and the following members were present:

Second Vice-President, Chas. A. Weidemann, M. D.; Treasurer, Edward C. Jones; Secretary, Wm. E. Krewson; and Messrs. Henry Trimble, Jacob S. Beetem and Thos. S. Wiegand.

A communication was read from Thos. H. Potts, President, regretting his inability to be present.

The Secretary also stated that Mr. L. E. Sayre had informed him that it would be impossible for him to be present to-day.

Wm. A. Ball, John E. Cook, Louis Genois, David W. Ross and Wallace Procter were also noted as being absent.

The minutes of the last meeting were read and approved.

Reports of Committees were now called for.

The Secretary then read the Report of the Committee on Microscopy, as follows:

Philadelphia, Pa., January 31st, 1883.

To the Executive Board:

Your Committee on Microscopy would respectfully report that the Class was duly organized on Friday afternoon, October 6th, 1882, and continued every week to the close of the course. The Class numbered twelve students, eight Seniors, two Juniors, and two Graduates of the College. Seven of the number were members of the Senior Quiz Class, consequently their tickets were $5.00 each, according to agreement. The two Graduates paid $10.00 each, and the three others paid each $7.50. The total amount being $77.50 from the sale of tickets, and add to this $9.72 for the sale of covers and slides, will make a total of $87.22 realized from the Microscopical Class.

The Instructor, as per agreement, received $5.00 for each student, making $60.00. The cost of slides and covers amounted to $10.50, and the printing cost $5.50, making a total cost of $76.00, leaving a balance of $11.22 as a gain to the Association.

The Committee held a meeting in the Alumni Room this afternoon, to make arrangements for the Spring Course on Microscopy, and resolved to hold the first meeting on Monday afternoon, April 2d, 1883, at 3 o'clock, for organization, the same to take the form of a microscopical exhibition, the same as at the commencement of the winter course.

They agreed to put the tickets at $10.00 for each applicant without limitation for the course of twelve to fifteen lessons.

The Chairman was authorized to draft a suitable circular, which the Secretary was instructed to have printed and circulated among the students, and also to send one to each member of the Association, with the notice of the next Annual Meeting.

They further agreed to pay the Instructor the same price as heretofore for each ticket.

They also authorized the Secretary to have a notice placed in the *American Journal of Pharmacy*, February, March and April.

Respectfully submitted,

A. P. BROWN, Ph. G., *Chairman,*
DR. A. W. MILLER, Ph. G.,
EDWARD C. JONES, Ph. G.,
L. E. SAYRE, Ph. G.
DR. CHAS. A. WEIDEMANN, Ph. G.,
Committee.

Attest,

WM. E. KREWSON, Ph. G., *Secretary.*

The Secretary moved that the report be accepted and spread upon the minutes. Carried.

It was also moved and seconded that the Committee be continued, and the suggestions made in their report be carried out. So ordered.

The report of the Committee on Quizzes was then read, as follows:

Philadelphia, Pa., February 1st, 1883.

To the Members of the Executive Board
of the Alumni Association of the Philadelphia College of Pharmacy:

GENTLEMEN:

Your Committee appointed at the regular meeting of the Board, held May 4th, 1882, to form Quiz Classes, under the supervision of the Alumni Association, would respectfully report that the Senior Quiz Class was duly organized at the commencement of the course, October 4th, 1882, and have been continued every Wednesday afternoon to date, and have proved very successful, both *financially* and in numbers.

Sixty-seven of the Senior Class made application and received their tickets, and upon their graduation in the College will become active members of the Association.

The Junior Quiz Class was duly organized on Thursday afternoon, October 5th, 1882, under the personal supervision of Mr. Henry Trimble, one of our Committee.

Only fifteen of the Juniors availed themselves of this opportunity to receive that necessary information which will be of so much use to them in their examination, on the 15th of this month, notwithstanding the tickets were put at the small sum of $5.00 each.

The amount received from the sale of the sixty-seven Senior Quiz tickets was $670.00, and from the fifteen Junior Quiz Tickets $75.00, making a total of $745.00.

The two Senior Quiz Masters will receive, as per agreement, $335.00, and the Junior Quiz Master, $75.00.

The expense of the Committee for printing tickets and circulars amounted to about $25.00, netting to the Association $310.00 clear of all expenses.

Respectfully submitted,

THOS. H. POTTS, *President,*
EDWARD C. JONES, *Treasurer,*
WM. E. KREWSON, *Secretary,*
HENRY TRIMBLE,
JACOB S. BEETEM,

Committee.

Mr. Henry Trimble moved that the report be received and spread on the minutes. So ordered.

Mr. Edward C. Jones then read the Report of the Committee appointed at the last meeting to give a microscopical exhibition during the holidays, as follows:

Philadelphia, Feb. 1st, 1883.

To the Executive Board:

The Committee appointed by the Executive Board to give a public microscopical exhibition during the holidays, respectfully report:

That there was held such a soiree on the evening of Thursday, Dec. 28th, 1882.

We had the use of fifteen microscopes, and were shown the following objects, viz: Foot of a spider, tongue of blow-fly, gizzard of cricket, section of clematis stem, section of blackberry stem, section of rosebush, section of black snakeroot, kinate of quinia, tartaric acid, crystals of gold, silver and copper, section of pine, aspharagin and phloridzin.

At the close of this entertainment, the company were invited up-stairs, and, through the kindness of Prof. Sadtler, were shown views of travels, process of making glass, iron and ice; crystals of· different chemicals, etc.

The Committee would return thanks to those gentlemen who loaned slides and microscopes, and trust this small beginning in this important research may stimulate all to the study and use of the microscope, and the sociability may make us feel that we have something more to enjoy than the confinement of the business of our stores.

Respectfully submitted,

A. P. Brown,
Dr. A. W. Miller,
Edward C. Jones,
Committee.

The Secretary moved that the Report be received and spread on the minutes, and the Committee be discharged. So ordered.

Mr. Trimble asked to be excused, in order that he might attend to his duties as Quiz Master to the Juniors, who were in waiting in the next room, which was granted.

The Report of the Committee appointed to represent the Alumni Association at the meeting of the American Pharmaceutical Association, held at Niagara Falls, September, 1882, was read by Mr. Jones, as follows:

Athens, Ga., Nov. 27th, 1882.

To the Executive Board:

The Thirtieth Annual Meeting of the American Pharmaceutical Association, was held at Niagara Falls, September 12th, 13th, 14th and 15th, 1882, in the Assembly Room of the Cataract House. Three members of the Committee appointed were present, viz: Messrs. G. W. Kennedy, Wm. Weber and Joe Jacobs. The Chair appointed Mr. Henry Trimble, of Philadelphia, and * * * * * in lieu of the two absent, (Messrs. John A. Witmer and Ed. S. Dawson).

The address of welcome by the local Secretary, Mr. Hiram E. Griffith, was brief, but cordial. Following this was the annual address by the President, Prof. P. W. Bedford, of New York, which contained a number of valuable suggestions, and its reading was listened to with marked attention.

Many circumstances contributed to the success of the meeting.

The papers read were eminently practical, and some of them evinced much labor devoted to their production, making this meeting, in this respect, one of the most important so far held. The result of delegating executive business, in a large degree, and the arrangement of entertainments entirely to Special Committees in practice was wise and satisfactory, the disappointments attending the latter feature of the meeting were undoubtedly owing less to the lack of forethought on the part of the Committee than to the shortcomings of the hotel proprietors.

At the second session, Chas. A. Heinitsh, of Lancaster, Pa., was elected President; John Ingalls, of Macon, Ga., First Vice-President, Louis Dohme, Baltimore, Md., Second Vice-President, and Wm. B. Blanding, of Providence, R. I., Third Vice-President.

A very fine exhibition of chemicals, drugs, pharmaceutical implements and of curiosities having a relation to pharmacy, had been arranged in the large pavilion in Prospect Park. The display proved attractive and instructive.

The entire meeting passed off harmoniously, proving a source of pleasure and profit to all who attended.

4

Washington, D. C., was selected as the place of the next meeting, on the second Tuesday of September, 1883.

Respectfully submitted,

> JOE JACOBS, *Chairman*,
> GEO. W. KENNEDY,
> WM. WEBER,
> HENRY TRIMBLE,
> *Committee.*

On motion of the Secretary, the report was accepted and ordered spread on the minutes, and the Committee discharged, with the thanks of the Board.

New Business:

The Secretary stated that he had received a postal card from Mr. W. C. Bakes, Secretary of the Board of Trustees, stating that the Annual Commencement would be held on Friday, March 16th, 1883.

The Secretary then moved that the Nineteenth Annual Meeting of the Alumni Association be held on Wednesday afternoon, March 14th, 1883, at 2½ o'clock, in the Alumni Room, and that the Nineteenth Annual Reception to the Graduating Class be held on the same evening, at 8 o'clock, P. M. So ordered.

The Secretary reported that he had received the following acknowledgments from those who had received the Eighteenth Annual Report:

From the Pharmaceutical Society, No. 17 Bloomsbury Square, London, Elias Bremridge, Secretary.

Also, the following Reports:

Transactions South Carolina Medical Association, 1882.

Proceedings of Third Annual Meeting of Illinois State Pharmaceutical Association, held at Chicago, Ill., Oct. 10-12, 1882.

Proceedings of the First and Second Conventions of the Western Wholesale Drug Association, Dec. 7th and 8th, 1880, and Nov. 9th and 10th, 1881.

Proceedings of the Convention of Druggists, and First Annual Meeting of the Massachusetts Phar. Asso., held at Worcester, Mass., May 17th, 1882.

Proceedings Wisconsin State Pharmaceutical Association, held at Oshkosh, Wis., Aug. 8th–10th, 1882.

Also, the first six copies of *The Druggists' Circular*, edited by our First Vice-President, L. E. Sayre.

The Secretary also stated he had received a communication from Wm. L. Mactier, Secretary of the Board of Trustees of the Presbyterian Hospital, requesting a full set of our Reports, which he had sent him. On motion, the action of the Secretary was sustained.

The Secretary stated that he had received the following communication, which he read:

Tenth and Coates St., Philadelphia, 11, 3, '82,

DEAR SIR:

I have on hand nearly a full line of specimens, both botanical and chemical, which I will willingly give to the Alumni Association, if you will tell me when and where to send them. Respectfully,

> F. W. E. STEDEM.

He further stated that Mr. Stedem is a member of the last Graduating Class of 1882, and that the specimens were in the possession of the Alumni.

Mr. E. C. Jones moved that a vote of thanks be tendered to Mr. Stedem, which was unanimously carried.

The following bills were presented, after being approved by the President and Secretary:

Craig, Finley & Co.—

Nov. 8th, 1882. For 300 postals, composition and printing, for second Social Meeting, .		$4 75
" composition and printing 3000 specimen blanks, ...		7 50
11th, " " composition and printing 100 postal cards, ...		1 75
Dec. 5th, " " composition and printing 300 postal cards for third Social Meeting, .		4 75
6th, " ". composition and printing 1000 gummed labels, ...		2 00
21st, " " composition and printing 400 postal cards for microscopical exhibition,		6 00
28th, " . " composition and printing 300 postal cards, fourth Social Meeting, .		4 75
Feb. 1st, 1883, " composition and printing 450 postal cards, fifth Social Meeting, . .		6 00
		$37 50

Jas. W. Queen & Co.—

Nov. 14th, 1882. For 5 turn-tables, ...	11 00	
" 1 gross smooth slides, . . .	2 50	
" 1 ounce $\frac{11}{16}$th circles, No. 2, . .	2 25	
		15 75

C. R. Morgan—

Dec. 20th, 1882. For reporting second and third Social Meetings, ...	10 00	
Jan. 27th, 1883. For reporting fourth Social Meeting, .	5 00	
		15 00

Edwin Morgan—

Dec. 28th, 1882. For composition and printing 100 cards for microscopical exhibition, . .	1 50

Aschenbach & Miller—

Jan. 11th, 1883. For 1 copy U. S. Pharmacopœia for 1880, in sheep, nett, ...	4 00

Secretary—

Feb. 1st, 1883. For postage and incidentals, . . .	3 62

T. H. McCool—

Feb. 1st, 1883. To filling in 13 membership certificates, @ 30 cts., ...	3 90

A. P. Brown—

Jan. 29th, 1883. To 12 scholars instructed in microscopy, @ $5 00, ...	60 00

Making a total of, ...	$141 72

The Secretary moved that the bills be paid. So ordered.

The following applications for membership were received and read:

Chas. N. Riggs, Class 1882, S. W. cor. Eighteenth and Chestnut Sts., Philadelphia.

Wm. C. Dockstader, Class 1880, Montclair, N. J.

C. B. Clapp, Class 1882, Danville, Vermilion Co., Ill.

The Secretary stated that they had all paid the necessary fee, and had received their Certificates of Membership.

The Secretary announced the death of Chas. Wm. Elkins, Class of 1880, who died at the residence of his parents, No. 2038 Frankford avenue, on Wednesday, November 1st, 1882, in the twenty-fifth year of his age, of consumption. Mr. Elkins joined the Association November 16th, 1881, and further stated that the Committee on Deceased Members would furnish the proper obituary.

The Secretary stated that the funds in the hands of the Trustee of the Sinking Fund were exhausted, and it would be necessary for the Board to take some action in reference to procuring the Alumni gold medal.

Mr. Jacob S. Beetem moved that Mr. T. S. Wiegand be authorized to have the usual gold medal struck off, to be presented to the member of the Graduating Class receiving the highest general average, and that he call upon the Treasurer of the Association for the amount necessary to defray such expense. The motion was seconded and carried.

It was moved and seconded that a Committee of two be appointed on Annual Reception, and to procure the usual prizes. So ordered.

The Chair appointed Edward C. Jones and Wm. E. Krewson as the Committee.

Mr. J. S. Beetem moved that the Secretary be authorized to have the Certificates of Membership filled up for the members of the Senior Quiz Class, who successfully pass the final examination in March next. So ordered.

There being no further business, on motion, the Board adjourned.

Attest,   WM. E. KREWSON,

Secretary.

Minutes of the Social Meetings.

FIRST MEETING.

Hall of the Philadelphia College of Pharmacy,
No. 145 N. 10th Street,
Tuesday Afternoon, Oct. 10th, 1882.

The First Social Meeting of the Alumni Association of the Philadelphia College of Pharmacy, was held this afternoon, in the Museum of the College, with an attendance of forty-two members and students.

The President, Thos. H. Potts, called the meeting to order at quarter of four, P. M., with a few well chosen remarks, inviting the co-operation of the students and others present in maintaining the Social Meetings during the present winter, and calling attention to the Junior and Senior Quiz Classes and the Class in Microscopy, all of which are under the auspices of the Alumni Association.

He then introduced Dr. A. W. Miller, Ph. G., of the Class of 1862, and Chairman of the Committee on Social Meetings, who read a paper on

"Emoluments of Pharmacy," which was listened to with marked attention. After which he read several extracts from various newspapers to the amusement of those present.

The President then introduced Mr. Lucius E. Sayre, who made a few remarks upon the paper read by Dr. Miller, and invited the students and those present to a discussion of the subject, which was participated in by Mr. Evan T. Ellis, Wm. H. Barr, Jr., Mr. R. F. Finck, Dr. Miller and the President.

Mr. Sayre then read a paper on "The Use of Ammonia in Baking Powder," which was attentively listened to by the audience.

Dr. Miller made a few remarks upon the paper, after which he exhibited a specimen of crystals deposited from distilling oil of white cedar. He then read a selection entitled the "Lawyer and the Cat," which was heartily enjoyed by those in attendance.

Dr. Miller then read his paper, entitled "The Attacks of the Press on Druggists."

Mr. Sayre introduced Mr. A. P. Brown, who made a few remarks in reference to the analysis of urine.

Dr. Miller then read an amusing piece from choice selections, by Phineus Garrett, which was enjoyed by those present.

The Secretary moved that a vote of thanks be extended to Dr. Miller, Mr. L. E. Sayre and Mr. A. P. Brown, for their services in making the meeting so interesting, which was duly seconded and carried.

Mr. Genois and Mr. Sayre read several amusing extracts from newspapers, which were heartily enjoyed.

The President then announced that the Senior Quiz Class would be held hereafter every Wednesday afternoon, from 2 to 3 o'clock, by Mr. L. E. Sayre, and 5¼ to 6¼ o'clock, by Mr. Louis Genois, instead of from 2 to 4 o'clock, as heretofore.

He also announced that the next Social Meeting would be held on Tuesday afternoon, November 14th, 1882, at 3 o'clock, and Dr. Chas. L. Mitchell, of the Class of 1872, would deliver a lecture on "The Germ Theory."

On motion of the Secretary, the meeting adjourned.

Attest,   WM. E. KREWSON,
                                                  Secretary.

SECOND MEETING.

Hall of the Philadelphia College of Pharmacy,
No. 145 N. Tenth St.,
Tuesday Afternoon, Nov. 14th, 1882.

The Second Social Meeting of the Alumni Association of the Philadelphia College of Pharmacy was held this afternoon in the museum of the College.

The meeting was called to order at a quarter to 4 o'clock, P. M., by the President, Thos. H. Potts, with fifty members and students present.

The President then excused himself from presiding this afternoon, and invited Dr. A. W. Miller, Chairman of the Committee on Social Meetings, to take his place.

Dr. A. W. Miller then took the chair, and called for the reading of the minutes of the last Social Meeting.

The Secretary then read the minutes, which were approved.

The President *pro tem.* called the attention of those present to the book for registering the names of all those in attendance. He then called upon Mr. Robt. F. Finck, a member of the Senior Class, who gave an original selection, entitled "A Reminiscence," which was listened to attentively by those present.

Dr. Miller made a few remarks, explanatory of a materia medica specimen box which he had invented some years ago for the use of pharmaceutical and medical students for the better preservation of specimens, also the label, with blank spaces, for the officinal and botanical names, natural order, dose, etc., of the specimens, samples of which he distributed among those present.

The Chairman then introduced Miss F. Lizzie Pierce, the distinguished teacher of elocution, who gave a recitation, entitled "The Swiss Good-Night," which was received with marks of high approbation, and, upon receiving an *encore*, she recited "The Bugle Song," which was likewise well received.

The President *pro tem.* then expressed his thanks, as well as those of the entire meeting, to Miss Pierce for her magnificent performance.

Dr. Miller then announced that, as in previous years, the Committee had prepared specimens in the same manner as they would have them placed before them in the eventful month of March for recognition.

They were as follows :

No. 1. Tinctura Lobeliæ.
" 2. Vinum Ipecacuanhæ.
" 3. Acidum Phosphoricum Dilutum.
" 4. Tinctura Gentianæ Composita.
No. 5. Extractum Taraxaci Fluidum.
" 6. Pulvis Jalapæ Compositus.
" 7. Ammonii Bromidum.
" 8. Zinci Oxidum.
" 9. Belladonnæ Folia, English.
" 10. Hyoscyamus, "

The specimens were then handed to the students.

Dr. Miller then announced that some weeks ago he was advised, as Chairman of the Social Meetings, that Dr. Mitchell was willing to deliver a lecture on the "Germ Theory" at one of our Social Meetings, and he wrote to him, asking him whether it would suit him this afternoon to give the lecture at this meeting, and he received an affirmative reply; but, on Friday last, he received a letter from him, which he read as follows :

Nov. 9th, 1882.

Dr. A. W. MILLER, *Chairman Entertainment Committee*
Alumni Association, P. C. P.

DEAR SIR :

I have just learned, through a number of the *American Journal of Pharmacy*, that my lecture next Tuesday is to constitute a part only of the programme, and is to be accompanied by an elocutionary entertainment. This arrangement is quite a surprise to me, and not at all agreeable, and as I feel that I have, perhaps, mistaken the character of the exercises, I would prefer not to lecture upon the occasion named.

I am, etc., yours, respectfully,

CHAS. L. MITCHELL.

Dr. Miller further stated that when he received the above letter he acknowledged it to Dr. Mitchell, and succeeded in prevailing upon a friend of his to deliver a substitute of that lecture on the same subject.

He then introduced Dr. Louis J. Lautenbach, Ph. D., who delivered a very interesting discourse on the "Germ Theory," which was listened to attentively by the audience.

The President *pro tem.*, then announced that he had been handed a prescription which was actually presented at the store of one of the members of the Alumni Association a few days ago. It consisted of twelve different articles, and was written in very fine Latin, and he would read it, showing the absurdity of combining so many remedies.

The prescription read as follows:

> R Potassii Bromidii, ℥ii.
> Ammonii Bromidii, ℥i.
> Hydrarg: Bichloridi, gr.i.
> Aq. Cinnamoni, ℥iv.
> Tinctura Aloes.
> " Rhei, āā ℥ij.
> " Verat Viridis.
> Elix. Bismuthi Sub Nitratis.
> "   Lactopeptin, āā ℥i.
> "   Cinchonæ, ℥i.
> Tinctura Hyoscyami.
> Liq. Potassii Arsenitis, āā ℥ij.

Fiat Mistura.
Signa: Take a teaspoonful in water after each meal.

Dr. Miller remarked he wished them to remember that there was twelve different articles, and each one of them for a different complaint. The name of the physician was suppressed.

Dr. Miller then called the attention of those present to the request of the Alumni Association for specimens for the Alumni Museum, and assured those who might contribute that they would be thankfully received.

The students were then requested to give the names of the specimens which were handed around early in the meeting, which was done.

Mr. David W. Ross moved that the thanks of the meeting be extended to Miss Pierce, Dr. Lautenbach and Mr. Finck, for their attendance and the manner which they had entertained us this afternoon, which was duly seconded and unanimously agreed to.

The President *pro tem.* then announced that the next Social Meeting would be held on Tuesday afternoon, December 12th, 1882, at 3 o'clock, P. M., and requested the attendance of all those present on that occasion.

On motion, the meeting adjourned.

Attest,   WM. E. KREWSON,
                 Secretary.

THIRD MEETING.

Hall of the Philadelphia College of Pharmacy,
No. 145 N. 10th Street,
Tuesday, Dec. 12th, 1882.

The Third Social Meeting of the Alumni Association of the Philadelphia College of Pharmacy, was held this afternoon, in the Museum of the College.

The meeting was called to order at half-past 3 o'clock, P. M., by the President, Thos. H. Potts, with seventy-five members and students present.

On account of the absence of the Secretary at the opening of the meeting, the reading of the minutes of the last meeting were omitted.

The President, in calling the meeting to order, announced that this was the third of the Social Meetings of the Association for this course, calling the attention of those present to the different subjects that would be presented this afternoon.

He then introduced Prof. John E. Cook, Ph. G., of the Class of 1873, and an active member of the Association, who delivered an interesting lecture on Weights and Measures, which was attentively listened to by those present. (See Weights and Measures.)

After the conclusion of Mr. Cook's lecture, Dr. A. W. Miller introduced Prof. Stephen L. Adams, the Teacher of Elocution, who recited " The Apothecary," which was received with great applause, and after being encored, he again came forward, and gave a humorous recitation, entitled " Giving the Old Man the Royal Bumper Degree."

Dr. Miller then read a communication from Dr. C. C. Vanderbeck, Professor of Hygiene at the Wagner Free Institute, expressing his willingness to lecture before the Alumni Association at the next meeting in January, on the subject, " The Anchors of Health ; or, Good Health, How to Get It and How to Keep It."

The President then stated that the discussion would now take place, on the " New Pharmacopœia."

Mr. L. E. Sayre opened the discussion with extended remarks, and was followed by Dr. A. W. Miller, Ph. G., Dr. Lawrence Trumbull, Ph. G., Dr. F. E. Stewart, Ph. G., Messrs. Wm. McIntyre, Ph. G., Wallace Procter, Ph. G., Andrew Blair, Ph. G., C. Carroll Meyer, Ph. G., and others, occupying upwards of one hour in the discussion.

Mr. L. E. Sayre then moved that Prof. Adams be invited to give another reading. Agreed to.

Prof. Adams then came forward and recited a humorous piece, which was received with great applause.

Dr. Miller called the attention of those present to the auction sale of fancy goods, belonging to the estate of the late M. A. Fritsche, at his store, on Chestnut street, particularly the specimens of malachite and other articles, advising the students to inspect the same.

Dr. Miller moved a vote of thanks be extended to Prof. Adams for his entertaining recitations, which was unanimously agreed to.

After a few remarks from Mr. E. T. Ellis and Dr. Miller, upon the publication of the *Dispensatory* in this city, the meeting adjourned.

Attest,   WM. E. KREWSON,
                                                Secretary.

FOURTH MEETING.

Hall of the Philadelphia College of Pharmacy,
No. 145 N. Tenth St.,
Tuesday, Jan. 9th, 1883.

The fourth of the series of Social Meetings under the auspices of the Alumni Association was held this afternoon in the museum of the College.

The meeting was called to order by the President, Thos. H. Potts, at a quarter to 4, P. M., with forty-five members and students present.

The Secretary read the minutes of the last Social Meeting, which were approved.

The President announced that the subjects for discussion this afternoon would be the conclusion of the lecture on Weights and Measures, by Prof. Cook, followed by a lecture by Prof. C. C. Vanderbeck, M. D., on " The Anchors of Health ; or, Good Health, How to Get It, and How to Keep It," after this a discussion would take place upon the Spiritus and Wines of the New Pharmacopœia.

He then introduced Prof. John E. Cook, who gave an interesting lecture on Weights and Measures, which was a continuation of the lecture delivered by him at the Social Meeting in December, dwelling particularly upon the *metre*, giving a brief historical account of the introduction and adoption of the same.

The lecture was attentively listened to and appreciated by those present.

The President then announced that the next on the programme was the lecture by Prof. Vanderbeck, and requested Dr. A. W. Miller to introduce him, which he did in a few well-chosen remarks.

Prof. Vanderbeck then came forward, and delivered his lecture on "The Anchors of Health, How to Get It, and How to Keep It," which occupied about three-quarters of an hour in its delivery, and was very attentively listened to and enjoyed by all those present.

After the close of the address, Dr. Miller made a few remarks, and thought the lecture contained so many suggestions that it might be profitable to discuss them.

Several of those present spoke upon the various points touched upon by the lecturer, among which was the subject of over-work by the students of brain and muscle in preparing for examination, also the profits in the drug business, and attention was called to the article in the *Ledger* in reference to the report of a meeting of the Drug Trade Association of this city, which was held in this room a few days ago.

The President stated that the next Social Meeting would be held in this room on Tuesday afternoon, Feb. 13th, and it would be the last one of the series, and cordially invited all those in attendance this afternoon to be present.

Dr. Miller announced that Dr. Lawrence Turnbull, a graduate of this College, of the Class of 1842, had promised to be present at the next meeting, and deliver a lecture upon "The Therapeutics of the New Pharmacopœia."

He also announced that Prof. Carl Seiler, M. D., would deliver a lecture before the Pharmaceutical Meeting in this room next Tuesday afternoon.

On motion, a vote of thanks was tendered to Prof. Vanderbeck for his interesting lecture, which was carried unanimously.

The Chairman then announced that the discussion on the Spiritus and Wines of the New Pharmacopœia was now in order.

Dr. Miller suggested that this discussion be postponed until the next meeting, which was agreed to.

Mr. A. P. Brown then exhibited a machine for making gelatine-coated pills.

It was invented by Mr. Wm. C. Franciscus, of Lock Haven, Pa., and a member of the Senior Class of this College.

Mr. Brown stated he had one called the Porcupine machine, which was similar to this, and that this morning he had coated 1,800 pills in a very satisfactory manner.

Mr. Hancock also gave an interesting account of his experience with the same kind of a machine.

Mr. Sayre made a motion that the thanks of this meeting be extended to Prof. Cook, for his valuable lecture of last month and also this month, which was duly seconded and unanimously carried, and as Mr. Cook was not present, the Secretary was requested to inform him.

On motion, the meeting adjourned.

Attest, WM. E. KREWSON,
Secretary.

Hall of the Philadelphia College of Pharmacy,
145 N. 10th Street,
Tuesday, Feb. 13th, 1883.

The Fifth and last Social Meeting of the Alumni Association was held this afternoon, in the Museum of the College, with 107 members, students and visitors present.

In the absence of the President and Vice-Presidents, the Secretary called the meeting to order at quarter to 4, P. M.

The reading of the minutes of the last meeting was omitted.

The Secretary then introduced Dr. Lawrence Turnbull, Ph. G., of the Class of 1842, who delivered a lecture on the New Pharmacopœia (1880), with some points on Therapeutics. The lecture was very interesting, and attentively listened to by the audience.

At the conclusion of the lecture, Dr. A. W. Miller, Chairman of the Committee on Social Meetings, having arrived, took the chair and made a few remarks, saying that it was customary to discuss the subject when important papers were read, especially such as the one we had just listened to. "A great many interesting topics have been touched upon, and we will be glad to have a few remarks from any one who will favor us." He further stated "that in reference to the Class of Abstracts, of which we have heard so much this afternoon, he would call upon the author or originator of this Class (abstracts), who is present, and would be glad to hear from him concerning a few of the points involved in this important paper."

Prof. Jos. P. Remington then made some very interesting remarks upon the paper just read, and also spoke of the New Pharmacopœia of 1880 and of the criticisms of the same, after which the Chairman, Dr. Miller, endorsed what the former speaker had said, and stated that there was still some time left for any one else who wished to be heard.

Mr. Louis Genois having been called for, made a few pertinent remarks upon the subject, after further remarks by the Chairman and several of the students present.

Dr. Miller called upon Miss F. Lizzie Pierce, the Teacher in Elocution, who recited "Uncle Reuben's Baptism," which was received with a great deal of merriment, and being encored, recited the boy's composition on "Girls."

Dr. Miller then read a short paper upon Spts. Vini Gallici. He also handed around specimens of Holland gin, whiskey and rectified spirits prepared by himself.

Mr. Robert England moved that a vote of thanks be extended to Dr. Turnbull for his able address, which was duly seconded and carried unanimously.

Mr. Turnbull then made a few remarks upon the American Wines.

The Secretary then moved that a vote of thanks be tendered to Miss F. Lizzie Pierce for the recitations given, which was seconded and unanimously agreed to.

Dr. Miller announced that Dr. W. S. W. Ruschenberger, a life-long friend of the late Prof. Robert Bridges, and a member of the Centennial Commission, was present, and that we would be glad to hear from him.

Dr. Ruschenberger declined to make any remarks, on account of suffering from a severe cold.

Dr. Miller then exhibited to those present a large old-fashioned relic, it being a mortar made out of bell metal, which had been presented to the

College by a friend of Prof. Bridges, and his name engraved thereon. He further remarked that no doubt it had resounded in former years to the delight of many a student.

The Secretary stated that this was the last Social Meeting of the Alumni Association for this session.

The Chairman then thanked the students and others present for their attendance and the interest they had taken in the meetings during the winter.

· There being no further business, on motion the meeting adjourned.

Attest,   WM. E. KREWSON,
                                                    Secretary.

OPENING REMARKS

OF THE

PRESIDENT, THOS. H. POTTS,

At the First Social Meeting of the Alumni Association, held in the Museum of the College, Tuesday afternoon, Oct. 10th, 1883.

The President called the meeting to order, and spoke as follows :

GENTLEMEN :

As you are probably aware, this is the first of our Social Meetings for this session, and that they will be held hereafter on the afternoon of the second Tuesday in each month during the College Session.

The Alumni Association viewed with great pleasure the success of similar meetings, which were held in this College during last winter, and anticipate still greater success for the coming ones.

It seems to me to be an appropriate time to remind the students that are present, and who, no doubt, hope to become members of the Alumni in the near future, that it is to them we look for the successful issue of these meetings, and we trust they will lend us their presence, as well as those of their friends whom they may wish to invite.

I would also call your attention to the Quizzes, Senior and Junior, and the Class on Microscopy, instituted under the auspices of the Alumni Association, and trust you may make it convenient to give them your attention.

They were not created merely to make financial profit out of, but to promote the advancement of the students in those branches in which he is particularly interested.

EMOLUMENTS OF PHARMACY.

A Paper read by Dr. A. W. Miller, Ph. G., Class of 1862, at First Social Meeting, held Tuesday, Oct. 18th, 1882 :

Complaints, loud and persistent, are heard on all sides, that our profession is from year to year becoming less and less profitable. Statements so frequently repeated, and coming simultaneously from widely separated sections of our country, are worthy of credence, and hence they deserve our attention. To what causes shall we attribute this decadence of the profits of legitimate pharmacy ?

It is not generally asserted that the volume of business has diminished ; on the contrary, in very many localities this appears to be continually on the increase. Neither does there seem to be any marked difference in the profits realized in the compounding of prescriptions, nor in the sale of those drugs which are used as medicines.

On the other hand, drugs used in the arts are probably sold on closer margins than formerly, as we find in all the larger cities numerous establishments, whose sole business it is to supply drugs for technical purposes, as for instance dyers' materials, butchers', painters' and confectioners' supplies, photographers' chemicals, etc. Another important factor is undoubtedly the unprecedented increase in the use of proprietary articles, on which the average rate of profit to the retailer is not more than one-third of their selling price, while on drugs in general it will probably average double this ratio. We are forced to admit the existence of both these causes that tend to perpetuate the poverty of the proverbially " poor apothecary," but, unfortunately, they are both beyond any remedy that we can supply.

We cannot extirpate the technical warehouses, neither can we free the masses of the people from the heavy chains of superstitition, nor from the gullibility with which they swallow every new compound that is offered them. Alas ! the proverb of old, "*Mundus vult decipi, ergo decipiatur*," is but too true ; the world wants to be deceived, therefore it is deceived. We all know to our sorrow that even many highly educated physicians are readily taken in by the walking advertisers of elixirs, sugar-coated pellets, fluid extracts of Feejee Island herbs, and other elegant specialties. While the general public is treated to endless newspaper puffs and certificates of miraculous cures, interspersed with gorgeous show cards and marvelous fence paintings, the physicians are catered with profuse samples and the blandishments of the smooth-tongued travelling salesman. Not being able to cure either of these ills, we must endure them with as much patience and fortitude as we can command. But are those the only causes for the scanty rewards of pharmaceutical skill, or are there others that may, perhaps, be obviated by remedies intelligently applied?

The *Public Ledger*, of Philadelphia, in its issue of August 3d, 1882, in an article on " Co-operative Stores," makes the following statements : " In the aggregate these English establishments divided last year to their *purchasers* nearly ten per cent. on the gross amount of their *sales*. This is equal to sixty per cent. on the share capital ; a much larger per cent. than the private tradesman realizes, the greater profit arising from the fact that the co-operative stores are not required to go to any expense to get or retain custom, and that their business is so regular that they need suffer very little from dead stock. The sales to more than a half a million members amounted in 1880 to one hundred million dollars. These are not estimates, but the figures given in returns to the Government of actual business."

Without desiring to advocate co-operative pharmacies, the only reason assigned for the higher profits realized by these stores over private establishments, merits our most careful consideration. It is, in brief, the cutting off of a most important and wasteful drain on legitimate business, namely, the advertising expenses ordinarily indulged in for obtaining and retaining custom. The delusion which is so zealously fostered by every newspaper in the country, that in order to succeed in life, each merchant must vie with every other to outstrip every competitor in lavish expenditures for advertising, has fastened itself like a vampire on the productive industry of the land, draining its very life-blood. The present methods of conducting business are beyond all question entirely too profuse in their expenditures. First and foremost amongst these unnecessary expenses are the enormous sums consumed by the swarms of travelling salesmen which are now regularly kept on the road by most of the wholesale druggists and manufacturers of pharmaceutical specialties. The sums thus expended are out of all reason to the net·profit realized on the sales thus made, yet the salesmen are regarded as indispensable adjuncts to business, which without them could not increase. And yet the question may be fairly asked, do the combined efforts of all the salesmen in the United States increase the annual amount of business one single cent? Do they not rather actually retard business by forcing goods on reluctant buyers, which the latter subsequently find themselves unable to pay for?

Again, the immense outlays for advertisements in the daily papers, or in medical and pharmaceutical journals, most of which live merely on the revenue derived from their advertising sheets is just so much money thrown away. In the same category may be ranked the luxurious trade catalogues, got up regardless of expense. as well as the chromo cards and the decorative plaques donated by less pretentious establishments to their patrons. It may be difficult to suggest a feasible remedy, and in fact it is necessary first to fairly recognize the enormity of the evil before we can undertake to correct it. The fact cannot be disputed, that we should all do just as much business if salesmen and advertisements of all kinds were forever banished. This remark, of course, does not apply to patent medicines, but only to a legitimate trade in drugs and pharmaceutical preparations. The community requires these, as well as that long list comprised under the generic title of "Druggist's Sundries," and if they are not forced on the customer he will seek for them of his own accord.

Now, as to the retailer, he may flatter himself that he does not pay the extravagant salary and expenses of the salesman. It is equally true that, in all probability, the entire profit on his whole order will not amount to one-half of the money actually paid to the salesman for the time consumed in taking it. But would it not richly pay both purchaser and seller to dispense with the superfluous go-between? The wholesale dealer would certainly gladly sell to a purchaser who had assured him that he had firmly resolved to abstain absolutely from giving orders to useless middlemen for just one-half the usual margin. That one-half would then fairly represent a profit, while under the present system it is all absorbed by the salesman. Even if the pharmacist paid precisely the same prices in purchasing direct, he would still be abundantly repaid in the saving of valuable time now wasted in warding off the importunities of the ubiquitous salesman. This desirable object could be very readily accomplished by the display of a little sign bearing the inscription, "No Goods Purchased from Salesmen." A mute reference thereto would prove far more eloquent than words.

It would, indeed, be found to be a very valuable calculation to ascertain how much ready money is annually absorbed from the productive industries of the United States by the countless swarms of travelling salesmen who, in reality, are just so many drones that have to be supported by the workers, be they buyers or sellers.

Another evil consequence of this system of having salesmen continually on the lookout for new customers, is the facility of starting in business, and thus unduly increasing the number of stores in a given locality. Young men find it comparatively easy to start on stock eagerly furnished by competing salesmen. Having nothing to lose, they are comparatively indifferent to the success of their enterprise. In order to procure ready cash, they

are but too prone to sell standard articles below established prices, thus in-
flicting a double injury on those of their legitimate competitors, who pay
their honest debts promptly, " without defalcation or discount."

In conclusion, it may not be amiss to allude to the commissions paid
to physicians by many pharmacists, one of the severest and most cruel
drains of the poor apothecary.   We all know that this evil exists in spite of
all medical and pharmaceutical codes of ethics to the contrary.   Still, those
who are weak enough to submit to this species of extortion, deserve, in
place of our sympathy, the severest condemnation for the disgrace they
bring on the profession and the frauds they practice on the public.

In connection with the above paper the following discussion took place :

Dr. Miller continuing, said :

When I was in St. Louis the other day I picked up a paper and found
therein an advertisement which seemed to coincide so entirely with my
views that I tore it from the sheet, and as it has a direct bearing upon the
subject, I will take the liberty of reading it,

He then read an advertisement of a grocery firm, after which he said :

The grocery business runs into a much larger amount of money than
the drug business.   My own experience, and I believe it will coincide with
that of all my friends, is that the expense of selling drugs through a salesman is about ten per cent., to say nothing about the stock sold through the
intermediate salesman.

I have another extract from a salesman here.   I do not know what
paper it is from.   I have had it for some time.   It nevertheless has a very
important bearing upon the point that I am endeavoring to make.

He then read the extract.

The President then introduced Mr. Sayre as follows :

I merely wish to introduce to you a gentleman whom I have no doubt
is well known to most of the graduates of this College, and one of the
Alumni.   I have the same to say of him as I have said with regard to Dr.
Miller.   I refer to Mr. L. E. Sayre.

Mr. Sayre then arose and said :

The remarks of our worthy Chairman are entirely unexpected to me.
I have to read a paper—I am put down on the programme for that service ;
but previous to reading it I would say that it is our custom to discuss the
papers as they are presented, and as this should excite no little discussion,
I think that it would be a pleasure for us to hear from some of the members
of this Class.   I have my eyes upon a few young men that I know are competent to express themselves and probably can do so.

Now, this article as published has probably three or four points concerning it, and I think we can take up only one ; that is the travelling salesman.   Is it desirable to dispense with the intermediate man ?   Is he a useless person ?

Now let us hear the subject of advertising in the papers and the
starting of young men in business on no capital, and all that sort of thing.
I feel myself that the idea of starting in business on borrowed capital is a
poor policy.   There is no question about that; and possibly there are others
who would be willing to stock a young man so that they would have an

opportunity of seizing on him in case he would get into a bad fix; and that if there were less going into business on no capital at all these salaries of clerks would advance. We are continually told by the clerks that they get so very little money for the labor; but the fact is that there are so many stores started by new persons that it is impossible for them to employ a clerk, and if they do at all they get one at a very moderate salary. I think that if we would concentrate business more it would be better for the clerks and better for all hands all round. Let us ask the question whether it is better to dispense with the salesman. I think that there is another side of this question. Is not the salesman a valuable man? Let him like every other tub stand on his own bottom. When we see a man, as the salesman, making three and four thousand dollars a year, and even more, under an arrangement of this kind—that he will go into a house and sell goods on commission; that this house agrees to share with him the legitimate profit—if that house makes so much, for example, it is so much the better for him. In other words, is not there a value to these men from the trade they bring? I claim, sir, that the intermediate salesman is a valuable one. If I had a preparation to introduce, I should select a man who is wide awake, and I would possibly give him a good salary. I should say, "Here, my success is with yours. I am perfectly willing to share with you. If you can create a demand for this article worth ten thousand dollars a year, I will share with you the profits." If the sales of my goods amount to ten thousand dollars a year, I give it over to him most gratefully, and am glad of it. It only shows the value of these men. Now, let us hear Dr. Miller, who I have no doubt will knock the pins from under my feet with the final argument. Let us hear from the Class and have an expression. I have no doubt that many of these young men—in fact, the most of them—may enlist themselves in this department, and I do not wish to discourage them at the outset. I claim, sir, that the intermediate man is a valuable one.

Mr. Evan T. Ellis made the following remarks:

Mr. President, I can only give a little experience. In my own house, the house of Charles Ellis, we never employed them. About the year 1865, I think it was, I told my father that we should either have to employ salesmen or else go out of business; that the times had changed; that everything was done in that way. My father replied that he did not like it; that he thought our ways of doing business in our store and our stock ought to bring customers. I then dropped the matter, knowing that it was useless to say anything further. The business was continued on until 1875, when we went out of business. The result was that we retained a larger volume of the old business than any house of the country; we had customers that all the drummers of the United States could not get away from us as our friends. But you know our customers would die, and then too they would go out of business. The consequence was we were left with a decreasing trade; so much so that after my father's death I felt called upon to give the thing up. We did keep all we had, there is one thing, but we did not get any new ones.

Dr. Miller then said:

For my own part I would say in reference to the subject of the argument that I feel very glad to have been confirmed in what I said by Mr. Ellis as I have been confirmed. I have no special arguments to advance in opposition to what Mr. Sayre has stated. I like the theory very well. I coincide with it excepting this, as I have found, and I give my experience, salesmen are not satisfied with half the profit, but they take all of it; they absorb every cent of the profit there is in the business, and you will often find that they want something in addition. You will find that you are far better off without any business brought in in that manner than you are with it.

Mr. William H. Barr, Jr., a student, then said:

I think with Mr. Sayre that in certain branches of business travelling men are a necessary evil. Still I do not think that a firm's business depends entirely upon it. I have worked for our house—the business has been established for 30 years—and they have never employed a travelling man. They started a small retail business, and they now have worked up to a large wholesale business. Within a year they have put on one travelling salesman. I guess they begin to feel that they are a necessity. The section of the country that this man has been travelling over is the northern part of Wisconsin and part of Michigan. It is a country where there is a great deal of mining done, and those people spend money freely, and buy good goods, and pay big prices for them. To get that trade it is necessary to have a man to travel for the house, because the men who travel through there travel hand and glove with the merchants. They go out and drink with them; they play cards with them, and lose a little money occasionally, and that is the way they keep their trade. There is one firm that is represented in the town I come from, and that one firm has been doing business in that section of the country for several years. When they send a new man into that country they say to him, "You cannot sell goods. You do not keep any stock. The firm in Milwaukee from whom we buy our goods buy goods by the car load, and you cannot sell goods alongside of that firm." And that is just the impression that they seek to convey among a great many retailers. The idea is conveyed by the travelling men that the houses for which they travel buy large quantities of goods, and consequently they can sell them cheaper than small houses; but the fact is that the travelling men sell at the same price as other houses. This fact is not known, however, to the trade. They have their samples to show them and they catch their trade and they sell their goods.

The President then remarked as follows:

As far as my experience goes, I can readily see the good side as well as the bad side to the question of a travelling salesman. I think in the case of the country dealers the travelling salesman is a God-send. It saves the expense of a trip to the city. The samples are shown, and if they are not as represented the retailer can send them back. In the case of a man in the city it has its good side also. Where the druggist is left without a clerk, he is saved the annoyance of losing half a day to obtain new goods. On the other hand, it has its objections where four or five of these drummers come into the store in a day and stick themselves on to you. They are then a nuisance. There are certainly two sides to this question.

Dr. Miller:

The President has given us one side. There is another side to this same question. Houses that employ travelling salesmen, and are doing a great deal of business, want to increase their trade and do more business, and the more trade they do the more they want to do. A salesman is put on for the purpose of increasing the trade. Oftentimes goods are pushed on to the customers that lie on the shelves and are never sold. I am perfectly willing to admit the necessity of a salesman in certain lines of business. In the case of manufacturers, where they have new goods to introduce, where they are not known to the public, there, I say, the utility of the salesman will be manifested, but that is more than counterbalanced from the fact that manufacturers make a large profit on their goods. As for a merchant who buys and sells, I deny the necessity of any service whatever. I fail to see the force of the argument of the President—namely, that it is a great convenience to the druggist who is without a clerk. I cannot see why such a man could not send a postal card as rapidly as having a salesman. All he has to do is to write down his order and send it by post; he can then get his goods without any trouble. This would be much more convenient than having a travelling salesman call upon you. In case of any error it could be corrected probably much better than with a travelling salesman, and there is much less liability of error when the order is written; so that I think that drugs can be as well ordered by mail as through a travelling salesman. I do not see any advantage to the country dealer in being visited by a salesman. We know the same evil exists in the country, and merchants there very frequently are pestered by two or three travelling salesmen in a day, and by salesmen who fairly fight for the orders of the country merchants. The country merchants are much annoyed from this solicitation on the part of the salesmen. The salesmen urge that they have gone to a considerable expense to visit them, and therefore they claim the order as a matter of right. There seems to be an advantage in having salesmen in the line of druggists' sundries, and where there is an opportunity like that it can be utilized—samples can be displayed; but in that case there is a liberal profit, and the same objection does not hold.

The President further remarked:

The objection I referred to is this, that when a salesman calls at a store there is an opportunity of buying one pound or five pounds. This opportunity is presented by the salesman. When the druggist orders one pound or two pounds, the salesman will suggest, "Why do you not buy five pounds?" And the druggist sees the advantage of buying five pounds instead of two, and he gains in that way and this is to his advantage. The question again comes where rare drugs are required, and it will take a great deal of time to obtain them by means of a postal card, when the salesman could tell you in a moment whether they had the article, or whether they could furnish it, and where it could be obtained, and also the price. I think there is an advantage of having a travelling salesman.

Mr. Sayre:

Stopping over one evening in Maryland, I visited a druggist, and he was telling me the way he carried on his business. He said it was not necessary for him to leave his store, and he was at very little expense for clerk hire; that the Baltimore wholesale druggists would send up a salesman with samples, and if he wished to purchase cinchona bark or rhubarb he could see samples in the store, which would save him the cost of a trip, and yet he could have the accommodation as much so as if he were to go to Baltimore. So it does seem that in the purchase of rare drugs and all those articles which have a steady demand there is a value in our having a travelling salesman. It is true that it might be argued that for these articles alone it would not pay, but the salesman could carry other things that did pay.

I am a member of a little organization which has a requirement which is enforced upon the members that they should speak, and that they should

5

give their views upon any subject. We are well drilled in this matter, so that there is no backing out; and as there is one of the members of that meeting here—I hope he will forgive me—I will call upon him to express his views. If he does not know anything upon the subject, let him say so. I will call upon Mr. Finck to express his views with regard to this subject.

Robert F. Finck, a student, then spoke as follows:

I have been called upon to speak by the gentleman who last addressed this august assembly. An incident occurred to me in December last, at the time of the great pageant here, the reception of General Grant. Reading his life, which was given in the Philadelphia *Press*, he said how much, seemingly, influence does. Touch a man's pocketbook and how quickly his principles and his views are conveyed away and how they all change. Before the war he and his wife had lived and he had voted for Buchanan and was a Democrat. After the war, and what occurred in it, he was made a Republican. And so it is with trade, or with a certain aspect of it. I do not wish to oppose the gentlemen who have spoken before me upon this question as to travelling salesmen; but I would say that there is a certain subject on which I can speak, and that is as regards advertising. I come from a body whom I represent as a tyro or embryonic journalist, and standing by my friends, I would say that I believe it is the duty of every merchant to advertise in the daily newspapers, because if you were not to advertise you would not be known. Chicago is a place in point, and St. Jacob's oil is known all over the country. Why? Because on every board fence and on every street car you will see St. Jacob's oil advertised. Even in the circus ring it is considered as a standing joke, and is given forth by the clown. He advertises St. Jacob's oil, and in that way the nostrum is sold. That is the way it is done with that patent medicine, and if it is true with that, why should it not be true as to any genuine article which we think should reach suffering humanity, and which we know will alleviate the sufferings of the sick of our country? The district or village in which I live has a newspaper, and in that newspaper all the new remedies which have been discovered in the large marts—cities like New York, Philadelphia, Boston and Chicago—are advertised; and with these few remarks I close.

Dr. Miller:

I would like to inquire of my friend Finck what would be the result if his argument were carried out, and if every merchant were to advertise? Would not life be too short for us poor mortals to read all of their advertisements?

Mr. Sayre:

I believe it is not customary for us to make any decisions upon these debates, and I will proceed to read an article which I have prepared for this meeting that will illustrate so much of the argument or of the debate as has taken place. I step aside from a strictly pharmaceutical subject—indeed, I propose to have a little relief from pharmaceutical study and try to have the meeting partake as much as possible of a social character. It is in regard to an article that I have seen going the rounds of the papers, originating in the *Scientific American*, copied from that into other journals, and finally into the *Pharmaceutical Journal*. The article is headed "Popular Science—the Use of Ammonia in Baking Powder."

THE USE OF AMMONIA IN BAKING POWDER.

A Paper read by Lucius E. Sayre, Ph. G., Class 1866, at the First Social Meeting:

An article has been going the rounds of the papers ascribing wonderful properties to ammonia as a culinary agent. This application of it is spoken of as a recent discovery, as will be seen from the following quotations:

"Old methods are giving away to the light of modern investigation, and the habits and methods of our fathers and mothers are stepping down and out, to be succeeded by new ideas with marvelous rapidity.'

"Among recent discoveries in this direction, none is more important than the use to which common ammonia can be properly put as a culinary agent, and which indicate that this familiar salt is hereafter to perform an active part in the preparation of our daily food."

"The bakers and baking powder manufacturers producing the finest goods have been quick to avail themselves of this useful discovery. The handsomest and best bread and cake are now largely risen by the aid of ammonia, combined, of course, with other leavening materials."

"It will prove a boon to dyspeptic humanity, and speedily force itself into general use in the new field to which science has assigned it."

After seeing this article we were reminded of the knowledge gained in our boyhood which led us to think that this was not such a new discovery after all. Large quantities have been sold over the country by ourselves to bakers as well as by our preceptors before us. In all probability hartshorn has been thus used for a score of years at least, as the receipt book of the bakers and others of that date would indicate. As the statement has been repeated so often it may be well to ask how long this application has been practiced. At least thirty, and probably fifty years ago, bakers taught the art of combining ammonia with and substituting it for leavening material. As to the leavening properties of ammonium carbonate, it is plain to us all that this is a misnomer. The gases comprising the carbonate of ammonium, nitrogen and hydrogen, united as NH_3 and carbonic acid gas (CO_2), will, when liberated in the dough, by the aid of heat produce an aerated form of bread or cake, but not a leavened form. Leavening, chemically speaking, is a fermentation. The yeast added to the dough converts a small portion of the sugar which the meal naturally contains into alcohol and carbonic acid. The gas evolved as a consequence produces a sponge-like mass out of the tough and adhesive material. The mass is still further expanded by the heat of the oven, which at the same time dissipates the alcohol.

Carbonate of ammonium will lighten, it is true, but not produce this fermentation. Hydrochloric acid and sodium carbonate have been used to produce this effect. Still another method has been used which is by far the best, namely, by agitating the dough in a strong vessel with water saturated with carbonic acid gas under pressure. When the dough thus treated is subsequently released from the pressure and exposed to the air, it lightens the mass as effectually as by the process of fermentation. This last process has an advantage over all the above methods. Over fermentation, because the danger of going too far is inseparable from this when a disagreeable sour odor and taste is communicated to the product, over either of the chemicals, because the free carbonic acid gas leaves no residue which might be detrimental to health or might make the product unpalatable.

Again the article reads: "The handsomest and best bread and cake are produced." We admit it may be the *handsomest*, but certainly not the *best*. We do not advocate *this* artificial method of lightening dough or batter, especially when ammonia is made to do the duty of eggs and good yeast, the evil is still greater. There is a growing tendency in this direction of this species of *adulteration*, which should be discouraged rather than praised. We may add just here that when carbonate of ammonium and other substitutes are made to take the place of eggs, the deception is made more complete by the use of the well-known coloring material, tincture of curcuma. This is mixed with the batter, and gives to the cake the appearance of having been raised after the method of our good old mothers. But, though we may deceive the eye, the palate soon detects the adulteration. Not satisfied with the harmless coloring of turmeric, we have lately had proof brought to our notice that occasionally the pernicious and poisonous material, chrome yellow, is used by bakers to simulate the appearance of eggs. *En passant*, we would suggest to our friends, the students, that the solubility of chromate of lead in the gastric juice would be a subject for a thesis that might merit a gold medal. We still cherish a vivid recollection of the disappointment experienced when partaking of some beautiful sponge-cake, apparently made by the old and proper method, to find it intensely alkaline from carbonate of sodium. This offensive product had been undoubtedly made by one of the disciples of the above theory. Notwithstanding the very delicious and tempting appearance of the cake, its taste proved to be most atrocious. We may say of this so-called "boon to dyspeptics," we would prefer taking our dose of ammonia, as an anti-dyspeptic, separately. Nine-tenths of the cake made by the use of carbonate of ammonium has, after the baking process is finished, a residue of this alkaline salt remaining, oftimes in such quantities as to be offensive even to the least fastidious. How can such a character add to its digestibility? We consider that the growing use of this salt in the manufacture of bread and cake should be deprecated, and classed among the ingenious means of adulteration favorable to the producer at the cost of the consumer. Instead of having our fathers and mothers stepping down and out, let us step up and in to their good and wholesome way, until we can show some real and genuine progress and improvement.

We have just ascertained that one of our wholesale dealers of this city has contracted for a monthly delivery of ten casks of ammonium carbonate during the present year. As the average weight of a cask is about 600 pounds, this amount represented 72,000 pounds for one year distributed from one establishment, almost solely for the purpose above described. This statement serves to prove the enormous consumption of "hartshorn" by bakers.

Dr. Miller then made the following remarks:

In verification of one allusion made by Mr. Sayre in his admirable paper, I might state that a few weeks ago a clerk came into my office and told me a customer wished to have some stuff to put into cakes for coloring them yellow. He had forgotten its name. I suggested to him that it was probably turmeric that he wanted. He had already been shown turmeric and it did not meet his requirements. I told him to show him a sample of annatto, thinking that that was what he wanted, and in half an hour or so I saw the clerk and he said that the customer had seen the chrome yellow and said that was what he wanted, and he bought two pounds of it and went off with it.

I have a specimen here that was produced from the distilling of cedar shavings. I will pass it around for inspection.

Mr. Sayre remarked :

This is quite interesting. Suppose that we discuss the product of it and ask the question what the proper composition of it is. Cedar contains resinous substances. We know that resin when boiled with water gives us abietic acid and resinous substances containing this anhydride of various substances. Couldn't this be a chrystalline substance somewhat of that character ? In distilling yellow cedar do you not use the cedar shavings or tops, cutting them fine and putting them in the still and then running the water over them, and the oil being extracted goes over with the steam and is collected in that way ? In this case we use merely cedar sawdust. We had a large quantity of the red and whi'e cedar sawdust. The red cedar produced no deposit ; the white cedar produced this deposit. I would say as to the red cedar that was distilled that it was very odorous. I have heard it said that druggists have used it for the purpose of diluting the oil of sandal wood.

ATTACKS OF "THE PRESS" ON DRUGGISTS.

By Dr. A. W. Miller, Ph. G., at same Meeting.

For a number of weeks past the Philadelphia *Press* has been devoting a portion of its space to a denunciation of pharmacists, accusing them of sophistications, adulterations and other improprieties. Old reports on these subjects made years ago to the American Pharmaceutical Association have been ransacked, and all the blame of frauds committed in the remotest corners of the earth has been heaped upon our city druggists. While the original motive of these articles may have been to put the public on guard for their own protection, we must concede that very many absurd and foolish statements have been made, which must necessarily weaken the arguments presented. In addition to this they do infinite harm to the commercial reputation of our city. It is hardly to be expected that reporters and editors entirely unacquainted with the mysteries of our profession, could intelligently write up a subject which is entirely too intricate for them. We have reason to think that of late professional chemists have been employed to examine and report on test preparations, which have been compounded by certain pharmacists suspected of practicing sophistications such as for instance the substitution of cinchonidia for quinia. Presumably no respectable member of the profession will object to the weeding out of those who sanction these nefarious actions. We all know that our profession is overcrowded, chiefly from the insane desire of so many young men to display their own " shingles " and thus to be relieved of the irksome supervision of an employer.

But we do object most emphatically to the wholesale method of indiscriminately placing the stigma of fraud on all the pharmacists of our city. " *The Press* " ought to remember the vast chemical industries, the numerous importers of drugs, and above all, the many medical, pharmaceutical and dental educational establishments of our city, all of which will be somewhat affected by assaults of this kind, uttered audaciously, copied and disseminated broadcast over all our country.

In order to give an idea of the harm thus engendered in remote quarters, we translate almost verbatim the following editorial from an obscure

German paper of the West, the *Belleville Zeitung*, of August 30, 1882, published in Belleville, St. Clair county, Ill.

Philadelphia is the central depot for the drugs used in the United States. The adulteration of these important articles has assumed such proportions there, that the attention of physicians and druggists has for a long time been directed to it. The press and public opinion is now expressing itself with indignation on this subject in the city of brotherly love. Cinchona bark is prepared by saturating the bark of ordinary trees with a weak solution of chinoidin ; chicory is sold for dandelion ; unmixed rhubarb can scarcely be obtained ; anise is falsified with clay, and asafœtida with calcium sulphate. Ground sand is mixed with gum arabic, lead with opium, fish oil and croton oil with castor oil, and paraffine oil with olive oil. Of all the essential oils not a single one enters into commerce from Philadelphia pure and unadulterated ; the same remark applies to the acids. It has gone so far that almost all drugs in Philadelphia are adulterated with noxious and worthless substances. so that no physician can depend on the efficacy of the medicine which he has prescribed.

'" Throw medicine to the dogs, I'll none of it,' says Macbeth, and thus it will eventuate if the doctors and druggists throughout the land do not energetically oppose the machinations of the wholesale swindlers of Philadelphia."

"We know that many of our foods and drinks are adulterated, but when we call in the physician to restore the maltreated machinery to its normal function and thus only introduce new sophistications, how can we, then, successfully resist pernicious influences pouring into us from kitchen and cellar, and especially from the drug store ?"

"The least that the doctors and apothecaries outside of Philadelphia ought to do in order to wean the druggists of this city from their swindling operations, would be to examine every drug coming there most carefully, and to return the same promptly if they find a trace of adulteration."

We may smile at the strange absurdities of our Western friend, at the very few grains of truth sprinkled in here and there for seasoning, at the feeling manner in which he speaks of his favorite beverage, but we must not overlook the sober side of the question. Absolute nonsense, as much of the above undoubtedly is, it will nevertheless be eagerly seized upon by our active competitors to prejudice purchasers, as well as students, against our fair city, in which, we feel quite confident in saying, there is relatively less adulteration and sophistication practiced than in any other city of the United States. We therefore appeal earnestly, to the patriotism of the managers of *The Press* to rectify many of its statements, and thus to remove the stigma they have cast on our profession.

A LECTURE ON THE GERM THEORY.

Delivered by Dr. Louis J. Lautenbach, Ph. D., at the second social meeting, held Tuesday afternoon, November 14th, 1882. Dr. Lautenbach spoke as follows :

MR. PRESIDENT AND GENTLEMEN :

When spoken to last Saturday evening I thought there was but little connection between the germ theory of disease and the students of the Philadelphia College of Pharmacy ; but in the interim having given the subject more thought I consider that a lecture on this subject would be appropriate, not only because it was the subject chosen by the gentleman who was to lecture to you to-day, but also because the public demands of its pharmacists a broad, general education to which is essential an intimate knowledge of the now popular theory of disease.

Probably yon all know that the germ theory of disease is not of recent origin. It is a theory which originated some 320 odd years ago; but the first absolute statement of the germ theory in the words that disease is most likely caused by certain germs, was made somewhat over 200 years ago by Father Kircher. He said that the plague was probably due to a small living creature invisible to the eye. Within a few months the public prints have taken up the subject with a degree of energy which would have been surprising fifty years ago. Taking into consideration the fact that upon the germ theory very much of human life depends, the lecture which I propose to deliver to you will, I hope, prove of interest.

For centuries upon centuries the causation of disease has interested mankind, and has been a subject of discussion and investigation, but it is only 'of late years that there can be said to have been any substantial progress made. It is no longer supposed that disease is evidence of the disapprobation of the gods, nor that the sick person is possessed of an evil spirit, which must be driven out before the individual can get well. Man having sought for some more tangible cause, has, as a result of his labors, probably succeeded in finding the cause of disease, and not only succeeded in this, but also in that greater desideratum—the prevention of disease.

Until lately three theories explaining the causation of disease were prominently before the scientific world. These were the chemical theory, the germ theory and the bioplastic, or graft theory.

CHEMICAL THEORY.

The chemical theory endeavored to explain disease to be but the result of abnormal chemical action occurring in the blood and tissues. When the fermentation process became known, the chemical action was compared to this process, and some even went so far as to say that disease was but the result of fermentation. This would explain it much more satisfactorily; but, in this process, the chemical action can be considered as determined by the organism, which we will show to be present in the different diseases. However, this theory has at present but few supporters, and is not generally believed.

GRAFT THEORY.

The graft or bioplastic theory claims that each individual protoplasmic mass can carry within itself the potentials of the entire organism and by contact with another organism can impress upon it the conditions present in the first. They consider that a cell of A, who is sick with some infectious disease, can be carried to B, and produce in him the same disease. It is just as easy to consider, and in fact much more reconcilable, that the cell transmits not only the entire potentiality of A's disease but his entire potentiality, which is absurd. This theory can be used to explain but one disease, scarlatina, and its originator, Dr. Lionel Beale, stands almost alone as its supporter.

GERM THEORY.

The germ theory explains that each of the miasmatic, infectious and contagious diseases is the result of a microscopic organism acting on individuals susceptible to their influence.

These microscopic organisms, as will be shown later on, are mostly of vegetable origin, in fact fungoid in their nature.

By the individuals being susceptible is meant that the system must be open for the reception of the organism, that it contain at the time of the exposure the proper food of the micro-organism and that the latter be allowed to multiply without disturbance.

We see that negroes very seldom contract either yellow fever or malaria, while they are especially liable to small-pox. One of the *peronospora*, the *Oidium Tuckeri*, although it originated in America, where it is comparatively harmless, yet has in Europe destroyed entire vineyards.

Having now stated the theory, we may perhaps think it of recent date, but it has existed in a more or less crude state for over two hundred years. It was somewhat over two hundred years ago when Father Kircher brought it clearly forward by advancing it as a hypothesis to account for the propagation of the plague.

Toward the close of the seventeenth century, the discovery of the spermatic animalcules, as they were termed, gave a decided impulse to this theory. They assumed that the spermatozoa were distinct organisms, and reasoned that if a man can have living bodies within his structure without creating disease, he may have other organisms which cause disease. When, however, the function of the spermatozoa was discovered, there was a decided reaction against the germ theory, and it was only after Helmholtz's experiments with the yeast plant, by which he proved that fermentation is directly dependent on the presence and multiplication of low organisms that the germ theory came prominently forward. Liebermeister, by some general propositions which he established, also did much to insure the adoption of the theory.

Liebermeister determined that the poisons of diseases preserved their energy for an indefinite length of time when stored away ; that the poisons of infectious diseases can reproduce themselves to an unlimited extent ; that the diseases always preserved the same invariable type, whereas the effects of cold, acids, etc., are not invariable, one suffering with cold has coryza, another facial paralysis, a third catarrh of the stomach, a fourth bronchitis, a fifth a general muscular rheumatism. "No individual or external influence ever decides the nature of an affection, and one disease is never under such circumstances changed into another." (Liebermeister.) "As surely as a thistle rises from a thistle seed, as surely as the fig comes from the fig, just so surely will the typhoid virus increase and multiply into typhoid fever, the small-pox virus into small-pox." (Tyndall.)

The germ theory having been fairly presented to the world it was not long before a host of investigators appeared, who, soon as a result of their experiments, served greatly to strengthen it, but it remained for the last few years to give to the former theory the unmistakable evidence of fact.

Fungi as we all know produce innumerable spores. The spores of a single puff ball have been estimated to be greater than the number of the earth's inhabitants. Whether this be so or not it is undoubtedly the case that the air is literally full of spores, but it remained for Prof. Tyndall to prove this by some most beautiful experiments. We all know that innumerable particles are constantly floating about the room ; that these particles are rendered visible by allowing a ray of sunlight to enter a small opening in the shutter. If the air was perfectly pure we would not be able to see the ray because there would be nothing to reflect the light ; this was beautifully demonstrated by Tyndall. He made the ray of light travel through volatile transparent media, such as steam, when the ray of light disappeared to the eye. He also took a long glass tube closed by glass plates and exhausted it of air, when on passing through it a ray of light from an electric light burner there was nought but darkness. He proved that the

bodies floating in the air causing the dispersion of light were organic particles by burning the air in a platinum tube, when on repeating the light test
the ray of light was not seen. To establish the plausibility of the germ
theory it is not absolutely necessary to suppose that all of these organic particles are living, but that a considerable number of them are, is proved by
the fact that so many of the lower forms of plants, especially fungi, develop
when the conditions are favorable, and the fact that substances sterilized,
that is deprived of all adherent germs, may be kept in a close receptacle
for an indefinite length of time without any growth manifesting itself;
whereas if exposed to the air they are soon covered with the lower forms of
plant life.

Having now proved the universal presence of low forms of vegetable
life, it will prove interesting to notice, first, whether any of these forms
of life are present in any disease; second, whether they are invariably
present; third, whether they are the only forms present; and, fourth,
whether these same diseases can be produced experimentally by inoculating with the particular organism. In order to do this, we will begin first
with some of the more common diseases of plants, following this by diseases
of animals and of man.

DISEASES OF PLANTS.

Contrary to an impression which generally prevails, we find that
diseases of plants are very frequent. One who is looking for diseased
plants will be struck by the large number he will see, in even a short
journey through field or wood, especially in the latter.

Our ordinary apple tree is a sufferer from no less than forty-five diseases, which are occasioned by the lower forms of plant-life; while there
are, in addition to this, quite a number of diseases occasioned by insects.
All the higher plants are sufferers from diseases occasioned by various
forms of fungi.

That these diseases are destructive to the plant or the fruit, or to both,
is evident. The potato rot, which, by its destruction of the potato tuber and
vine, has occasioned so much misery in Ireland; the wheat rust, which at
various times has caused absolute destruction of the wheat crop; the corn
mould, which has been the cause of much sickness; the ergot disease,
which, destroying the oat, wheat and rye, but especially the rye crop, and
being taken into the human system as bread, causing various diseases,
especially gangrene,—all these diseases are sufficiently familiar to give to
you some idea, not only of the destruction of the plant and its product, but
also of the danger which these diseases entail on animal life.

We have already mentioned the vine mould which attacks the entire
plant, even the fruit. This disease is due to the growth of the fungus *Oidium
Tuckeri*. If the spores are destroyed by burning all parts of the vine where
the mould has appeared, the disease is checked, but just as soon as any of
the fungi are brought into the vine-growing region it reappears.

The potato rot is exceedingly destructive. It is due to the fungus
peronospora infestans. All potatoes suffering from this disease, which have
been examined, contained this fungus and no other. Experiments made
on healthy plants by sowing the fungus prove that a disease is produced identical with the original both in general and in microscopical characteristics.
We have in this case a most perfect exemplification of the proposition that
disease is produced by lower organisms.

In Southern India we have a disease of the coffee plant due to the fungus *hemileia vastatrix*. This disease only appears when the plant has been
weakened by the production of its crop. This liability to disease of the

berry-bearing plant corresponds very closely to the predisposition of the human being.

Corn mildew is cosmopolitan, and in all countries has proved very destructive. This disease is caused by the *puccinia graminis*, a fungus which, during its life history, is at one time a dweller on berberry bushes, and at another period has for its habitat the corn. A village in Norfolk was formerly noted for its mildewed corn. After various expedients had been tried, some one bethought himself of the berberry bushes, which were forthwith destroyed and mildewed corn disappeared..

Medicinal ergot, as you all know, is but diseased rye, the second stage or the sclerotium of a fungus, the *claviceps purpurea* replacing the grain. This disease is always more or less present, but some years it is much worse than others. In this section of the country it is not present to any extent, but in some of the Western provinces of Russia whole communities have been required to use bread largely composed of ergotized rye, this being the only grain which their fields brought forth. As a consequence of the eating of this bread, much sickness and not a few deaths have occurred in these provinces.

The high price of hops this year has been owing to the fact that a fungus, the *Spaerotheca Castagnei*, has caused the almost total destruction of the crop in some parts of this country and in Southern France. This disease first appears as whitish blotches on the leaves, which soon turn brown at the same time penetrating through all the tissues of the leaf.

We all know that otto of rose is almost indispensable, at least in the eyes of many ladies. In order to extract the oil the rose is necessary. This industry is a very important one in Southern France and in some parts of India, and to the cultivation of the rose thousands upon thousands of acres. of land are devoted, and thousands of people are directly dependent on this industry. The rose is very subject to the attacks of several fungi, *the Phragmidium mucronatum*, the *Asteroma rosae*, the *Spaerotheca pannosa* and the *Peronospora sparsa*. The two latter of these are, when once introduced into a rose field, very hard to eradicate.

The ordinary smut of Indian corn, which is apparently eaten with so much relish by the cow, is but a mass of threads of a fungus, the *ustilago maidis*.

The *Puccinia Apii* spoils beds of celery by attacking the leaves.

The above instances are but a very few of the very many diseases of plants which are caused by fungi. But, in order to show what difficulties frequently are encountered in studying these diseases, we will call attention to but one more disease of plants, namely, the wheat rust—the *Aecidium Berberidis*, formerly known as the *Puccinia Graminis*, whose life history is complex, it being completed on two different plants—one the *Berberis vulgaris;* the other some graminaceous plant. The first stage, beginning with the rusty appearance of the wheat, is the uredo stage. Examining a speck of *rust*, we find it consists of a mass of spores, around which you see a torn edge of epiderm. These spores originated from mycelial threads, which ramify under the cuticle. These threads give off a mass of branches, pointing toward the cuticle, which they rupture. The upper ends of the branches enlarge, and each produces a spore—the uredospore. Allowed to germinate, it protrudes two germ tubes, of which one soon stops its growth, the other continuing until the whole of the yellow endochrome is passed from the spore into the end of the growing tube, which now twists, taking a spiral shape, a septum at the same time forming, cutting off the empty spore-case. Now, this germ tube can enter into the interior of wheat or other grain through the stomata, producing mycelial filaments, and these reproducing the uredospore. This production of uredospores could go on forever; but, as the life of the host plant is limited, the fungus must have some more tangible hold on the wheat than a spore which can only live for one or two months, and for this purpose the fungus has the resting spore—the *Puccinia*, or mildew—the second stage of its history. This resting spore has the power of lying dormant through the winter.

The resting or teleutospores are produced in a precisely similar manner to the uredospore, but they are different in structure. They are club-shaped bodies of a rich brown color, and are divided by a septum into two compartments. Each spore has an elongated stem attaching it to the host plant, and germination only occurs after a lapse of several months, and consists in the protrusion of a germ tube which gives off three branches, each bearing an oval spore. These spores again germinate by sending out a germ tube, and if this be placed on the *Berberis vulgaris* the germ tubes bore through the epiderm and produce *mycelium*, which soon produces an *aecidium*, or cluster cup, the third stage. There is produced a collection of minute cluster cups which are filled with golden yellow spores, the aecidospores These spores are developed from the *mycelium*, and when ripe germinate in the same manner as the uredospore, and the spores then produced falling on a grain leaf enters the *stomata* producing mycelial threads, but falling on the berberry leaf dies. Besides these three stages there is another part to the life history of the *æcidium*, the *Spermagonia*, which is usually termed the fourth stage. This is probably but a part of the third stage. In connection with the cluster cups there are developed on the opposite (the upper) side of the berberis leaf, flask-shaped bodies which are made up of exceedingly fine threads and which in the interior bear on their ends chains of spore-like bodies, the *spermatia*, which seem to play the part of a male organ.

A most interesting and important fact in connection with the wheat rust is the wonderful difference in the effects of the mildew when derived directly from the berberry, and when derived from the uredospore which has reproduced itself through several generations. The first laying waste whole districts, while the latter is continually present without creating trouble. This fact serves to corroborate Pasteur's conclusions in regard to successive cultures, which will be spoken of later on.

A further proof, if any were needed, of the causation of disease of plants directly by fungi, is found in the fact that carbolic acid, locally applied, has been of such great use in plant diseases, and is even said to prevent the *Hemileia vastatrix* in the coffee plant.

Having now proved satisfactorily, I hope, that diseases of plants are produced by lower organisms, frequently fungoid, it yet remains for us to prove that the diseases of animals are produced through a similar agency. The fact of plant diseases originating from the invasion of micro-organisms is a strong point in favor of the germ theory, for, if diseases of plants are so produced, why not diseases of animals?

DISEASES OF ANIMALS.

In the common house-fly we find a beautiful illustration of the germ theory. Every one must have noticed that, during the fall months, great numbers of flies are found adhering to the windows. They have been attacked by the *Empusæ muscæ*, which, when once a spore has been sown, pervades their entire body. If another fly comes within the endemic range of the dead fly, it also becomes diseased and dies.

The silkworm is attacked by a fungus—the *Botrytis Bassiania*—which at times has caused great havoc.

The vegetable wasp is gradually killed by a fungus—the *Torrubia sphecocephala*.

Fish are also destroyed by some of the lower forms of plant-life. Gold-fish in aquaria are very frequently attacked by a mouldy fungus, which almost invariably kills them.

Coming now to the vertebrates, we will find that the number of diseases to which they are liable are not a few, that many of their diseases have been distinctly proven to be due to micro-organisms.

In rats, cats, and mice we have the *tinea favosa* disease, due to a fungus attacking the skin and hair follicles.

In the horse we have a similar fungus attacking the epidermic layer of the skin.

The swelling in the horse's heel, known as grease, appears to be due to a low organism.

Glanders is a contagious disease, occurring in the horse, ass and mule, and is communicable to man. It assumes two forms, the lymphatic and the nasal form, generally termed farcy. In this disease examination of the lymphatics, of the nasal mucous-membrane and of the blood has revealed the presence of *Bacteria*.

Before going further it may be best to indicate the position which these micro-organisms, *Bacteria*, *Bacilli* and *Micrococci* occupy in the vegetable world. They are all members of that sub-division of the fungi termed the *Schizomycetes* or cleft fungi, are unicellular plants which at some part of their life are aquatic. *Micrococci* are globular in form and excessively small. *Bacteria* are larger and are elliptical in shape, while the *Bacilli* are rod-like.

Tinea favosa, scald head, is a disease of the hair follicles, the hair or the surface of the skin, produced by the fungus *Achorian Schoenlini*. The fungus can always be found by examination of the diseased skin, and if a spore be sown on another individual it will produce the same disease.

Tinea circinnati, ringworm of the body, is a disease of the epiderm occasioned by the *Tricophyton tonsurans*. *Tinea tonsourans*, ringworm of the scalp, is due to the same fungus, its situation being different. If the fungus attacks the beard it causes the disease termed *Tinea sycosis*, or barber's itch.

Tinea versicolor, chloasma, is due to the action of the *Microsporon furfur* on the surface of the skin.

Scabies, occasioned by the *Sarcoptes scabiei* and *Phtheiriasis pediculi*, serve to show that several skin diseases are due to animal parisites.

The madura foot of India has been traced to the ravages of a fungus, the *Chionyphe Carteri*.

There are found in the human ear two forms of aspergillus, the *aspergillus nigricans* and the *aspergillus glaucus*, both of which cause disease. If a spore is taken and deposited in another ear, if the conditions are favorable, that is if there is present a certain degree of moisture, the disease is reproduced.

In thrush we have a disease of the mouth which may extend to any extent along the intestinal tract, in which the only lesions are small white or whitish yellow patches, these patches being composed of a fungus, the *oidium albicans*.

The mycelial filaments of fungi have been found in the dejections of dysentery, and in the blood of relapsing fever patients the mycelium of the *spiroceta* was observed.

In yellow fever patients Drs. Richardson and White discovered in the *Uriniferous tubules* of the kidney fungus growths; *micrococci* were also found in the blood.   Several other experimenters, among them Klebs and Klein, found *Bacteria* in the blood of yellow fever patients.

. Profs. Thorne and Klobe, and Drs. Hallier, Simon and Harris, believe in the fungoid 'character of cholera contagion.   The presence of *mycelium* and spores has been demonstrated in the rice-water stools.   Vevey says that cholera must be due either to an organic poison or to a living organism   An organic poison would not be accompanied by fungoid growths— in fact, it would tend to their destruction.

Pyæmia is believed to be due to the *microsporon septicus*.

Puerperal fever is now believed to be due to a *micrococcus*, very likely the *micrococcus diphtheriticus*, it having been found in the uterus.

Bacteria have been found present (Coze, Feltz, Klebs, Burdon-San-derson, Klein) in the blood of patients suffering with typhoid fever, small-pox, scarlet fever and puerperal fever.

In caries of the teeth there has been found present, by Leber and Rottenstein, the *leptothrix buccalis*, a fungus not found where the teeth are healthy.

We all know the fact of the disease *trichinosis* being produced by the migrations of the *trichina spiralis* derived from the hog.   This disease, not of vegetable, but of animal origin, is so important in its bearings on the germ theory as to require mention.   Without the microscope we would not know the true cause of this disease, and would most likely think it to be due to the action of some chemical poison.

An objection to the germ theory which undoubtedly has suggested itself to you is, may not the *Bacteria* be but the result and not the cause of the disease.

To disprove this we will, for the present, only mention that malaria, septicæmia, pyæmia, small-pox, measles, scarlet fever, typhoid fever and a host of other diseases have been reproduced by inoculation with their respective *Bacteria*, and that wheat rust never prevails unless the *æcidospore* from the berberry is brought to the leaf of the wheat.

In some experiments of Drs. Zahn and Liegel on septicæmia they inoculated animals, with a liquid made from the blood of animals who had died with this disease and reproduced the disease.   They then filtered the parasites from the liquid, and on inoculating animals with this, caused nothing but slight feverishness.   Koch, experimenting upon septicæmia finds the introduction of one kind of fungus always produces the same results.

. The experiments of Dr. Salisbury on malaria would go to prove that the malarial germ had been isolated, but some researches made since his communication appeared, do not support this.   He collected some upturned marshy soil and placed it in a sleeping room 300 feet above the sea level, and produced the disease in all the occupants.   The attacks were broken by quinine.   He found that the sputa contained long, elongated cells which were the same as those he collected by placing plates over still water containing vegetable remains; an *algæ*, the *palmella*.   Hannon, during the examination of some fresh-water *algæ*, not in a malarial district, was attacked with an intermittent fever of six weeks' duration.

Somewhat later than this Dr. Salisbury endeavored to establish the *puccinia graminis* as the cause of camp measles.   He inoculated himself and some eight others with *puccinia graminis*, and produced a disease, the symptoms of which were apparently identical with camp measles.   This has since been disputed by Dr. Woodward.

In *mycosis intestinalis*—a rather rare disease—we have a local expression of the splenic fever, or charbon of the lower animals.   In this disease the parasite is found in the mucous membrane of the intestines and in the blood. The disease can be occasioned by inoculation with the *anthracoid bacillus* (the *bacillus anthracis*).

Coming now to the investigations of the past few years, we will find that the proofs of the truth of the theory have increased wonderfully, and that the work has been done by but a few experimenters, at the head of whom stands Pasteur.

The experiments of Pasteur on chicken cholera proved that *bacteria*, or, as he terms them, *microbes*, existed in the blood of the fowl, and that these *microbes*, carried even to the one hundredth culture, provided the cultivations, follow rapidly enough, one upon the other, are capable, when inoculated, of producing death by chicken cholera as quickly as if they had been inoculated with the original bacterial blood.

If the interval between the successive cultures was increased, the less virulent would the poison become, and by increasing or diminishing the interval between the successive cultures, he could obtain any degree of virulency he desired.

Drs. Wood and Formad arrived at the same result in their investigations on diphtheria. They found that the longer the interval between the successive cultures of the *micrococci* of diphtheria the less they had the power of multiplication, and, consequently, the less virulent did the poison become.

Pasteur further found that fowls, which had been rendered sufficiently ill by attenuated virus, suffered an illness of a passing character when inoculated with virulent virus.

What makes the virus which has not been actively sown so attenuated? The oxygen of the air. In order to prove that the attenuation is due to some constituent of the air, probably oxygen, produce a culture in a tube and seal the ends; leave for any length of time, when, upon opening it, it is found to be as virulent as ever.

The oxygen of the air would seem to be a modifying agency of the virulency of the disease. May it not be a general law, and be applicable even during an attack of sickness, and would it not be better to have air and ventilation in a sick room, instead of the patient suffering from the stifling atmosphere so universally present?

As Pasteur's experiments on splenic fever, the charbon of the French, the Milzbrand of the Germans, are of great importance not only as concerns this disease, but also in regard to other diseases, we will briefly call attention to them.

He found that in splenic fever the *anthracoid microbe* was present in translucent filaments, and that by culture he could reproduce the *mycelium*. If this *mycelium* is exposed to the air for forty-eight hours he had formed a germ dust. If these corpuscles germinate the new culture reproduces the virulence of the original thready form, and this result is observed even after a long contact with the air. He then endeavored to prevent the *anthracoid microbes* from producing the corpuscle germs and then to keep them in contact with the air. By keeping the culture at 42°–43° C. in contact with pure air he succeeded in producing a *mycelial* culture of the *bacteria* free from germs. If this culture is exposed for 4–6 weeks it dies and no effect is then produced by inoculation. If we examine the culture during the interval we will find that long before this time the microbe has lost its virulency, and that between this and the point of most active growth there are all degrees of virulency present. What lends increased value to this, is the fact that all the grades of attenuated virulency can be reproduced by culture.

As charbon usually does not attack an animal a second time, we see that our attenuated *microbe* constitutes for the virulent *microbe* a vaccine, that is a virus capable of producing a milder attack of the disease.

In order to prove this Pasteur vaccinated 25 sheep with the attenuated virus of charbon and afterward inoculated them, beside 25 sheep who had not been vaccinated, with the most virulent *anthracoid microbe*; the 25 unvaccinated sheep all died within 50 hours while the other 25 all resisted the infection.

The experiments of Dr. James Law on swine plague indicate that *bacilli* are everywhere present in the diseased animal, that when the *bacilli* are inoculated they produce the disease in healthy animals, but that if inoculated after the *bacilli* have been exposed to a temperature of 130° Fahr., for half an hour, the effect produced on the animal is but slight.

. The experiments of Dr. Koch on tuberculosis are exceedingly interesting as well as important.

The reason why the *bacillus* of tuberculosis has escaped all former observation appears to be due to the fact of the staining fluids as well as the illumination being inadequate. Dr. Koch uses a double staining method which colors the tissue of a light brown, while the *bacilli* are blue, and he also uses means for excessive illumination, the oil immersion lens and the Abbé illuminating apparatus. He has found that the *bacillus* of tubercle and the *bacillus* of lepra are the only *bacteria* which stain blue in his process.

The *bacillus tuberculosis* he has found to be abundant in tubercular neoplasms, in the sputa, in the walls of tubercular cavities, in degenerated scrofulous glands, and in the bones of tuberculous cattle. Are these *bacilli* the cause of tuberculosis? It appears at least to be very plausible. Koch endeavored to prove them the cause, by his culture experiments. He sterilized blood serum, which he used as the feeding ground of the *bacillus tuberculosis*, by heating it to 58° C. for an hour on six consecutive days, and on the seventh day to 65° C., until the serum became of the consistency of gelatine. Now he introduced a small fragment of tubercular tissue into the sterilized menstruum. Soon spots and streaks were seen on the surface of the serum. This is the first culture. From this he could make a second culture, and from this latter a third, and so he could go on to any number he desired. If from any of the successive cultures, even the ninetieth, a speck be taken and introduced under the skin of a white mouse, guinea-pig or rabbit the exact pathological products of tuberculosis are obtained, and these, in turn, can be used to inoculate other animals.

Baumgarten, in a communication published soon after the appearance of Koch's article, confirmed his results.

The *bacillus tuberculosis* is a rod-like body, its length being about one-third the diameter of the red-blood corpuscle, while its width is one-sixth its length.

Erysipelas is due, according to Koch, not to a *bacillus* but to a *micrococcus*.

Coming now to diphtheria we find that the false membrane is impregnated with a *micrococcus* which cannot by its appearance be distinguished from the *micrococcus* of the ordinary furred tongue, and yet the fact of the diphtheria being directly the result of the *micrococcus* was enunciated by Oertel in 1868. In fact he even went further than this and said, "the intensity of the disease is proportioned to the degree in which the tissues are penetrated by the parasite."

It follows from the experiments of Drs. Wood and Formad that the *micrococci* of diphtheria are identical in appearance with the *micrococci* usually found in the mouth, but that they differ from them in the fact that while the latter have but little tendency to grow, the former are much inclined to growth, the degree of growth depending on the malignancy of the case; that the *micrococci* of diphtheritic membrane long exposed to the air loose their power of growth; that by prolonging the intervals between the culture the malignancy decreases; that inoculation with diphtheritic virus almost invariably produces diphtheritic pseudo-membrane.

Having now, we hope, gone over the ground sufficiently at length we will call attention simply to a few facts which we think have been proved.

First.—That there are numerous diseases of plants which are directly the result of fungoid growths.

Second.—That there are several diseases of the skin for which no other origin is claimed than that of the parasites, and when the parasite is destroyed the disease is at an end.

Third.—That in almost all infectious diseases there are invariably present certain low organisms, each disease having a particular organism.

Fourth.—That by absolute separation of these organisms and their inoculation in healthy individuals, the original disease is reproduced.

Fifth.—That by means of attenuation of the virulency of the various specific germs, we have at our command one of the most effectual means for the prevention of disease.

This subject is one about which a great deal can be said, both pro and con; but we have seen that the proofs are entirely on the side of the germ theory, not as the cause of every disease, but that many diseases are caused by germs. Of course, there are diseases simply the result of inflammation, the result of external causes, it being possible for a single cause to give rise to most diverse conditions, whereas the disease caused by a germ is always the same. We have a common instance of this in a cold, which in one case produces a coryza, in a second a bronchitis, in a third a facial neuralgia, and in a fourth a general rheumatism. There are also various diseases of the skin produced by physical causes.

Beside a general idea of the relation between germs and disease, what else can we learn from these studies? We learn that America, if she wishes to retain her position as one of the most enlightened of nations, must be up and doing, there is no time for waiting. Already the names of other nations are chiselled on this branch of study, but has America her accustomed position? No! It is true that with the investigations of Drs. Law, Wood and Formad to her credit, that the work is already in hand. What has been the cause of this seeming apathy on the part of her investigators? It is the want of Government encouragement. It is the want of that moral and substantial encouragement which the European countries are so ready to accord their workers. It would have been utterly impossible for Pasteur to have experimented to the extent which he has without the direct aid of the Government. Other governments while they possibly have suffered from some such measures, as our "River and Harbor Bill," yet also appropriate money liberally for scientific investigations.

You all must see the direction in which the germ theory is opening an avenue of health, the inoculation by attenuated virus, or what may be called vaccination. You all know the benefit which vaccination has been in arresting the progress of small-pox. At the present time, the cattle of Europe are being extensively inoculated with the attenuated virus of anthrax, to guard against the splenic fever, which was so wide spread and so quickly fatal. We are already in receipt of intelligence that hydrophobia is to succumb to the advances of science. Unfortunately, however, the immunity from consumption, which was apparently half accomplished, is not yet within reach, nor does any avenue appear which gives any promise. It is true that a bacillus has been found associated with the disease which is probably its cause, but it gives no promise of affording any protection ; it appears as if it were impossible to attenuate the virus.

WEIGHTS AND MEASURES.

A lecture delivered by John E. Cook, Ph. G., Class of 1873, and assistant to Prof. J. M. Maisch, at the third Social Meeting of the Alumni Association, held Tuesday, December 12th, 1882.

GENTLEMEN:—The subject on which I am about to speak to you, "Weights and Measures," may, perhaps, be a little foreign to the part that I generally take in the College, but my object in drawing your attention to this subject is not to teach you what weights and measures are, because you have already studied them from your schoolbooks. As to the weights and measures you use in your stores, they have a distinct and definite relation to each other. This is a subject which has been thoroughly presented to you by the Professor of Pharmacy, and I do not propose to infringe on his department in that respect, but simply to go a little deeper into it, and to give you the manner in which measures, and of course weights, are actually obtained.

In starting in business you buy and use measures and weights, and the inquiry then arises, where do they come from ? Of course you went to the maker and you bought them. But where does he get them ? You may say he makes them. But how does he make them ? He has certain standards to work by. But where do those standards come from ? No matter how far back you go, the question resolves itself into this : What is the original standard, and how are these weights and measures actually made ? We will suppose that you want to make a yardstick, or a pound weight, how would you go to work to do it ? I had intended to have my notes thoroughly prepared for this meeting, but illness has prevented me from such a thorough preparation as I could have wished, and I ask your indulgence, as I shall only be able to give you an introduction to-day, at this time, of my subject, and at the next meeting I will give you the mechanical operations involved in making these weights and measures.

In this connection I may state that the term " weights and measures," or the phrase, rather, is a very loose one. In many books you will see that they come under the head of weights and measures—certain weights and certain measures. Now this may be a trifling thing, but it is important to notice. We have currency, weights and measures, and let us see how they should all be included under that one term. If we come to consider what is the unit with which we begin, we shall see presently that it is a standard of length.

We start with a straight line. How long is that line ? So many yards. What is a yard ? A yard, you say, is thirty-six inches. But what is an inch? Three barleycorns. But what is three barleycorns ? Just as I told you before, no matter how far back you go, you have to stop at some certain fixed standard or unit of length that is used in measuring ; so that we say that it is a certain length, and contains the unit or standard so many times. If we say three yards it contains the yard three times, and so with three feet, three inches, or three barleycorns. No matter what it is, we will see that the standard of length is the standard that we start with. Now we will make this into a surface (indicating). There we have a rectangle, at least intended to be a rectangle, but it is not a perfect rectangle as it stands on this board, but it will do for illustration. We want to find the area of it. How do you find the area of it? You multiply the length by the breadth; that is, you multiply the length in one direction by the length in the other direction; and there you .fall back again on the unit of length. We will now make this into a solid, and find the solidity or volume or capacity of that. How do you do it? You multiply the length of it by the breadth, and the product by the thickness. In other words the length in three directions. Now we have three lengths to multiply and we start with a unit of length again.

Take weights. What is weight? Or to what is weight compared? No matter whether you use troy, avoirdupois, or the metric weight, it is referred to the weight of a certain volume of water at a certain temperature —in the case of troy or avoirdupois weight a cubic inch; that is, an inch in either direction; there again, you have to use the unit of length. In the case of the metric system the unit of weight is the weight of a cubic centimetre of water. What is a centimetre? Here we must again make use of the unit of length.

Take time; what is the unit of time? What is a day? It is a space passed through in a certain time by the earth; it is a certain distance, and there you have it again—you have the unit of length; so that you see the unit of length is the most important thing that you have to study. You have got to understand that thoroughly, because it is the foundation of measurements. You have then a surface measure, the measure of volume or capacity, the measure of value which depends on weight, the measure of weights and time.

Now there is another thing in this connection that I want to draw your attention to, and it is this: Notwithstanding the fact that you are weighing and measuring all the time in your business, it is a point that even practical mechanics, and in fact all who have anything to do with weighing or measuring are apt to loose sight of, and that is the difference between indications and measurements; indication is one thing and measuring is another. If I have two bars of metal it is the easiest thing in the world to tell whether one is longer than the other. But to take one bar of metal and to tell precisely how long it is is the most difficult thing; to tell the theoretically precise length of a bar of metal or its weight is simply impossible, but we can approximate. There is a machine used for measuring made by a party in Wilmington, and it is an excellent measuring machine, it will show the difference between indication and measurement, it will *indicate* a difference of the 25,000th part of an inch, but it will only give you an approximation of the *measurement* to within .0001 part of an inch. You will say that this is unnecessary—to measure to the .0001 part of an inch. It is not. I will give you an illustration to show you that it is infinitely more important than even those who are using these things all the time may suppose. A correspondent of one of our periodicals made a visit to the repair shops at Altoona. He found the workmen fitting crank-pins to the hubs of driving-wheels of locomotives. The idea occurred to him to ask the workman how close he worked. He asked him when fitting those pins: "How close do you come?" "We come within a bare sixty-fourth of an inch, and that is near enough for all practical purposes." "Well," said the visitor, "let me see what is your idea of a bare sixty-fourth. We will take the calipers, an instrument of this shape (indicating), and apply them to the crank-pin and measure between the points." He then told the workman to separate those points a bare sixty-fourth—so as to show his idea of a bare sixty-fourth. The workman did so and said "that is about it." A paper was inserted until a perfect fit was made again, and the paper was measured by a micrometer guage, and he found his bare sixty-fourth was just the .005 part of an inch.

Another workman was tried in the same way, in order to ascertain his idea of a bare sixty-fourth of an inch. That workman made the very best kind of work; both of them were engaged in fitting, and they worked very accurately. The result was the same. I tell you this instance to show you that the general idea of the finer divisions in measurement is so vague.

Now I will give you another illustration, showing you how important it is to come within that amount of fine division in construction, and show you that the .001 part of an inch is not to be sneered at.

Take a piece of metal with a half-inch hole in it, then fit a spindle, three inches long, to that hole, but making the spindle the one thousandth part of an inch smaller than the hole—that is, instead of making it five thousandths (.005), make it four hundred and ninety-nine thousandths (.499) of an inch in diameter, and insert it one-eighth of an inch into this hole, and allow the other end to stick out. (Indicating). It will then be found that the bar or spindle will move through an arc of three-sixteenths of an inch. To do that, or better than that, is what an ordinary workman tries to do, and generally succeeds. So that the thousandth part of an inch, you will find in many cases, on careful inquiry, is no useless refinement in measurements.

Now, there are two units of lengths which are in general use, namely, the metre and the yard. The yard has its origin in the length of the arm of King Henry VII. It was afterward the standard, or at least the yard was in actual use. It was referred to the length of certain metallic bars, and afterward the length of certain pendulums, and again, by further experiment, it was found better to refer it to the length of certain fixed bars, because the experiments made with the pendulum were found to have been subject to error.

The metre is the ten millionth part of the distance from the equator to the North Pole, as ascertained by actual measurement of an arc of the meridian.

Now I will first give you a synopsis of the history of the yard. During the reign of Henry I., an inch was declared to be of the length of three barleycorns, round and dry. It is indefinite as to how dry they should be, or how much of the end should be cut off to make it round. No record, however, exists of the actual construction of the standard of units based upon use of barleycorns, but Acts of Parliament were passed for the purpose of securing some uniformity among the ordinary measures, in accordance with which certain standards were placed in the Exchequer, with which all rods were required to be compared before they were stamped as legal measures. The oldest standards date from the time of Henry VII, but those have long since been disused. There, was another small rod called an "ell," equivalent to a yard and a quarter. Perhaps you will remember in the old books that five quarters, or a yard and a quarter, made an ell. It was to be used as a legal measure. It was regarded as one and a quarter yards. That remained until a rod half an inch square was placed there in the time of Queen Elizabeth. As one writer remarks, "this is about as good a standard as a poker filed at both ends." In fact, it was afterward broken, and then dovetailed together, and after that it would have made as good a pair of tongs as it would a standard of measure.

In the year 1742 some Fellows of the Royal Society and members of the Academy of Sciences at Paris proposed to have accurate standards of the measures and weights of both nations made and carefully examined, in order that the results of the scientific experiments in England and France might be correctly compared. They found several standards, one of them (at Guildhall) being an ell, and the others yard measures. The committee selected the standard (kept in the Tower of London), which consisted of a solid brass rod about seven-tenths of an inch square and forty-one inches long, on one side of which was a yard divided into inches. From this two copies were made and sent to the Academy of Sciences at Paris; on these was set off the measure of the Paris half toise. One was kept at Paris and the other returned to the Royal Society, but as it was not stated at what temperature the toise was set off, the comparison is now of little value. In 1760 a rod was finished by Mr. Bird by order of the House of Commons and declared to be the legal standard of all measures of length. This rod was marked "Standard Yard of 1758," and was a copy of the standard in the possession of the Royal Society. No further action was taken by the government until 1824, when a very thorough revision was attempted. These investigations resulted in the adoption of the imperial standards and measures under George IV., which took effect January 1, 1826; these standards were retained by the enactments under William IV., which took effect January 1, 1836. In the imperial measures, the yard copied from the standard of 1760 was to be of brass, and measured at the temperature of 62° F., while its length was further defined by declaring that the pendulum beating seconds of mean time in the latitude of London at 62° F., in a vacuum at the level of the sea, should be 39,1393 inches of the above standard. In 1838 a commission was appointed, who, in 1841, reported that serious errors had been made in the experiments with the pendulum, and that the condition that the yard was to be a certain brass rod was the best that could be adopted, and that by the aid of the Astronomical Society's scale, and a few other highly accurate copies known, the standard could be restored without sensible error. Mr. Baily was selected to prepare the new standard, and after his death in 1844, Mr. Sheepshanks continued the necessary observations, executing, himself, in the course of his labor, about 200,000 micrometric measurements. He prepared several copies, each being a square inch bar, consisting of copper, zinc and tin, 38 inches long, with half-inch wells sunk to the middle of the bar and one inch from each end, in which the lines defining the yard are drawn on gold plugs. These standards were legalized in July, 1855. One of them, marked "Bronze 19," was selected as the parliamentary standard yard, and "Bronze 11" was presented to the U. S. Government.

There is one point I wish to draw your attention to, and which will be necessary to understand before you can take up the consideration of the relation between the metric system and the inch or yard system. The points I wish to give you will be, I think, rather detrimental to the metric system.

All civilized nations of the present day use the Arabic system of notation, but it is so familiar to you that I need not describe it. Other systems of notation can, however, be used; and, although the decimal system has advantages, still, at the same time, it has defects. The binary method counts by twos, and has but two figures, viz, 1 and 0. The ternary counts by threes, and has three figures, 1, 2 and 0. The quaternary counts by fours, and has four figures, 1, 2, 3, 0. The quinary counts by fives, and has five figures, 1, 2, 3, 4, 0.

It will be seen that these systems all use the cipher, while the number of significant figures is indicated by the name of the system. Where a greater number of figures than 9 is required, the additional ones are represented by letters of the alphabet.

In addition to the systems already named, we have the senary system, that counts by sixes. Its figures, of course, would be 1, 2, 3, 4, 5 and 0. Then there is the septenary system, which I do not think has ever been used. It counts by sevens; its figures are 1, 2, 3, 4, 5, 6 and 0. Then the octary system, counting by eights, and the nonary, counting by nines, and the decimal system, counting by tens. Then there is the undenary system, counting by elevens, and the duodecimal, counting by twelves, and the vicenary, counting by twenties, and the tricenary, counting by thirties. Now how are all these used? In this way: I set down any number, say 1256, in the decimal system—that is, one thousand, two hundred, fifty and six; or, one thousand two hundred and fifty-six altogether. You see that the figure 6 occupies the first place to the right, and the figure 5 is one remove to the left, and the figure 2 is two removes to the left, and the figure 1 is three removes to the left. The figure 5 has ten times the value it would have in the first place, and the figure 2 a hundred times the value it would have in the first place, and the figure 1 a thousand times, and so on. In *all* systems, the first place to the right is the place for units, but the value of the other places depends entirely upon the system of notation used. Thus, in the binary method, we have, commencing at the right and going to the left, units, twos, fours, eights, sixteens, and so on. In the quinary method, we have units, fives, twenty-fives, one hundred and twenty-fives, etc. In the decimal system, we have tens, hundreds, thousands, etc. In the duodecimal system, we have units, twelves, one hundred and forty-fours, seventeen hundred and twenty-eights, etc.

Now the principal advantage of the binary system lies in the fact of its capability of continual bisection. This operation you can practically perform without using any measuring apparatus whatever.

Decimal fractions are much more convenient to use than regular fractions, and here we have an advantage of the duodecimal system over the decimal, as the following table will plainly show, the former system requiring fewer figures.

Decimal Scale.		*Duodecimal Scale.*	
$\frac{1}{2}$	= .5	$\frac{1}{2}$	= .6
$\frac{1}{3}$	= .333+	$\frac{1}{3}$	= .4
$\frac{1}{4}$	= .25	$\frac{1}{4}$	= .3
$\frac{1}{5}$	= .2	$\frac{1}{5}$	= .2497
$\frac{1}{6}$	= .166+	$\frac{1}{6}$	= .2
$\frac{1}{7}$	= .142857	$\frac{1}{7}$	= .186A35
$\frac{1}{8}$	= .125	$\frac{1}{8}$	= .16
$\frac{1}{9}$	= .111+	$\frac{1}{9}$	= .14

In using the duodecimal scale it must be borne in mind that .6 is not six-tenths but it is six-twelfths, .4 is four-twelfths. As stated previously, when a system requires a greater number of characters than ten, the additional ones may be represented by letters of the alphabet; hence the duodecimal .186A35.

Now this subject is a foundation of comparison. I shall give you a history of the metric system and the method of comparison of the metric system with the old system, and the manner in which measures are made, at the next meeting.

Conclusion of the lecture on " Weights and Measures," by John E. Cook, Ph. G., at the fourth Social Meeting, held Tuesday afternoon, January 9th, 1883.

At the last meeting I gave you a short historical account of the yard measure, and also of the various systems of notation. At this meeting I shall give you a brief history of the metre. The metric system was suggested as long ago as 1528 by Jean Fernal, a physician of Henry II., of France, but the suggestion did not take a practical turn until 1790, when Prince Talleyrand distributed among the members of the Constituent Assembly of France a proposal for the formation of a new system, upon the principle of a single and universal standard. A committee of the Academy of Sciences, consisting of five of the most eminent mathematicians of Europe —Borda, Lagrange, Laplace, Monge and Condorcet—was subsequently appointed, under a decree of the Constituent Assembly, to report upon the selection of a natural standard; and the committee proposed, in its report, that the ten-millionth part of the quarter of the meridian of Paris should be taken as the standard unit of lineal measure. Delambre and Mechain were appointed to measure an arc of the meridian between Dunkirk and Barcelona. This arc, comprising about 10° of latitude, was measured trigonometrically and compared with the arc measured by Bouquer and La Condamine in Peru in 1736, and the length of the quarter of the meridian, or the distance from the equator to the pole, was calculated. This length was divided into ten million equal parts, and one of these parts was taken for the unit of length and called a metre, from the Greek word *metron*, a measure.

If the arc of the meridian is calculated from the result of French researches, the metre itself is equal, in English measurement, to 39.37079 inches; and, multiplying this length by ten millions, the length of the quadrant of the meridian when converted into feet, will be 32,808,992 feet. Sir John Herschell estimates the length of the quadrant of the meridian at 32,813,000 feet; so that, according to his calculation, there is a difference between the French and the new estimate of the quadrant of 4008 feet, and therefore the French length of the quadrant is $\frac{1}{8194}$ too short, and the metre is $\frac{1}{208}$ of an inch less than the length of the ten-millionth part of the quadrant. It will be readily seen from this that the metric measurements are just as arbitrary as the yard and its divisions, and in case the actual metre should be lost there would be as much difficulty in replacing it as there would be in replacing the yard.

Now suppose we wish to *make* a yard or metre measure, how shall we proceed to do it? A metre measure is in the possession of the Conservatory of France, and one is also deposited in the Archives of Paris. The original yard measure is held by the government of Great Britain, and copies are held by other governments, including the United States. Of this forty copies were made and distributed to various governments, the United States receiving the one marked No. 11.

The standard yard is a bar of bronze, 38 inches long and 1 inch square on the cross section, the length being taken at the temperature of 62° F. The yard itself (36 inches) is the distance between two lines drawn on gold plugs, which are sunk in wells near each end of the bar. The reason of these plugs being sunk in the metal is as follows: If a bar of metal be suspended by its extremities, it will swag down in the centre, the particles of matter in the upper surface being compressed and those in the lower surface being extended. Midway between the two surfaces is a line in which the particles are neither compressed nor extended, and this is termed the neutral line. Hence the plugs are placed in depressions deep enough for the lines to be on this neutral axis.

The standard metre is a bar of platinum, differing from the yard in two important particulars, viz: the length is taken at the temperature of 32°, and it is an end measure—that is, it is exactly one hundred centimetres from end to end; it is also two and a half centimetres broad and one centimetre thick.

We will now proceed to show how a comparison may be made with the standard, or rather with a copy of the standard. The original is not used, as too much handling would injure it. Two blocks of hard wood, of the shape of a right-angled triangle, have a semi-circular depression made in the perpendicular side of each of them, and two fine threads are stretched across these depressions. The standard copy is then placed upon a perfectly plane piece of wood, which is somewhat longer than the copy. One triangular block is placed at one end of the copy, so that the end (in the case of the metre), or the line drawn on the gold plug (in the case of the yard), is directly under the threads crossing the depression in the block. The other block is similarly placed at the other end, and the copy is then removed. The bar that is to be marked is now carefully laid between the blocks, and the position of the lines to be drawn is determined by sighting down the double threads on the end blocks. This is, of course, a rough mode of proceeding, but it shows the principle of many comparators, or instruments for comparing the length of any given rod or bar with that of the standard.

The Richards' measuring machine consists of an instrument in which the distance between two "centres" is determined by means of bars of a known length at a certain temperature. The bar to be measured is then placed between the "centres," and, if it be longer or shorter than the standard bar, the amount is indicated by the forward or backward motion of a micrometer screw, which actuates one of the "centres." It will be seen that this instrument indicates differences of length, and not the actual length. The Rogers' system consists of a pair of microscopes sliding on "ways," between which is placed the bar to be measured. It is obvious that if the portion of the instrument supporting the bar is not perfectly flat that the measurement will be worthless, for if there should be any horizontal or vertical curvature, the ends of the bar will be thereby brought nearer together. To obviate this curvature, set-screws are used, by which the necessary corrections may be made. The importance of paying attention to temperature is shown by the care with which Prof. Rogers made his observations. Through the co-operation of the President of the college (Harvard) he was allowed the privilege of fitting up a special room in the basement, and, although the change in the temperature of the outside air varied from 10° to 30°, he found, by accurate observations in this room, that in three weeks the range was considerably less than 2°. In making comparisons with the official standards, he made but six observations at a time extending over a period of not more than about fourteen minutes; he then allowed the room to rest for about a day and a half, so that the temperature of the room would be restored, and the standard would resume its original length.

We now arrive at a very important part of our subject, namely, the division of the yard or metre into parts. It must be understood at the outset that there is no such thing in existence as a Government foot, inch, or centimetre; that is, that there is no such division of the yard or metre in the actual possession of any government. The only standards that are recognized are the yard (by Great Britain and the United States), and the metre (by Continental nations). Any division of these, even if it is made by any department of the Government, has no more value than a division made by a private individual, unless it should be made more accurately.

The simplest and easiest way of dividing the yard or metre is by hand, making use of the binary system; that is, by continual bisection. This is done in the following manner: Take a line, which in the present instance will be 36 inches or one yard long. Taking each end as a centre, describe two circles each of two feet radius.

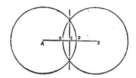

Then erect a perpendicular passing through the points of intersection of the two circles. This bisects the lines, as may be proved in the following manner: As the two circles are made with the same radius, therefore A D=B C. Now C D is, of course, equal to itself; therefore, A D—C D= B C—C D; that is, A C=B D. Now, by construction, C E has been made, equal to D E. But A C=D B; therefore A C+C E=B D+D E; that is, A E=B E; hence the line A B has been bisected. In the same way A E and B E may each be bisected, and the process continued until the whole line A B has been divided. In actual practice the division is made by means of a cutter set on the periphery of a divided wheel, which constitutes what is termed a dividing engine.

The object of the dividing engine is to reduce the error of subdivision to the minimum, and it is done as follows: The circumference of the index wheel is divided into a large number of parts, say 200. The cutting instrument is applied to the bar that is to be divided, and a mark is inscribed. The wheel is then turned to the next division, and another mark is made, and this process is continued until the wheel has made an entire revolution. The excess or deficiency of the markings is then ascertained, and the necessary correction is made. Thus, if after the wheel has made a revolution, the last division is found to be $\frac{1}{100}$ of an inch too large, this shows that each division is $\frac{1}{200}$ of $\frac{1}{100}$ of an inch too large; that is, that the error is $\frac{1}{20000}$ of an inch, an error that amounts to but little in actual practice.

DISCUSSION

Which took place at the Third Social Meeting, held Tuesday, December 12th, 1882, on the New Pharmacopœia of 1880.

Mr. Lucius E. Sayre remarked as follows:

Mr. President:—Having been called upon to introduce this very important subject, I would say that I am aware of the fact that it is possible for me to lay out too wide a scope for this discussion. The Pharmacopœia contains a vast number of formulæ, and we could spend profitably several hours in the discussion of the Pharmacopœia without going into very great detail. When we approach the criticism of it we should bear in mind that while such a book may be subject to a considerable number of just criticisms, we will all admit that this work shows, however much we might object to certain parts of it—illustrations of the progress of pharmacy in the United States. You can readily see that we are in keeping with the age. We are in a state of progression, and this book, as we have it before us to-day, we can point to as we can to pharmacy itself, with pride.

Now, in bringing before you this book, we cannot help but say some few words in regard to certain introductions and omissions. We see omitted from the list of the Pharmacopœia 230 articles, and we have introduced about 250. Out of the 230, I must say that I regret to see a number of preparations familiar to us omitted. For instance, Sol. Morphia and

Deshler's salve. Then there are a number introduced which seem to me unnecessary, but they are used in another part of the country, though not much used in Philadelphia. It was necessary to provide for the wants of the whole country, and when we take into consideration the vast extent of it, we may safely say that the selections that have been made in the articles introduced and placed in the Pharmacopœia have been very wise. It is not unnatural, at the beginning of a criticism of this kind, to throw out many compliments. A speaker feels generally safe in doing so. But we must take these things before our minds and criticise them honestly. That is the object of our coming together, of our pharmaceutical meetings, and of our work. We are to take the Pharmacopœia in our own hands and individually criticise it, and we should communicate this to the journals. Let your criticism be fair and concise—let it be pointed. I hope that many of these gentlemen present will help in the next decade, undoubtedly they will improve our present standard. It is before you now, and there is a work to do before 1890, and the work we have to perform is this, to bring our standard into greater simplicity. We want a standard that is very simple. We have, for instance, certain classes of preparations which cannot be easily calculated. They are either ten, twenty or fifty per cent. representatives of a drug, as the case may be. Let us have simplicity, that is what we want. The aim has been to arrive at this in the Pharmacopœia just issued. We may come short of it in many cases. Take the tinctures. We have a vast variety of tinctures that come up in our minds as students and physicians, and owing to the diversity existing it is difficult to recollect the exact percentage of their strength. We have aconite of a certain percentage, and we have valerian of another, and so on. There is no need of encumbering ourselves by too much detail. We meet at the outset in the U. S. Pharmacopœia with the term "abstract." That is a point that I think would be worthy of discussion this afternoon, and if we took that up we would have as much to do in discussing it as the time would allow.

I would call your attention to the solid extract of Ergot, and how easily it is prepared, by the simple evaporation of the fluid extract, and the introduction of the other portions, which is a point well worthy of our comment. I have found that for dispensing such a powder is a very convenient thing to handle—especially the alkaloids, such triturations are especially desirable. If we have strychina, four grains in a hundred, let it be to twenty-five per cent. trituration. One grain would therefore represent a quarter grain; a half grain would represent a one-eighth and so on. Now, it is very much easier to weigh out this triturated material. When we wish an eighth or a sixteenth, it is easier to weigh it out than it would be to divide it using the pure alkaloid. I think that the triturations are a very valuable addition, and that we are soon to become very familiar with them. I think the use of the absorbent cotton simplifies the making of the medicated waters very much. Phosphate of lime and carbonate of magnesia, will separate the globules of the essential oils, but absorbent cotton seems to be a very simple way for this purpose, as you will find in the U. S. Pharmacopœia. Without taking up too much time in this matter, Mr. President, I would bring up another point, which is a practical one, and one which, as I have stated in a previous meeting, is of importance—it is, with regard to the use of "parts." "Parts" have, to some minds, no value, and to good practical laboratory workers it is hard for them to get into the use of "parts." In the introduction in the new formulæ of this term—in the Pharmacopœia—there is a considerable difficulty; a person who would otherwise be fully qualified to compound, not being a good arithmetician, which is a common failing, is apt to make some mistake, and these cases of error we must guard against. I will illustrate this: We have the formula for liq. potass citratis, thirty grains citric acid, and forty grains bicarb. potassium (about) to a fluid ounce of water. If we desired four fluid ounces the calculation was easily made—the numbers 30 and 40 were simply multiplied by four.

The New Pharmacopœia calls for citric acid, six parts; bicarbonate of potassium, eight parts; water, sufficient quantity to make eighty parts. It will be seen at once how much more difficult the calculation is in the latter problem. To make the necessary calculations for four fluid ounces of the new one, we are obliged to resort to a considerable mental arithmetic and apply the rule of three, thus: as eighty is to six so is 32 (the number of drachms in four fluid ounces) to the quantity of citric acid required, and so on. Now although one may be a perfect druggist, there is a chance of his making an error in his calculation especially. And what is an error, what its effect? It is the ruination of a business oftentimes. A man may be ever so prominent in his business, the more prominent he is the greater the downfall if he makes a single error. So I say that everything should be done with great care. A single error may be disastrous. We cannot do the compounding ourselves, but we must delegate it to good men. It is necessary to have a good level head and accurate calculators. To the young men I would say you must not only know the characteristics of the drugs and chemicals and articles used, but must be also level-headed. That is certainly to be desired, but it is a common failing as I have pointed out. Without dwelling any longer upon the subject, I would simply leave this matter in your hands for discussion.

Dr. A. W. Miller said:

The object of bringing this matter up for discussion was not so much that of hearing extended remarks from any particular individual, but to draw out the thoughts of students and visitors. We have a number of distinguished gentlemen here, some of the College graduates, whom we should be very glad to hear from. I should be very glad now to hear the voice of Dr. Turnbull on the New Pharmacopœia. No doubt he has some thoughts which will be of use to us.

Dr. Turnbull:

I would be glad to give my views in regard to the matter, and I would say that I have glanced over it, but have not studied the matter, and I come here to listen, and not to speak.

The President:

I think it would be a good idea to call upon some of the senior members of the Class. I think that they could discuss the subject thoroughly. It is certainly a very important subject to them. We would be pleased to hear from any of you, gentlemen.

Dr. Miller:

There was one point that I would like to call attention to, namely, in reference to the centesimal scale. I see a great advantage in committing it to memory. Heretofore it was necessary to remember carefully not only the active ingredients, but also of the amount of the diluent and all other different materials. Now, according to the new plan, if we simply charge our memories with the relative amounts it is sufficient. For instance, solutions of arsenic are one per cent. solutions; they contain one per cent. of arsenic, whatever the diluent may be. Formerly we had to remember so many kinds and so many ounces of diluent. It was different for every one of the solutions of arsenic. I believe they are all now brought to a uniform strength. I see a marked advantage in these labor-saving appliances, so far as the student is concerned. In looking over the book I was notably struck with the marked influence that the Germans had in its construction. There are a great many preparations of drugs introduced that heretofore have been only in use among the Germans. These have been used by the German physicians and German pharmacists in Germany and in this country. It is, no doubt, due to the fact that the book was published and largely prepared in New York, where the Germans seem to have a greater influence than with us. For instance, calendula flowers, and a number of other drugs of this kind that are in use by them, have been introduced. Now, as to the triturations alluded to by Mr. Sayre. It seemed to me as though this was an approach to homœopathy. I fully coincide with what has been said, and I see no especial harm, and no especial objection to learning from homœopathists, or our enemies, if we may so style them. Other things have been learned from them. Physicians no longer give the enormous doses that they formerly gave, and that much has been obtained through their influence—through the influence of this recognized system. Then, I am not as yet aware whether the attention of the gentlemen have been called to an error in the Pharmacopœia. I refer to the opium preparations. This is an extensive fault. There is a difference in the strength of the tincture of opium. It is stated to be ten per cent. greater than in the old Pharmacopœia, while it really is about fifty per cent., according to Squibb's statement. The method of analysis is defective in not fully indicating the per centum. The same is true with reference to other preparations of opium.

I am also unaware as to whether iron has yet been lectured upon to the present class. The phosphate of iron, as we have found out, is now an entirely different preparation from what it formerly was. The phosphate of iron, as we were accustomed to see it, was an insoluble slate-colored powder. That prescribed by the present Pharmacopœia is of a bright green appearance—bright green scales, similar to the pyrophosphate of iron. It is also soluble. It is a phosphate of iron held in solution by the acetate sodium. It is therefore a citroferic orthophosphate. It is a very much more eligible preparation than the former one. There is another preparation of iron which we have which I conceive to be a very valuable one for certain purposes. It is a very great advantage over the ordinary form as it does not cause any loss of time in preparing it. In making up the ordinary antidote for arsenic, we are aware that it must be freshly made. In order to have it freshly made; it must be precipitated and washed with water to remove the caustic alkali, and to avoid this the present Pharmacopœia prescribes a mixture of calcined magnesia in the proper quantities and mixed together, well shaken, to be administered to the patient. It must be administered at once to the patient. The preparation of this article can be completed in a few moments. In this it has an advantage over the old preparation for administration in cases of poisoning by arsenic. Arsenic is a strong corrosive agent, and if any effects are to be obtained from the antidote it must be administered promptly.

Now, I have read a story somewhere of the prophet who desired to have the mountain come to him, and he prayed and prayed violently and vigorously for a long time, but the mountain would not approach him, and when he found that his prayers were of no avail, he did the other thing, and he himself went to the mountain. Now, it seems to me that the patent medicines of the Pharmacopœia are almost in the same position ; that they all should be considered. We have now in the Pharmacopœia many of these so-called patent medicines. We have the emplastrum capsici and heavy magnesia and others. It seems to me that that is legalizing patent medicines ; indeed, I think that there may be some few others. These are the only ones that occur to me at present. I hope that this subject will be continued by some of the gentlemen in the room—the special subject of the New Pharmacopœia.

Mr. Sayre :

My attention has been called to a formula for the Mistura glycyrrizæ composita, which is a comparatively clear preparation, while previously it was muddy, and we were obliged to put "Shake the vial" upon the labels. The preparation is one which will please the physician and with which he will have very little trouble. For a long time, until we have fully digested the Pharmacopœia, it may present some difficulties in our making new preparations. In the course of a few months it will come into general use. It is a pity that a certain fixed date was not agreed upon, before the Pharmacopœia was issued, between the pharmacists in this country when the old book should cease to be used and the new one take its place, say March, 1883, as the date for the universal adoption of it. Then we would have had an opportunity of preparing ourselves, and getting rid of the old preparations, and would have had time to make the new ones.

I intended in the course of my former remarks to state that a very convenient balance has been devised by Henry Troemner, for the working of the "parts" of the New Pharmacopœia. By means of a sliding weight a bottle or beaker can be easily balanced, the accompanying metric weights are conveniently arranged in sockets in front, at the base of the scale. The metric weights will be necessary in using the parts. It will be better to dispense entirely with the use of the avoirdupois and troy weights in the laboratory. In working the parts I would suggest that we throw away almost as unnecessary the avoirdupois and troy weights, and work on the metric scale. We can then work the parts very well much more easily.

Dr. Miller :

I have been very much interested in the remarks that have been made, and I would say in reference to compounding prescriptions by weight that one soon learns to do it, and after it is once acquired the results will be more accurate than those obtained by measuring. •

Mr. Sayre :

I should like to hear an expression as to whether the Pharmacopœia has put into use the patent medicines, or whether we are having lessons from homœopathy. These are two points, I think, which are worthy of our consideration.   •

A Member :

This question which has been referred to, I think, is an important one, and should receive attention—the question of patent medicines.

Dr. Miller:

I do not know, Mr. Chairman, whether it is worth while to discuss what are known as patent medicines, as I presume, we all understand what patent medicines are. I, for one, would define a patent medicine as being a medicine the formula of which is held as a secret and the article is sold under a proprietary title. I am aware that this may include a great many things that are not generally so regarded.

Mr. McIntyre:

. As to the first point that was spoken of—the question of abstractum—I should like to ask what portion of this country this abstractum came from, or the practice of using it. It was certainly not from my section. We have had no call for them heretofore. I would also say that I think there is a wide difference between what we have understood as triturations in the drug store and the present list of abstracta. To be very explicit, we have all had triturations of morphine and triturations of strychnia. Such preparations act as a measure of convenience to the apothecary, to aid him in more rapidly dispensing small portions of medicine. The abstracts seem to be preparations of this kind.

Dr. Miller:

I think—if I am entitled to speak twice—that I would like to say that the abstracta originated in the adjoining room. When the College of Pharmacy appointed a committee to make a preliminary revision of the Pharmacopœia, Prof. Remington was one, with myself and another member to do the work. When Prof. Remington offered the title "Abstractum" in the adjoining room, a broad smile appeared on the countenances of those present, but the name appeared to be pleasant, and there seemed to be no objection to it, and we soon became accustomed to it, and rather liked it, and now it appears to have met with the sanction of the Pharmacopœia Committee.

As to the fact that they are not yet prescribed, I think that is due to the fact that physicians have not as yet become acquainted with them. They embody several points of value, and I think that they are likely to come presently into use. This matter of the relation of the dose to the crude drug is a matter of importance. The strength of the crude drug being one-half of the strength of the fluid extract, it is easily calculated. There will be no trouble in ascertaining the dose or the quantity to be administered.

The fact, also, that the abstracta can be dispensed in the form of powders is another thing which is of advantage. They are not liable to deteriorate in any manner. I was present at a meeting of physicians, some few weeks ago, and I there made some remarks upon the New Pharmacopœia. I referred especially to this class of abstracta. I think that there were several gentlemen present who heard those remarks, and one of the physicians present took occasion the next morning to write a prescription for the abstract of something. His object was, as he expressed it, to paralyze the adjoining druggist, which he did effectually.

Mr. Sayre:

In regard to the second point, there has been an article written in *The Medical Journal* calling attention to this matter—I mean as to the position of pharmacy at the present time.

Dr. Turnbull:

I would like to say a word in reference to the Pharmacopœia, and that is, that there seems to be very little in it for the physician, and thus the physician loses his interest. A very good thing has been done by Dr. Phipps, Professor of Materia Medica, and that is the preparation of a commentary for the physician as to the way of compounding several materials, and he has given a book on the Pharmacopœia, including the therapeutical qualities of the agents used in the preparations. I hope, some time in the future, to give such a synopsis myself; if I get the time I shall do it. Such a work would be of great interest to physicians, but the Pharmacopœia, as at present written, contains not a word as to therapeutics. Now the Dispensatory is a book that we refer to constantly; but, with regard to the Pharmacopœia, it is a book that is very little used by physicians.

Mr. Procter:

The matter has been brought up a number of times, and there was much difference in opinion as to whether therapeutics should be introduced, and it was the decision of the committee that it would be better not to raise any opposition in that way. I think that, if my recollection is correct, that was the way it was decided.

Dr. Turnbull:

There is another matter which is of importance, and that is the terminology. It is a matter of great importance, and I think should be discussed. I think that Dr. Miller will agree with me in this matter, that had the Pharmacopœia been prepared by physicians, in company with pharmacists, that this matter would have been arranged, and that we should have had more therapeutics in the volume. I think that it is a great mistake.

Dr. Miller:

While I agree entirely with the remarks made by Dr. Turnbull, I think that I can answer the points. In addition to what Mr. Procter has stated in reference to therapeutics, I would say that the book has been more especially prepared for druggists throughout the country. There are many druggists, especially in the country, who prescribe more or less, and it would be well if they were posted up on the therapeutics of the drug. There were reasons, and powerful ones, why therapeutics were absolutely excluded from the Pharmacopœia. Whilst they are sparingly dwelt upon in this college, yet they are mentioned to some extent. The reason is that we do not wish to encourage counter prescribing.

Mr. McIntyre:

The question of therapeutics is a question which interests the retail druggist to some extent. Whilst it is not absolutely necessary for him to know the whole subject thoroughly, it is necessary for him in his business to be able to supply the wants of citizens who apply to him. It is necessary for him to know, therefore, the therapeutic effects of the medicines to some extent.

Dr. Miller:

Dr. Turnbull has alluded to another feature of the Pharmacopœia, and that is the nomenclature. This will be troublesome to some, but I see no special reason why it should not be quickly learned. For instance, we have quinine and morphine and strychnine instead of quinia and morphia. The name of alkaloids which terminates in " a " have been changed. I take it that this is simply due to the effect that I have alluded to, the influence of the Germans of New York. The Germans have made all alkaloids, terminate in " in," and in order to harmonize with Continental Europe the Committee have changed the termination. There are some other changes which we have not now time to notice in detail. For instance, manganese is called " manganum," and we have " mangani sulphas " and " mangani oxidum,' and so on, a number of others. We have also chrysophanic acid. It is a change which is of value, as it renders everything uniform and harmonious. There are several other articles changed. For instance gamboge. It is now called " cambogia," and there are quite a number of others of greater or less importance.

A Member :

I do think that the Pharmacopœia is going to take away from the pharmacist the preparation of his own preparations, on account of the trouble there will be found in manufacturing the preparations. Every pharmacist cannot provide himself with a laboratory that has every detail necessary. Knowing how hard it is to make the preparations, the tendency will be to send to the laboratory of the manufacturing chemists for all preparations, instead of making them at home, as they now do.

As far as homœopathy is concerned I think that we take arnica from the homœopaths, consequently I think it would be nothing but fair to add that to the Pharmacopœia and give them the credit for it. Now we have also triturtations and all the alkaloids which we now use.

Dr. Miller:

I must add that I am not in harmony with the remarks of our worthy friend. There has been a good deal said about what is called the American fashion of measuring liquids. We contend with a great deal of force, that it is far less troublesome and takes far more time to measure the majority of drugs than it does to weigh them. On the other hand it is plain that they can be weighed much more rapidly than they can be measured. That a person expert with one system, and another equally expert with the other, doing the same thing, there will be a gain by the method of weighing. I think that this will be found to be the case, with the use of "parts" as now laid down by the Pharmacopœia weighing, will soon be the only way of dispensing medicine.

Mr. Andrew Blair:

I would like to add a word with regard to the difficulty of making preparations by the New Pharmacopœia. It has a good many objectionable points, but I do not propose to take them up in detail. This tendency in the Pharmacopœia will undoubtedly deter many pharmacists from using many of the preparations. It is a very scientific book, more so than any that we have ever had before. If it is to be a book to be put into the hands of the thousands of pharmacists throughout the country, with the expectation that they will make use of it and make their own preparations I think that there will not be many followers. There are many good points about it, but I think that there is also a great deal of intricacy about it. There are many processes which are much more simple than those given in the New Pharmacopœia. I think that it has been one of the greatest advantages to that class of manufacturers throughout the country, which we, as pharmacists, are interested in, that we are not recognized as dealers,   We are pharmacists, manufacturing pharmacists, but the tendency of the New Pharmacopœia will be to reduce our profession to that of one dealing in commodities which are purchased over the country. The effect will be to send the small dealers to the drug manufacturers. As merchants, where there is a great deal of competition, of course we are all anxious to buy goods as cheaply as we can. Take an example—the fluid extract of buchu, which is twenty-five cents per pound cheaper than that prepared by some one else, presents a great temptation to buy it. I will only say in one instance in reference to this subject, that is the price of making camphor water, which some present have heard a short discussion upon. The process of making it by the New Pharmacopœia is much more complicated than before, much more than it used to be. It is a question in my mind, even with the introduction of the new process, whether it is not altogether too scientific. There are thousands of young men throughout the country who will be expected to use it, and this is a consideration which seems to me has been overlooked largely by the framers of the New Pharmacopœia. That the book is practical is without doubt, but as I say, in the United States and throughout the country, there are comparatively few pharmacists, even in cities, who have had opportunities to thoroughly study the New Pharmacopœia, and it is a question in my mind whether it is going to be of the advantage that it would be if written in a more simple form. I think it would be desirable for every pharmacist to make his own preparations, even the most difficult. But when he makes his own preparations he wants to know all about them. The pharmacist should prepare these preparations himself and not leave them entirely to the manufacturing druggist.

Mr. Sayre :

Speaking of the manufacture of medicated waters, great care should be taken in their preparation ; the process should be thoroughly understood. No matter how carefully you conduct the present process a part of the oil will yet remain in the cotton. That has been my experience, and I have tried to do it repeatedly.

Mr. C. C. Meyer :

I believe that the intention of the Pharmacopœia is that the oil shall not be entirely dissolved, but simply that the cotton is to be saturated with the oil. The point is to divide the globules of oil with the cotton.

Mr. Sayre :

With regard to the remarks of our friend, I should like to say that I thoroughly coincide with those views--that we want to keep the work of preparing medicines in our own stores, and not delegate it to manufacturing chemists, as they have been called. The more we can encourage, by any means whatever, the having of this work done in our own stores, the more a desirable end is accomplished. I was rejoiced one day by a physician coming into my store and saying, "Have you got Wistar's Cough Lozenges? Do you make them yourself?" "No, sir." "I don't want them." I can make them for you in a short time, but they will not look as nice as those made by the manufacturer, but they will have the proper quantity of morphia in them." "That is what I want," he said, "and that is what others want. They want to know that what they get contains the proper constituents and the remedy prescribed."

Mr. McIntyre:

There is something that should always be borne in mind, and that is this: That it is no matter what the Pharmacopœia presents, or what the druggist makes, or what the doctor orders, but it does matter what the sick man gets. The sick man wants medicine that will produce a cure, and it is important that he should get that quality of medicine. It is in the interest of humanity. I think we will all acknowledge this.

ANCHORS OF HEALTH.

A lecture, by Dr. C. C. Vanderbeck, Ph. D., Professor of Hygiene at Wagner Free Institute. Delivered at the fourth Social Meeting of the Alumni Association, held Jan. 9th, 1883.

GENTLEMEN OF THE ALUMNI ASSOCIATION, AND STUDENTS OF THE PHILADELPHIA COLLEGE OF PHARMACY :—I feel as if I owe you an *apology* for offering such a subject for lecture, " The Anchors of Health." What have we, as doctors and pharmacists, to do with that science that is to lead people to a better type of living and rob us of our earnings? I am no prophet, yet I dare to predict that many of you seated here this afternoon will see the time when sanitary science will receive universal sanction by professional men as well as laymen, and a new order of business springing up by reason thereof. I desire *not* that this lecture discourage any student here, and cause him to wonder whether he had better not at once retire from the *Collegiate race* and to the *farm and plow.* Fear not! Pharmacy and Medicine have a future even more glorious than the past, and if you are doing your duty in preparation, you may well be thankful to belong to either profession. If you are not suited to them; if you are ill-prepared, there is a tribunal right at hand--your Professors and Examining Committee, and they will kindly tell you whether your future is a *mortar* or a *plow.* But the pocket-book, the pocket-book, tell us of that. Glory won't make the mare go, but CASH will. Where can you make a $20 drug store exist in the face of all that you hope Hygiene to accomplish? It is almost needless to attempt to sway the hearts of American men on ordinary occasions except by the means of the clink and the clang of the almighty dollar. To cause them to forsake business, to expect less income, less profit by the cry of glory, honor, humanity, is inconsistent with the American make-up. We are recognized abroad as a nation of *money-makers*, our castes are largely based on money, and wealth is the key to position and honor, and a cloak for a multitude of sins. This is not exactly due to the causes mentioned by the Irishman when the Frenchman asked of him, " How is it that your countrymen will fight for money and ours for glory?" Pat answered, " I suppose we both fight for what we most need—*we money, you glory.*"

It is not so much our need of money, but it is the American's possibilities, the chances for the poorest boys to accrue golden heaps. It is the incalculable undeveloped wealth. The rivers and soil teem with precious stones and metals. Crest after crest of mountain ranges hold in their embrace all kinds of metals and gems. The growing cities and budding plains invite energy into their midst and repay in shining, glittering gold. In the face of all this can we expect the drug man to be moulded of different clay? Is his life's work to be a drudgery, unrepaid? God forbid. He who becomes almost a fixture of the store, changed only to air and refreshen, at it

early and late, pulled out of bed for a postage stamp, and cursed· at for for-
getting to say " Thank you." He who yet has it in future to see Chestnut
street by electric light, and could not see the Jersey Lily ; the poor hard-
worked, overworked five-cents-a-pop-drug-man—God forbid that I say he
should ever take in less than $10.00 a day, and make it $50.00 if he can.
But now back to the subject: Hygiene WILL advance. *Put that down as a
fact.* Now if the over-heated rooms of our stores have not dried up our
brains and made them too hard to think acutely, we must meet this fact
squarely. There will be tons of drugs used for generations to come. Even
when Hygiene is an every day study at school, the fools will still be abroad
and disobeying the laws of health, call upon doctors and drug stores. Yet
these laws will be so acted upon by many, that the work of both doctor and
druggist will be to a degree modified. He is a wise man who laughs not at
these truths and wins the golden reward of being first in the ranks of the
new order and getting the cream of wealth and honor.

Let us examine what this new order of business may be, and in this
way one object of my lecture will have been accomplished, *i. e.* to urge the
importance of penetrating the future, seeing its probabilities and possibilities and work already for the reward it holds for those who are ready for
them. Another object is to gain your friendship for this grandest of
sciences that you may not consider it your enemy. I think that in the
future, preparations will be seen upon our shelves—marked well, we'll
say Tinct.—of—*Bugicide, i. e.* the germ theory, though rather over-esti-
mated in my opinion, has much truth in it, and to conquer disease we
must meet it in its *incipiency.* We must seek it in its *haunts.* What
scientific man here to-day who does not thrill with delight as he thinks the
dark, black cloud of obscurity is being penetrated, and he can, like a man,
meet disease causation in its very den, and give it fight while yet in its
infancy, before it becomes a grim monster, prowling about our fair earth
from the cradle with our blossoming little ones, our dearest and fairest com-
panions. *Fie* on the man who cannot bless the microscope and the keen
·eyes of science in their rooting out of pestilence and death ! Practically,
gentlemen, there is a future for substances to *positively* and *surely* destroy
or modify the life history of germs. This implies my doubt of carbolic
acid and kindred articles. Present disinfectants do have a certain use,
but the *ultimatum* is not yet reached. Every well-regulated drug store in
the future will have a department for approved health foods, and the
·doctors will be so wedded to the practice of hygiene that small and inex-
pensive *ozone generators* will be largely bought and used in every sick
room. We can sell cheap *spirometers* for household use. Chest expanders
(here is one of homœopathic origin), be careful that we are not left behind.
Little things like little powders often take. Solutions for wet friction baths
will be more called for. Bath gloves will be daily sales. Perfumes will
drop off a little, the extra care taken of the skin demanding less of perfume
to cover the smell of dried and decomposing sweat. This will be more than
made up by the increased sale of tooth brushes, tooth powders and fine
soaps. Cosmetics as ladies' powders, etc., will be out of style ; a few only
will be kept in a drawer with some articles seldom called for. Narcotics
will be less sold. Sundries for sick-room use and for the aid and comfort
of the patient will be greatly in demand, and a wide field of undeveloped
possibilities lies just here. Thus what is lost in *one* way is made up in
another, and the aggregate sales of the future store will be just about the
same to those who do not growl at progress and meet its demands. Gentlemen, if I understand these social gatherings, they are for culture, for
widening your views, lifting you for a time into new roads of thought and

out of old ruts. Allow me, then, to drop the drug-store connection of hygiene and worldly gain, and talk to you of sanitary science for its own pure sake. Trusting to your progressive spirit to herald it as a *friend* to suffering *down-cast humanity—a friend* to YOU, to ME and to ALL ALIKE. Lend me now attentive ears while I speak first of the meaning and scope of hygiene, then of such applications as our limited time will admit, which applications I have designated

ANCHORS OF HEALTH.

What is hygiene? It is the department of knowledge which inquires into the influences which surrounding agents, both moral and physical, have upon the human body, and to present the best means for developing the system and preserving its functions in a state of health.

The word hygiene is derived from classic mythology—the Goddess of Health—the daughter of Æsculapius. Æsculapius appears in Homer as an excellent physician of human origin. After a time he becomes the God of the Healing Art, having two sons and three daughters, one of whom was Hygeia. The followers of Æsculapius are called Æsclepiades, who inherited and kept the secrets of the healing art; or, assuming that Æsculapius was merely a divine symbol, the Æsclepiades may be regarded as a medical priestly caste, who preserved as mysteries the doctrines of medicine. Hippocrates is said to have descended from the Æsclepiades of Cos, who traced their descent, on the mother's side, from Hercules. Hygeia was the Goddess of Health of the Greeks; the Romans called her Salus. From these two words are derived the English words "hygiene" and "salutary."

It is true that the art of preserving health was not unknown to the ancients, in fact, it has been practised from earliest times. Even before Hippocrates, the great father of medicine, there were treatises on hygiene, which the great master embodied in his wonderful and incomparable works. Nevertheless, hygiene did not reach the dignity of a science until recent modern times. It was formerly based upon empirical rules, simply on observation of what seemed good or ill for health, but the revelation between the amount of food taken and of the mechanical force produced by it, the effects of different kinds of air, water and soils on health, etc., were either slightly or not at all understood. The ignorance of *chemistry* prevented, in fact, any great advance in this direction. The history of chemistry tells us that though the Egyptians preserved dead bodies from decay, fixed colors in silks by means of mordants, prepared many medicines and pigments, also soup, beer, vinegar, metallic alloys, common salt, vitriol, sal-ammoniac, glass, enamel, tiles, etc. Though the Chinese were early acquainted with the processes for dyeing and the preparation of metallic alloys, the fabrication of nitro sulphur, gun-powder, borax, alum, porcelain, verdigris, paper, etc., yet the first germs of a real science of chemistry did not appear until the end of the seventeenth century. After this the science rapidly advanced. It is obvious that the hygiene consideration and of the respiratory organs must have been imperfect, *unscientific*, before the *composite* character of the atmosphere was understood, and this fact remained hidden until 1724, when Hale published researches on the air and aeriform bodies, showing that the carbonic acid evolved during fermentation, respiration and by the action of acids on chalk, was different from atmospheric air. Nitrogen was discovered by Rutherford in 1772; oxygen by Priestley in 1784. The same remark holds true about the effect of different kinds of water and soil on health, ignorance of the true chemical science of geological chemistry and of mineralogy, precluded the examination, to any degree of perfection, of the elements, often potent agents generating and propagating disease. Hygiene then is now a science but not by any means an exact, fully developed one, for the simple reason that the sciences on which it depends are not exact. Chemistry, as just mentioned, is one of the basic sciences of hygiene, but this branch of knowledge is far from being perfect. Vast, unexplored regions are in the shadowy distance. Who has shown us the germs of malaria? Who has gathered the first specks of an epidemic poison? We can put up lightning rods that will protect us from the thunderbolts, but what chemist has shown us how to put rods that will protect us from a foul atmosphere. You can drain morasses that you can see, but you cannot free the atmosphere from impurities that you cannot see. The deadliest poisons are those for which no test is known; there are poisons so destructive that a single drop insinuated into a vein produces death in three seconds and yet no chemical science can separate that virus from the contaminated blood and show the particle of poison glittering palpably and say "Behold, it is here!" In the drop of venom which distills from the sting of the smallest insect, or the spikes of the nettle leaf, there is concentrated the quintessence of a poison so subtle that the microscope cannot distinguish it, and yet so virulent that it can inflame the blood, irritate the whole constitution and convert day and night into restless misery. There is no question that many mysteries of nature are yet to be revealed by chemistry and kindred sciences, but it is well to accept the fact that many mysteries will ever be locked from mortal here, and that the ages of eternity wil be partially spent in unraveling the intricacies of a vast universe made by an omnipotent and omniscient Creator. Science tells us that the activity of opium is due to morphia; that the virulency of nux vomica depends upon the presence of strychnia, that the terrible malignancy of the wourari poison with which the savages of the Amazon impregnates their arrows is corrovalia, a poison so persistent and terrific that though exposed to the air for many years it will, upon application to the slightest puncture, destroy the most robust animals in a few minutes. But after all, what is morphia? strychnia? corrovalia? A combination of carbon, hydrogen, nitrogen, and oxygen, elements similar, excepting the nitrogen, to those that exist in starch, sugar cane, grape sugar, etc., containing precisely similar elements as indigo and some other coloring agents.

It is needless to pursue the difficulties presented by inorganic and organic chemistry to the rapid progress of hygiene. The human intellect cannot fail to stagger in endeavoring to grasp the vastness of the unknown. Prime remarks, in his "Studies of Nature:" "I propose, therefore, to begin my work when I had ceased from observing and collected all the materials necessary to a history of nature, but I found myself in the condition of a child, who, with a shell, has dug a hole in the sand to hold the water of the ocean. Again, physiology is another science upon which hygiene is now based. This is in direct contrast to the school of alchemist and iatrochemist, who endeavored to increase, strengthen or indefinitely perpetuate life by the discovery of an elixir of life. Physiology teaches the various functions of the body, and the laws of life are being applied more and more to the prevention of disease. It endeavors not so much to apply some rejuvenating, vivifying substance, as it does to protect and ward off manifold injurious influences surrounding man on every hand. Physiology applied to hygiene demands no remedial life-growing elixir, but seeks to keep the harmonious workings of the beautiful system unmolested. It is obvious that, as accuracy is acquired in the knowledge of the functions and relationship of each and every part of the human economy, so must a more intelligent idea be obtained of the numerous deviations from normal action, and, and, the more perfect this becomes, the more firm is the basis upon which intelligent scientific hygiene rests.

WHAT IS DISEASE?

Many difficulties are yet in the way. Physiology, like chemistry, has many unploughed fields. As Park says, " If we had a perfect knowledge of the laws of life, and could practically apply this knowledge in a perfect system of hygienic rules, disease would be impossible." This happy state of affairs will probably never exist in this world ; indeed, it may be safely considered that a degree of sin, evil and sickness will continue to the end of time. Let us now, for a few moments, look at the scope of hygiene. It covers an immense field, for, taking the word in its largest sense, it signifies rules for culture of mind and body. " For a perfect system of hygiene we must combine the knowledge of the physician, the schoolmaster and the priest, and must train the body, the intellect and the moral soul in a perfect and balanced order." Hygiene, then, deals with the whole man, his body, mind and soul, and calls from its students and workers the highest powers of the intellect.

Let us now examine some of the chief laws of health for the gaining and keeping of good health—or figuratively the " *anchors of health.*"

The sheet anchor of health is cleanliness. Holding in mind the composite character of man, this law applies to his whole being. For a clean *conscience* I refer you to next Sunday's church. For a clean mind, one healthful and strong, with errors eradicated and one built up to make you all successful men, I refer you to the communion with books and men of superior minds. For *a clean body*, I ask you to widen your ideas from simply the *bath-tub* and a *piece of soap—skin cleanliness*—to the wideness of import that the word cleanliness is capable of bearing. It would be a waste of your valuable time to formulate for you laws of bathing. You are scientific men, more or less acquainted with the laws of physiology, and you know that skin, kidneys and lungs act with one another in ridding the system of waste materials, and unless the skin is kept sweet and clean and active, too much work is thrown upon the lungs and kidneys, and thus the way is paved for the two dread scourges of humanity—consumption and Bright's disease.

The great law of cleanliness is hygiene—means far more—it asks for your *stomach* clean, pure and wholesome food. It asks for your *heart*, for your *tissues*, bone and muscle, *nerves* and *tissues* clean, pure blood. It asks for your *lungs* and system at large clean, pure air. It demands clean clothing, clean houses and bed-rooms, clean streets and cities, clean water, clean sewers. It requires the removal of dirt of all kinds. It questions the right of factories to impregnate our water supply with refuse. It asks what is smoke, and can it harm a city's healthfulness. It pierces with keenest vigilance every possible source of disease, and asks for purity for disinfection—for the quick suppression of all filth, decay, dirt, darkness, dampness, and all that your mind suggests as being unclean.

Verily this is the sheet anchor of hygiene. Again, you are careful to a man about pure, clean food, and if the law of health is broken in this score, you are not at fault—your butcher or your market man deceived you—and this is your *misfortune*, not your fault, and you agree at once that we should have active food-regulating laws, to protect us from decaying, disease-breeding foods.

But now, dear hearers, I strike the key-note of an evil that sounds its chords in a thousand avenues of life. The disgustingly vile, the terribly unhealthy habit of living on our own and other refuse. What do I mean?

I mean you would resent with vigor the idea of drinking your own and your clerk's urine. You would not lick the sweat off your patient mortar-grinder's forehead. But—but—

You will, you do, devour his and others' worn-out, refuse breath. The *first breath*, the *inspiration*, of man should always be clean, pure, sweet; the *second* is, by nature of used-up air, more *unclean*, air more *poisonous*, often holding in its grasp decayed matter from old, carious teeth, cells from consumptive lungs. This we eat, we breathe, without one murmur. Sweet as it may be to sip the honey from the fair young damsel's lips, back of the *honey* lurks a *sting*. The moral is easily told—do your courting in a ventilated room. Did you ever see a glass of milk returned that held a hair? a cup of coffee that held a fly? a plate of soup with a mouse in it? a knife with yesterday's fish on it? a spoon that told of eggs? Do you like to see each gravied knife go into the butter-dish? What think you of the common soup-bowl, *a la mode* Chinese, each John dipping from the communistic tray. Horrors! By what line of thought, then, can you make it pleasant in closed-up shop, in sitting in sleeping-rooms, in hall or car, to breathe an air that has just been bathing the insides of perhaps some foul and syphilitic wretch? We may possibly make a little allowance for the before-mentioned lover, who will sip away at his sweetheart's mouth, not objecting if he sucks away the spittle, that he will not object to just breathing some air that has been deep down in the recesses of his darling's bosom. But, for the most of us, we will choose—at least, I hope we will—clean air. I have but time for suggestions, trusting to awaken thought in these matters. I pass on to another *anchor*.

REST.

We need to hear something of this in America. The great trouble with hygienic lecturers. Exercise is a very essential element of securing good health, but we do not hear enough of the extremes and opposites. All good things can be abused; there is an extreme to all laws. Alcohol is a boon, and yet it is a curse. Mercury gives health and life, and is one of our *materia medica's* best gift, and yet how extreme is the prejudice.

To many a closely confined man, it is not so much more exercise he needs as more air and change. We start out each day with a morning capital of energy. If we use it up at the books, in selling, in business, we have but little to spare for severe exercise, as heavy weights, dumb bells and gymnastics, to many a man, has proven a snare and a *death*.

Finally, the only anchor time will permit me to notice now is

GRIT.

Here is a strange message for you. It may seem unorthodox. Hygiene means care of health, Yet I say to you be not too careful. Here again extreme may be in error. The everlasting "take care" can be made a device by which existence is converted into a prolonged weariness. Life becomes a white elephant. Constitutions differ like faces. Is each face alike and numbered in the forehead? So rules must be for individuals. The pains taken to prolong life may actually shorten it. It is the blowing off of all the steam of an engine in the whistle. The pursuit of health may be like making a violent effort to go to sleep. The effort keeps us awake. Let none of us be too willing to accept the name of a delicate person. Be proud of saying I am grandly well; out upon the doleful sympathizer who says you do not look well.

This kind of sympathy seems at once to strike the chord of human nature that responds with an amen. The world don't want such people. If they continually croak and complain, out with them. Shove them off on the sidings of the main track of industry and traffic, thought and work. ·

Let us be full of *grit*. Even when disease comes along. Gentlemen, for your kind and close attention to me, on a subject so foreign to your usual study and thought, may I hope that a passing hour has left some seed behind that will fructify into an abundant harvest.

LECTURE.

Delivered by Dr. Laurence Turnbull, Ph. G., Class of 1842, Aural Surgeon Jefferson Medical College Hospital, on the New Pharmacopœia (1880); with some hints on Therapeutics, at the. Fifth Social Meeting, held Tuesday afternoon, February 13th, 1883.

Pharmacy is the art which teaches the knowledge, choice, preservation, preparation, and combination of medicine, so as they shall produce their full results. Without some knowledge of pharmacy a physician must be at a loss, for although therapeutics are distinct from pharmacy, some acquaintance with the latter is necessary to a correct application of the former.

The basis of both these studies is a knowledge of materia medica, or the substances employed in medicine. In every civilized country there is some recognized work of standard drugs and their preparation, known as the Pharmacopœia. In all European countries it is prepared at the expense and has the sanction and authority of the government and becomes a law at a certain fixed date ; while, in this country, it is the voluntary action, both in its preparation and adoption, by a representative convention meeting every ten years. At a recent visit to Boston, at the centennial of the Massachusetts Medical Society, I had the pleasure of examining a complete series of all the Pharmacopœias of the world; the first which was issued in this country was by the same society in 1808, and the second by the New York Hospital in 1810; these never extended beyond their respective States.

The first United States Pharmacopœia was published in Boston, December 15th, 1820, just sixty-three years ago ; a second edition of this same appearing in 1828. ·

In 1830 two Pharmacopœias were published, one in New York and one in Philadelphia,.owing to some misunderstanding on the part of the presiding officer. With the view of giving the various medical interests of the United States Government (which had not been done before) a proper representation in the convention of 1840, the Surgeon-General of the army and the Senior Naval Surgeon at Washington were invited to participate in the proceedings. The convention appointed a Committee of Revision and Publication consisting of seven members, three to form a quorum, and the meeting of the committee to be held at Philadelphia. To this Committee were referred all communications received by the convention from the various organizations represented.

The Committee was authorized, for the first time, to request the cooperation of the Colleges of Pharmacy in the United States. Valuable assistance was rendered to the Committee by the Colleges of Pharmacy of Boston, New York and Philadelphia, especially the latter. At their suggestion and recommendation, the process of displacement, or percolation, was introduced for the first time. The work was not published until 1842, and the Latin version was omitted. Then followed the revisions of 1850; a second edition 1855, 1863 and 1873. Then followed the call of Dr. James M. Morgan, the assistant secretary, and last surviving officer of the convention of 1870. Here let me pause, and for a few moments take a retrospective glance at the great and good men of our city, both of the medical and pharmaceutical profession, now deceased, who devoted their time and talents to this work, such as Drs. G. B. Wood, Franklin Bache, Joseph Carson, Robley Dunglison and Robert Bridges; and, on the other hand, Daniel B. Smith, William Procter, Thomas H. Powers, Edward Parrish, William Hodgson, Jr., Augustus Duhamel, now passed from us, but leaving the remembrance of their devotion to their high calling and the true work of good men to the cause of medical science and philanthropy. May we who remain emulate their virtues, and " whatsoever our hands findeth to do, do it with our might, for the night cometh, when no man can work."— Ecclesiastes, ix., 10; John, ix., 4.

The convention for the sixth decennial revision of the Pharmacopœia of the United States of America met at the city of Washington, D. C., on the fifth day of May, 1880, and the work was compiled and published under the guidance and supervision of a committee of revision and publication. The volume has 488 pages, issued by William Wood & Co., of New York, in 1882, which is now before us. In its general character and tone it is pharmaceutical rather than therapeutical. That is owing to the pharmacist having done almost all the work. The divisions of the Pharmacopœia of 1870 into primary and secondary lists of drugs and preparations have been abolished, and single alphabetical arrangement adopted, similar to the British Pharmacopœia. The drugs derived from the vegetable and animal kingdoms are briefly described as to their physical structure and chemical combinations, but not a word of physiological action, medical uses, doseage or toxicological effects. Processes for preparing chemical compounds have been omitted. This is proper where expensive apparatus and large quantities are required to be made, but not in the case of small preparations, as the iodide of mercury, etc. Except in a few cases, each chemical is described, its physical properties, chemical reaction, and impurities and tests of purity. For pharmaceutical preparations definite quantities of weight and measure are not employed, but by expressing the quantities by their relation to each other, except in the preparations of pills, the quantities being given in grains and grammes. Fluid extracts only grain weights are given, and for solid and liquids, except that the final product is to measure so many cubic centimetres.

The following table from the work exhibits the differences of strength of preparations made according to the Pharmacopœia, 1870, and the present, 1880.*

(A copy of which I have placed on the black-board.)

Name of Preparation.				Number of parts of active constituents to 100 parts by weight of the preparation.	
				Phar. 1870.†	Phar. 1880.
Acetum Lobeliæ,	.	.	.	13	10
Acetum Opii,	.	.	.	16.3	10
Acetum Scillæ,	.	.	.	13	10
Acetum Sanguinàriæ,	.	.	.	13	10

* This table embraces all changes which can be considered sufficiently great to require notice, and all changes of above one per cent. in the strength of preparations used internally. It does not note trifling changes in the composition of preparations intended for external uses.

†For liquid galenical preparations the figures in this column are only approximately correct, as the calculations into parts by weight involves the specific gravity which is subject to considerable variation.

Name of Preparation.	Number of parts of active constituents to 100 parts by weight of the preparation.	
	Phar. 1870.	Phar. 1880.
Acidum Aceticum,	35	36
Acidum Aceticum Dilutum,	4.5	6
Acidum Hydrochloricum Dilutum,	7.8	10
Acidum Nitricum Dilutum,	11.6	10
Acidum Phosphoricum Dilutum,	9.8	10
Acidum Sulphuricum,	About 100	96
Acidum Sulphuricum Dilutum,	12.1	10
Acidum Sulphurosum,	About 6.4	3.5
Alcohol Dilutum,	39	45.5
Confectio Sennæ,	8.33	10
Extractum Aconiti,	Leaves	Root
Extractum Conii Alcoholicum,	Leaves	Fruit
Ferri et Quininæ Citras,	16 Quinine	12 Quinine
Liquor Acidi Arseniosi,	0.87	1
Liquor Ferri Chloridi,	35	39
Liquor Potassæ,	5.8	5
Liquor Potassii Arsenitis,	0.87	1
Liquor Sodæ,	5.7	5
Opii Pulvis,	10 or over	12 to 16
Opium,	About 8	9 or over
Opium Denarcotisatum,	——	14
Spiritus Anisi,	6.8	10
Spiritus Camphoræ,	14	10
Spiritus Cinnamomi,	8	10
Spiritus Juniperi,	2	3
Spiritus Lavendulæ,	2	3
Spiritus Menthæ Piperitæ,	6.4	10
Spiritus Menthæ Viridis,	6.4	10
Spiritus Myristicæ,	2	3
Tinctura Aconiti,	47.6	40
Tinctura Aloes,	3.3	10
Tinctura Aloes et Myrrhæ,	Each 12	Each 10
Tinctura Arnicæ Florum,	23	20
Tinctura Asafœtidæ,	16	20
Tinctura Calumbæ,	15	10
Tinctura Cannabis,	36*	20*
Tinctura Cantharidis,	3.5	5
Tinctura Capsici,	3.5	5
Tinctura Catechu Composita,	7	12
Tinctura Cinchonæ,	25	20
Tinctura Conii,	Leaves	Fruit
Tinctura Cubebæ,	15	10
Tinctura Gallæ,	15	20
Tinctura Guaiaci,	23	20
Tinctura Guaiaci Ammoniata,	23	20
Tinctura Humuli,	17.5	20
Tinctura Lobeliæ,	15	20
Tinctura Myrrhæ,	12	20
Tinctura Nucis Vomicæ,	3.5 or less †	2†
Tinctura Opii,	9‡	10‡

* In reality 6 of the extract, which is equivalent to about 36 of dry Cannabis Indica.
† Of dry extract.
‡ The actual morphine strength is increased nearly one-half.

Name of Preparation.	Number of parts of active constituents to 100 parts by weight of the preparation.	
	Phar. 1870.	Phar. 1880
Tinctura Opii Deodorata, . . .	9	10
Tinctura Quassiæ, ...	6	10
Tinctura Rhei, ...	10	12
Tinctura Serpentariæ, ...	15	10
Tinctura Stramonii, ...	15	10
Tinctura Valerianæ, ...	15	20
Tinctura Valerianæ Ammoniata, . .	15	20
Tinctura Veratri Viridis, ...	55	50
Tinctura Zingiberis, ...	31.8	20
Unguentum Acidi Carbolici, . . .	12	10
Unguentum Acidi Tannici, . . .	6	10
Unguentum Belladonnæ, ...	12	10
Unguentum Gallæ, ...	12	10
Unguentum Hydrargyri Ammoniati, .	8	10
Unguentum Hydrargyri Oxidi Flavi, .	8	10
Unguentum Stramonii, ...	12	10
Unguentum Zinci Oxidi, ...	16	20
Vinum Ergotæ, ...	12.5	15
Vinum Opii, ...	13	10
Vinum Rhei, ...	14	10

It will be noticed in the above table that there has been changes in the strength of the liquid opium preparations, all of which, except pare-goric, are made so as to contain ten per cent. of opium, whilst the wine and vinegar are reduced from wine, 13 to 10 ; vinegar, 16.3 to 10. If the direc-tions of the New Pharmacopœia are strictly followed out, the result will be a tincture which will contain on an average six grains of morphia to the fluid ounce, whilst our old laudanum has about four grains to the ounce.

If, therefore, the full anodyne dose of the tincture—deodorized tincture, or compound solution of opium,—has been 24 minims, or 38 drops, repre-senting a quarter of a grain of sulphate of morphia, the corresponding dose of the new preparations will be 16 minims, or say 25 drops. This is an important change, and might be dangerous if not recognized, and, even if it did not produce poisonous results, would be attended with headache, nausea, etc., as observed by Dr. Squibb.* In physicians' prescriptions, for example, if deodorized tincture of opium is ordered, the figures "1870" or "1880" should be added, and he should give the dispensing pharmacist the liberty of using whichever preparation he might have, in the proper proportions of 1½ to 1, until the change becomes established. That is, if the 24 minims of the "1870" should be ordered, the pharmacist should use instead, 16 minims of "1880," if he happens to have the new and not the old strength.

As the old preparation and the new are identical, excepting the mor-phia strength, it is only necessary to dilute two measures of the new prepa-ration with one measure of menstruum to reduce them to the exact strength of the old preparation. For diluting the tincture of opium, or the deodor-ized tincture of opium, diluted alcohol should be used. For diluting the compound solution of opium, alcohol should be used.

The diluted mineral acids are made of a uniform ten per cent. in strength, except in the case of hydrochloric and sulphuric, the former of which has been increased one-fourth in strength, while the latter has been decreased one-sixth. This will alter the dose in both. We find an important

* In *Ephemeris*, by Dr. Squibb, Nov., 1882, page 151.

omission in Dover's powder; the sulphate of potassium is left out, while the name is changed from pulvis ipecacuanhæ compositus (1870) to pulvis ipecacuanhæ et opii (1880). Of the six important spirits, camphor has been reduced nearly one-third, while peppermint and spearmint have been increased nearly sixty per cent. Tincture of aconite root has been reduced one-seventh, and its name has been changed to simple tincture of aconite.

The dose should be from 1 to 5 minims, and not as is stated in some of the physician's visiting lists, from 5 to 15 minims; for three drops of a saturated tincture has proved fatal in a child. Compound tincture of catechu has been nearly doubled in strength; tincture of nux vomica, dose from 8 to 25 minims, has been decreased about forty per cent. Tincture of stramonum, dose 5 to 15 minims, and serpentaria thirty-three per cent., of veratrum viride ten per cent.; dose from 5 to 10 drops, not repeated oftener than three hours, owing to the tendency to cause nausea and vomiting with depression. Children should begin with one drop. While the tincture of ginger has been reduced about forty per cent, a more dangerous change has been made in the case of the extract of aconite, which is now to be made from the root instead of the leaves, although the old name, extractum aconite is retained. There are therefore three preparations to which the name may be at present applied by the prescriber or pharmacists: First, the old hydro-alcoholic extract of leaves (U. S. 1870); second, the fresh juice English extract; third, the extract of the root (U. S. 1880). The new extract is probably more than twice as strong as the hydro-alcoholic extract of the leaf, and at least six times as strong as the fresh juice preparation. The dose of the three extracts, whose name is the same, are respectively No. 1, one-half a grain; No. 2, one and a half grains; No. 3, one-sixth of a grain.

The "ferri phosphas" is entirely changed from the old green insoluble powder. It is now a compound phosphate, containing six parts of phosphate of sodium, and is in transparent bright green scales, having an acidulous taste, being made from citrate of iron.

The following aromatic waters: aqua anisi, camphoræ, cinnamomi, menthæ, piperitæ, and menthæ viridis, which in the Pharmacopœia of 1870 were made by triturating the oils with magnesia and then filtering them, are in the Pharmacopœia of 1880 made by adding so many parts of oil to absorbent cotton in small portions at a time, distributing it thoroughly by picking the cotton apart after each addition, then pack it firmly in a conical percolator and gradually pour on distilled water. Those of our pharmacists who have tested this plan differ as to the satisfactory character of the preparation as compared with the method in which magnesia was employed or by distillation. We find the following valuable preparations dismissed from the Pharmacopœia—carbolic and carbonic acid waters. This latter is a most valuable agent as a vehicle for many disagreeable drugs and also very useful in allaying nausea and gastric disturbances. Also two valuable officinal remedies—infusum senna and spigelia for the destruction of the round worm, are dismissed, which was a great improvement upon the old domestic remedy, the "worm tea." There has been substituted troches of "santoninate of sodium" in their place. This salt, as well as santonin, which is still retained, are poisonous, according to Prof. Wood. The first being soluble and the taste very disagreeable it must be employed with caution. It should be prescribed in doses not larger at first than 5 to 8 grains for an adult and 1 to 3 for children and taken at night, because its action is less interfered with and the yellow vision is not so apt to disturb the child. The following day a purgative should be given.

The majority of the Committee determined to spell the unit of weight gram, by adding *me* to it.

The Latin names of alkaloids have been made to terminate in *ina* and the corresponding English names in ine.   The so-called neutral principles have received the termination inum.   English—As examples (alkaloids), morphina, morphine; quinina, quinine.   Neutral principles—picrotoxinum, picrotoxin; santoninum, santonin.   The gender of the Latin nouns of salts is *as*, and *is* has been changed back to the masculine gender.   The following tables are introduced: List of reagents, tables of elementary substances, thermometric equivalent, tables of percentage and specific gravity, tables of solubility of chemicals in water and in alcohol, saturation tables, list of articles added and dismissed from the Pharmacopœia, tables exhibiting the differences of strength of the preparations as made according to the last and present Pharmacopœia, tables of weights and measures.   These will make seventy-five additional pages, increasing its size and cost, but are not all necessary, as most of them can be found in any recent work on chemistry or dispensatory and have no relation to the work as a standard authority to govern the medical or pharmaceutical profession.

The text of the Pharmacopœia, 1880, begins with *"Absinthium—Wormwood."*   This article the writer knows nothing of in medicine, having never seen it nor heard of its being prescribed in an experience of forty years, although it has been in the Pharmacopœia since 1840.   In this we fully agree with Dr. Squibb.*

ABSTRACTS.—This is an entirely new class of preparations and under a new name not before known in medicine.   The class is introduced by the committee at page 31 of the preface by the following paragraph: "To supply a demand which has arisen for dry powdered extracts a new class of preparations has been introduced under the title of Abstracta.   As will be seen on examination, these are just twice the strength of the crude drug or about twice the strength of the corresponding fluid extract."

The demand for a class of dry powdered extracts has, in Dr. Squibb's experience not been great, and what demand there was came from pharmacists rather than from physicians.

"The chief objection to them is that they require a troublesome, expensive, and hurtful process to effect so little in the way of concentration, condensation, and convenience."   "With the exception of belladonna and senega, all the abstracts could have been made much stronger.   Almost all of them could have been made to represent the drug in the proportion of one grain to four, and seven out of the eleven could have been made the strength of one to five as easily as they are now made one to two, and the main question as to their utility will be whether, therapeutically, it be worth while to go through such processes to gain so little.   The probable reason why many of them were not made of greater strength is that a few, one or two of them could not be made so, and it was considered best to sacrifice the nine to the two in order to have them bear a uniform proportion to the drug.   This may be good pharmacy, but it is bad theory or therapeutics, because the doses and uses are not materially improved by this uniformity nor benefited in any other way."

"Had these preparations been called powdered extracts, and had their processes been made supplementary to those for the officinal extracts of which they form a part and to which they naturally belong, and had each been made as strong as was practicable without injury, their chances of officinal permancy would have been much improved.

"Abstractum Aconiti (abstract of aconite).—U. S. P., 1880." The extractum aconite of the Pharmacopœia of 1870 was made from the dried leaf, while the extractum aconite of the present revision of 1880 is made from the powdered root.   When the powdered sugar of milk is added to

---

In *Ephemeris*, by Dr Squibb.

the fluid extract, and the mixture is set aside to evaporate, as directed, a very long time is required for this step. In a portion representing ten troy ounces of the powdered root five days' time was needed to effect the evaporation, although the mixture was frequently stirred, and it is doubtful whether this long exposure, even at the low temperature directed, be not hurtful or even more hurtful than a shorter exposure to a somewhat higher temperature. If the dish be shallow, the evaporation goes on rapidly enough until the mixture becomes a tough tenacious *mass* of a pilular consistence, but after this it dries very slowly indeed. It is far better practice to evaporate the fluid extract without sugar or milk and incorporate this at the end, for in this way a portion of similar size can be made in twenty-four hours, but the abstracts generally are not well made on a large scale, and are appropriate only to the dispensing pharmacist, at least until they prove to have therapeutic advantages to justify a general usage. Each dispensing pharmacist can easily make them for himself on the scale of his own demand by the following process: Take of fluid extract of aconite root 30 cubic centimetres, 480 grains of the root, powdered sugar of milk a sufficient quantity.

It is difficult to recognize the therapeutic uses and convenience of this preparation, and if it has no special value it is objectionable as complicating the pharmacy of a dangerous but very important drug.

"*Abstractum Belladonnæ* (*abstract of belladonna*).—U. S. P., 1880." When this is once fairly understood perhaps there is no danger of confusion. But the Pharmacopœia is now strictly alphabetical, and is referred to as a dictionary is, and a person who refers to the preparations of belladonna without going further than the title is not cautioned or reminded that there are two parts of the plant in use, the one much stronger than the other.

The first part of the above process is practically identical with the process for fluid extract, and, therefore, the process is shortened and simplified by taking an equivalent proportion of the fluid extract of belladonna.

These formulas and processes for abstracts are all alike in manipulations, and it was shown in the case of the abstract of aconite that it was very objectionable to add the sugar of milk before the evaporation, for reasons there given, and therefore, that the evaporations should first be completed or be nearly completed. By far the best way, however, is to make the abstract in small quantities, and avoid heat altogether, as follows: Take of fluid extract of belladonna root 31.5 c. c., if of the new official fluid extract, or 30 c. c., if of the older minim for grain strength,—either of these will represent 480 grains of the powdered root,—and of powdered sugar of milk a sufficient quantity.

The ordinary dose of belladonna root is about 2 grains or the equivalent quantity of 2 minims of the fluid extract, and in this dose is repeated, according to circumstances, every 2, 3 or 4 hours, until the pupils dilate and the mouth and fauces become dry. The equivalent dose of this abstract would be one grain, and it would be generally given in a capsule or a soft pill. Indeed, there is hardly any other way in which it could be given, and if so, the same capsule half filled with powdered sugar of milk, or any other absorbent powder, would receive and secure the equivalent 2 minims fluid extract and be given with equal facility and convenience, so that there really seems to be no necessity for this preparation when the extract, fluid extract, and tincture are supplied and already well known.

"*Abstractum Conii* (*abstract of conium*).—U. S. P., 1880." In the revision of 1880 the leaves are very properly dropped as feeble at best, and very uncertain and perishable. Then, by the rule of the preface, at page 28, the seed, being the only part retained, takes the title of conium simply, and from the seed all preparations are now made.   Hence it happens that all the preparations whose titles were heretofore extract of conium, tincture of conium, etc., and which were made from the feeble leaves, are now, without any change of title, made from the stronger seed, so that, without change of name, they are now more than five times stronger than before.

The process for this abstract is exactly like that for the foregoing abstracts, and all that was said there applies with equal force here, and the same simplified formula and process are applicable here only with still greater advantage over the officinal process, in the avoidance of all heating.   Of all drugs, conium is perhaps most injured by heat, and it is, therefore, almost certain that this preparation made by the officinal process, which requires heating to about 50° C. (equals 122° F.) for four or five days, would be inert.

The dose of conium being large, and the fluid extract being a rather nauseous preparation, there seems to be reason for some such preparation as this abstract, but these reasons would require the preparation to be as strong as practicable.   The doses of conium and its preparations are generally very much understated, and where such small quantities are given the medicine is useless.   Twelve to sixteen minims of a well-made fluid extract of the unripe fruit (called seed) is required to produce a moderate effect, and such a quantity is about a medium dose.   Six or eight grains of this abstract, if made without heat, would somewhere nearly represent such a dose.   Either of the quantities could be put into two capsules, and the dose would be thus more easily taken than the equivalent dose of fluid extract.   But it would still be more easily taken if of double the strength, as it should be.   The extract, if made without heat and given in pill, would, however, be still better, as a dose of 2½ grains would represent 15 minims of fluid extract.

"*Abstractum Digitalis* (*abstract of digitalis*).—U. S. P.,1880." The same objections occur in the practicable application of this process as was noted under abstract of belladonna, and the same substitute process is equally applicable, so that it is only necessary to refer to them.

The dose of digitalis is not over one or two grains, or one or two minims of the fluid extract, and such a quantity of the latter—which is by far the best preparation of this drug—is so very easily taken, either in water or dropped upon powdered sugar of milk in capsules, that the most fastidious persons would be satisfied with one or the other.   The reduction of such a dose to one-half the quantity does not seem to justify this addition to the preparation of digitalis.

"*Abstractum Hyoscyami* (*abstract of hyoscyamus*).—U. S. P., 1880." This formula and process are the same as that for belladonna, with only the change in the name of the drug and the additional direction that the hyoscyamus be recently dried.   The objections to the manipulation and the substitute process are both equally applicable here, and therefore need not be repeated.

The dose of hyoscyamus is universally very much understated, and its medicinal uses and effects are as commonly lost through the mistake of the authorities.   Long ago Dr. John Harley showed (see "Old Vegetable Neurotic," p. 330) that one fluid ounce of the British Pharmacopœia tincture is required to procure sleep.   This is equal to about 56 grains of the powdered drug, or nearly a fluid drachm of the fluid extract, or say 28 grains of this abstract when of the strength of one to two, and such a dose of a powder would be more difficult to administer than a fluid drachm of the fluid extract.   Neither would the abstract offer any special advantage in combining hyoscyamus with conium or with opium, since its great bulk or volume would still be very much in the way.

"*Abstractum Ignatiæ (abstract of ignatia)*.—U. S. P., 1880." According to the best authorities, this drug is a mere duplicate of nux vomica, containing the same active principles, but in a more variable proportion. This disadvantage does not seem to be counterbalanced by any known advantage over nux vomica, and, if not, then ignatia is a useless complication of the already overloaded materia medica.

"*Abstractum Jalapæ (abstract of jalap)*.—U. S. P., 1880." This formula and process for the abstraction of jalap is the same as that for belladonna, with only a change of the name of the drug. But there is no reason why they should be the same, as the conditions and results are so very different that the same process is not equally applicable. There is no necessity for wasting the alcohol in this preparation, nor of separating the percolate into two parts, nor of limiting the temperature of the evaporation. The old extract of jalap, with the single exception of the alcoholic extract of nux vomica, were far more frequently, as well as more largely, used than any other extracts with which the writer* has any knowledge or experience. Indeed with above-mentioned exception, they were more largely used than all other extracts together, for there are few substances in the materia medica which have stood their ground better, or with less advertisement, than jalap, for the reason that there are few of such general utility with smaller liability to abuse. It is a hydragogue cathartic, and although in such general and large use, it is rarely given alone. Hence this abstract or alcoholic extract presents a very useful form in which it may be combined in administration. The dose of officinal jalap alone, to give a full hydragogue effect, would be about 15 to 18 grains, but uncombined, and in such a quantity, it would prove irritating. The equivalent full dose of this abstract would be 7 to 9 grains, or of the alcoholic extract, 2.5 to 3.5 grains. But in the combination into which it enters with the most advantage, the compound cathartic pill for example, it enters in the proportion of 1 grain of the abstract, or say one-third of a grain of the alcoholic extract in each pill.

On page 444 it is found that extract of Jalap is dismissed, when in reality and in effect the process is improved under a new name. Then in looking at the "list of changes of officinal Latin titles," at page 447, no notice is found, although in effect it is really and substantially a change from *extractum jalapæ* of the Pharmacopœia of 1870 to *abstractum jalapæ* of the Pharmacopœia of 1880. All these points being known and recognized little inconvenience can arise, but it is feared that they are not generally known.

"*Abstractum Nucis Vomicæ (abstract of nux vomica)*.—U. S. P., 1880."— The abstract is a dingy or yellowish-white powder, and does not clog at all. But it only represents the nux vomica in the proportion of 1 to 2 where it might have been easily made to represent it in the proportion of 1 to 8. But of what use this abstract is to be in the presence of the officinal extract, which, if properly made, fully represents the drug in the proportion of about 1 to 12, the writer cannot see, especially as the better extract can be easily and safely made so as to rub into a powder. The demand for an extract of nux vomica of pilular consistence has very nearly ceased in the experience of Dr. Squibb, and the demand for a powdered extract will not be likely to be satisfied by this abstract of a strength of 1 to 2, when a powdered extract of the strength of 1 to 12 has long been supplied at a very much smaller proportionate cost, and a very much greater practical convenience.

The dose of good nux vomica is from 2 to 3 grains, and, therefore, the dose of this abstract would be half that amount for the same uses,

---

* I am indebted to Dr. Squibb for the facts in regard to the preparation of the "abstracts," etc.

while the equivalent dose of the powdered extract would be about one-sixth that of the abstract.   The abstract is too bitter to be well administered in any other way than in a capsule or in a pill ; and, if so given, it has no advantage over the powdered extract, nor, indeed, over the fluid extract, except that this latter preparation partakes more largely of the inequalities in strength of the different lots of the drug from which it is made.   Fluid extract, rubbed up with powdered sugar of milk in the proportion of 2 to 3 minims to 5 grains of the powder, can be about as easily filled into capsules as the abstract can, and will be as easily administered ; or, capsules half filled with powdered sugar of milk will receive 2 to 3 minims each of fluid extract from a minim pipette about as conveniently as they could be filled with equivalent weight doses of the abstract.   Hence an abstract of nux vomica appears to have been really least needed of any yet considered.

"*Abstractum Podophylli* (*abstract of podophyllum*).—U. S. P., 1880."   This preparation can certainly be of no practical utility or importance in the presence of an extract, a fluid extract and a resin, especially when the resin is known to be a perfect representative of the drug, while all other preparations vary with every variable quality of the root, no test having been adopted for the quality of the root.   It is well known now that the poorer the root the less resin it yields, and that the resin, like that of jalap, is practically the same, whether from rich or poor root, and hence there seems to be no real need or use for any other preparation than the officinal resin.   Then, if there be no use for them, they are not simply surplussage, but are objectionable from their greater liability to vary in strength with the quality of the drug from which they are made.   Indeed, judging from the root met with in the market, they can be rarely twice alike, and still more rarely of good standard quality."

"*Abstractum Senegæ* (*abstract of senega*).—U. S. P., 1880."   This formula and process is, with the exception of the name of the drug, exactly the same as those for extract of belladonna, and the same objections and the same substitute process are equally applicable here.   But senega is not well exhausted with alcohol.   Indeed, Procter states (see *American Journal of Pharmacy* for 1860, p. 150,) that polygalic acid is the chief active principle of senega, and that this dissolves in boiling alcohol, but the larger part separates upon cooling.   These statements have never been controverted, and Dr. Squibb believes that no better menstruum has ever been proposed for exhausting senega than that proposed by Prof. Procter at the time when he so thoroughly investigated the subject.

This consisted of two parts alcohol and one part water, such a menstruum has been used for more than twenty years in Dr. Squibb's practice with good results and it has now been adopted in his revision of 1880 for fluid extracts, and why a different and probably very inferior and more costly menstruum has been ordered here is not comprehended.   No good reason can be suggested except that the alcohol rejects the pectin and other gummy matter to a greater degree than the more dilute menstruum, and therefore yields a smaller amount of extract, yet such a reason would have little weight in the Committee against the fact that the strong alcohol is not a good solvent for the active principle.

The extract of senega of the revision of 1870 is dismissed.   It was a very imperfect preparation, though quite susceptible of improvement and might easily have been so improved as to dispense with this abstract.   Indeed the abstract when well made is only the extract of 1870 improved, and this is another instance of a title being dismissed or dropped when the improved preparation is present under a new name without any intimation in the list of the real character of the change.

" Now, however, this abstract of senega is one of the most important of the abstracts and may prove very useful in the absence of a better extract. The dose of senega to be effective is quite large and it is quite acrid, producing a lasting disagreeable effect upon the mouth and throat. These have stood very much in the way of its useful application, while its importance as a remedy is very generally acknowledged. Some 12 to 15 grains of the powdered root repeated three or four times a day is about the effective adult dose. The equivalent dose of the abstract would be of half that, say six or seven grains, and this quantity can easily be put into one or two capsules, and be thus got into the stomach without the disagreeable acridity of the fluid extract or the syrup.

" *Abstractum Valerianæ (abstract of valerian).*—U. S. P., 1880." With only a change of title this is exactly the formula and process of the abstract of belladonna, and the same remarks and substitute process are equally applicable here. But the preparation when finished has ʾlost so much of the sensible properties of the valerian with which the process is commenced, that it must be nearly inert and almost useless for the purpose to which valerian is applied. Dr. Squibb made the preparation with great care, and with all the skill of which he is capable, and yet the resulting preparation was unsatisfactory when compared with the fluid extract from which it was made. The 30 c. c.—1 fluid ounce of the fluid extract on spontaneous evaporation as directed gave 2.88 grammes—44.14 grains solid extract equal to 9.2 p. c. of the valerian root represented. This required 190 grains of sugar of milk to make up the 15.55 grammes, 240 grains of abstract, and the result was a very handsome looking powder, but very defective in odor and taste when compared with the fluid extract—so much so that it can hardly be doubted that powdered valerian root would, weight for weight, be stronger in medicinal value. It seems, therefore, to be the least successful of all the abstracts. We are glad to see the introduction of hydrobromic acid but see no good reason for so much diluting of the acid as that can so easily be done at home. We much prefer Dr. Squibb's original article, as we have tested both the dilute and the preparation made by Dr. Squibb, and find his so much superior.

The only objection to the use of this in any form is that it is apt to produce dyspepsia and should always be associated with a stomachic or bitter tonic.

USE OF HYDROBROMIC ACID AND HYDROBROMIC ETHER IN TINNITUS AURIUM AND VERTIGO.

For about four years I have been testing the use of hydrobromic acid in cases of diseases of the ear, and also in cases in which I considered it useful, in certain nervous diseases of a part or of the whole nervous system. The first preparation which I employed was made by the formula of Fothergill, which has been most generally employed. It is given in his " Hand-Book of Treatment," Am. edit. of 1877, p. 569. This formula is loose and inaccurate, yielding a complex solution containing much tartaric acid and potassium, and only containing between eight and nine per cent. of hydrobromic acid, and as the dose is stated to be ℨss to ℨi. By weight, it is only equivalent of from four to eight grains of potassium bromide. During 1878 and part of 1879, I used many ounces of this preparation, obtained from one of the very best drug houses in Philadelphia, but I could only say that I derived benefit from the drug in very few cases—some twenty-eight cases out of one hundred. After I visited Dr. Woakes, of London, who introduced the drug into use in the treatment of certain forms of tinnitus aurium, I told him of my want of success, and he informed me that he

8

had also a like difficulty with certain forms of the acid sold in London, and when he obtained a strong and pure article his success was very gratifying. On my return home I had a consultation with Mr. Charles Bullock, the able chemist, of this city, when we discussed the subject, and he advised my employing that made by the most accurate process, as described by Dr. Squibb in the pamphlet before referred to, which he kindly sent me. The formula and process for making an acid of the proper strength is as follows :

> Take of Potassium Bromide six parts.
> Sulphuric Acid, seven parts by weight, Sp. Gr. 1.838 at 15.6°C, (60° F.)

Add to the sulphuric acid one part of the water and cool the mixture ; then dissolve the potassium bromide in six parts of the water, add the diluted sulphuric acid and set the mixture aside for twenty-four hours to cool, when a decomposition takes place into hydrobromic acid and the sulphate of potassium. I will not go into all the details ; suffice it to state that a troy ounce of the acid obtained by this process contains exactly 400 minims (401.48) and the fluid ounce of 480 minims weigh almost exactly 574 grains (573.8+); a drachm of it, therefore, would contain 50 minims, and would be the bromide equivalent of 30 grains of potassium bromide. A gramme of the acid is equal to 12.86 minims, and therefore 4 grammes would be 51.44 minims, equal to 30.86 grains of potassium bromide,—a sedative dose. I commence with ten drops in ten teaspoonfuls of water and one tablespoonful of sugar, which makes a pleasant lemonade and is gratifying to a feverish patient. I increased the dose gradually until I arrive at thirty drops, when, if the tinnitus aurium headache or vertigo or epileptic convulsions are not relieved, and I find some disturbance of the heart's action, I either diminish the dose or employ in conjunction small doses of tincture of aconite, repeated until the heart is relieved. In some cases I combine the potassium bromide with the acid only when the urine indicates too much acid in the system, or it produces too much irritation of the urinary passages. In case of great debility with a severe vertigo, I advise the combination of the acid with lithium bromide which salt contains nearly ninety per cent. of bromine, or more bromine and less base than any neutral salt. It is suggested by Dr. Squibb to saturate the acid with lithium carbonate and adjusting the volume of the solution to the dose required, and experiments bear out the idea that bromine when combined with lithium proves more active than when combined with potassium.

Another objectionable preparation introduced is bismuth et ammonii citras, a soluble preparation of bismuth, which has no resemblance to any of the old salts of bismuth in their soothing the irritated stomach and intestines or allaying vomiting depending upon gastric irritation. This new preparation is a distinct astringent, and in small amounts irritating. Under the name of liquor bismuth et ammonia citratis, the British Pharmacopœia recognizes a solution of the citrate of bismuth and ammonia which was introduced some few years ago as an astringent in chronic diarrhœa. The preparation has not, however, met with favor in this country, and has been found as an irritant instead of soothing the mucous membrane. Some other additions, which it would have been as well to have tested them a little longer before introduction, as the bryonia, menispermum (Canadian moonseed), picrotoxin staphisagria, pulsatilla, calendula, frangula (buckthorn), and hamamelis, or witch hazel, etc., which would seem to indicate that the Committee desired the absorption of the labor of the homœopathist without due credit. At the same time we find a large list of articles introduced which are very valuable and have received the full sanction of the regular medical profession by constant use in practice. Indeed, we think that this whole subject should be in the hands of the general government and the next Pharmacopœia issued by it, so as to be able to enforce the uniformity in the preparations.

THERAPEUTICS OF THE PHARMACOPŒIA.

The subject of therapeutics of the Pharmacopœia is a comprehensive one, and, if fully carried out, would require many lectures, but this is not my intention. I simply have desired to offer some hints in reference to the action of certain agents employed in medicine, so that the graduates in pharmacy shall be incited and helped to study the subject for themselves, and shall be able to advise and act in concert with the physician ; not to take his place, except in an extreme emergency. A certain knowledge of the physiological and medical action of the drugs the pharmacist dispenses and their toxicological effects to which the antidote is absolutely necessary as a part of his scientific education. Physicians, owing to their peculiar avocation, are liable to preoccupation of mind, and this especially so if he is attending cases of critical diseases when much exhausted physically from overwork. He forgets at times the doses of certain articles and also their toxic action on the system. It is, therefore, well for him to have some one in haste to refresh his memory and prevent his making mistakes. Every one is liable to make mistakes, the dispenser, as well as he who orders the medicine. I am happy to state that the relations of the physicians and graduates of pharmacy in this city are of the most agreeable character. They are ready at all times to give their time, knowledge and original ideas for the benefit of each other. In no city of the United States are to be found a more highly educated and competent class of men.

THERAPEUTICS.

The term "therapeutics" is from the Greek, "I wait upon," "I alleviate," "I attend upon the sick ;" that part of medicine the object of which is the treatment of disease. We at the present day understand it as that department which comprises an explanation of the *modus operandi of medicine.* To be a good therapeutist, a man must be well versed in every department of medicine, and capable of observing and reasoning well. The old and tried method in therapeutics is that of clinical experience, founded upon a careful analysis of cases before and after the administration of a remedy, in a certain disease ; if the results be favorable, why not use it ? This knowledge has been handed down by the members of our profession, and many of the remedies have stood the test of two thousand years.

Another method is based upon the physiological action of individual drugs upon the human system in health and disease ; secondly, the action of the same drugs upon animals. This is considered at the present day the rational, scientific ground-work for the treatment of disease. We consider that neither plan must be absolutely adopted; we must use what is good in both. Long before any experiments were made on animals, there were certain facts known, such as the action that sulphate of sodium, Glauber salts, or sulphate magnesium, or Epsom salts, would purge ; that opium would relieve pain and induce sleep ; that wine, and the spirits distilled from wine, would cause intoxication, and that it would restore appetite and relieve fatigue, would take the place of food until the system was ready to receive it. Many drugs exert on the system antagonistic action, as, for instance, atropia (the active principle of belladonna) stimulates the spinal cord, but destroys the conducting power of the nerve-trunks; opium, in large doses, cause deep stupor and general relaxation, while, in the frog, letanic convulsions; monkeys are not susceptible to the action of strychnia, and the Virginia deer are fattended on the growing tobacco. It is a well-known fact that the goat eats with impunity the poisonous stramonium, and that pigeons are not impressed with opium. The plant hyoscyamus may be eaten without harm by hogs, sheep and cows, and has but little effect upon the rabbit, while barn-fowls and fish are poisoned by it. Should man, or his friends, the dog or cat, attempt to partake of it, it flushes the face, dries the mouth and throat, dilates the pupils, produces a drunken gait, loss of voluntary power, delirium and hallucinations, and, in large doses, comatose sleep, and, ultimately, death.

Poisoning by these powerful drugs is treated by evacuating the stomach by means of prompt remedies—emetics, as sulphate of zinc; or, when this cannot be had, copious draughts of warm water. If the stomach-pump can be obtained this is the most efficient means of removing the offending material. Warmth, by means of hot stove plates, or bottles of hot water, to the limbs and feet, while, at the same time, ice in bags to the head, or cloths wrung out of cold water. Hot whiskey punch, with ginger or pepper, or brandy, in hot coffee, should be administered, to keep up the circulation, and small hypodermic injections of morphine under the skin.

POISONS AND THEIR ANTIDOTES.

In this table will be found the chief poisons and their antidotes.

POISONS.	ANTIDOTES.
Opium .... *Calabar Bean*	Stomach-pump; emetics; cold infusions; counter irritation; strong decoction of coffee; hypodermic injection of atropia; electro-magnetism; artificial respiration.
Chloral.................	The same as opium, but the physiological antidote is strychnia, and artificial respiration is not to be employed.
Belladonna............. *Stramonium* .... *Hyoscyamus*............ *Dulcamara*.............	Stomach-pump; emetics; cathartics; cold infusions; hypodermic injections of amorphia-salt; electro-magnetism.
Tobacco .... *Lobelia* .... *Aconite* .... *Digitalis*............... *Conium*............... *Veratrum Viride*..........	After emptying the stomach, the diffusible stimuli, especially alcohol.
Alcohol.................	The same as for opium, except that ammonia is the physiological antidote.
Hydrocyanic Acid and Cyanides .... *Oil Bitter Almonds*........	Ammonia; chlorine; cold infusions.
Strychnia................ *Veratria*	Tannic acid; opium; conium; extract hemp; camphor; chloral; Calabar bean; bromide of potassium; atropia; inhalation of ether or chloroform.

POISONS.	ANTIDOTES.
Cream of Tartar..........	Sodium carbonates in solution.
Acids, Mineral and Vegetable...................	Magnesia; chalk; the alkaline solutions; the fixed oils. Emetics are not to be used.
Salt of Sorrel..............	Calcium salts.
Alkalies..................	Vinegar; lemon juice; citric acid; oils.
Alum.....................	Ammonium or sodium carb.
Baryta and its Soluble Salts.	Magnesium, sodium or potassium sulphates.
Arsenious Acid...........	Hydrated oxide of iron; hydrated magnesia.
Soluble Arsenites...........	Ferri subacetate.
Chromium Comps..........	Emetics; chalk or magnesium carbonate.
Corrosive Sublimate and Soluble Mercurial Salts.	White of egg; blood; milk; flour; ferrocupric salts; also ferrocyanide of potassium.
Soluble Zinc Salts..........	Albumen; sodium carbonates; magnesia.
Soluble Lead Salts	The alkaline or soluble earthy sulphates; diluted sulphuric acid.
Tartar Emetic..............	Tannic acid.
Nitrate of Silver...........	Chloride of sodium.
Sulphates and Chloride of Iron....................	Alkaline carbonates.
Bichromate of Potassium...	Magnesia; soap; alkaline carbonates.
Cantharides...............	Emetics; opiates and demulcents. Oils are objectionable.
Drastic Cathartics........	Opiates; demulcents; stimulants.
Phosphorus...............	Magnesia, and oil turpentine.
Iodine	Starch.
Bromine	Ammonia.
Chlorine Gas..............	The cautious inhalation of ammonia.
Creasote..................	Albuminous and mucilaginous substances.
Carbolic Acid..	Cold infusions; electro-magnetism.
Asphyxiating Gases........	Artificial respiration.

TOXICOLOGY.

Aconite and its various preparations, with its active principle aconitia, to which we have before referred to, are all powerful poisons. The active principle in the 100th of a grain causes tingling and dryness of the mouth and over the whole body, if the dose is increased, so as to obtain its full physiological effect, the symptoms are languor, giddiness, sleeplessness, hazy vision, nausea in the erect position, disphagia (or difficulty in swallowing), pain in the back of the neck and behind the jaw, a glowing, tingling feeling over the whole body and burning heat in the gullet.

Aconitine and pseudo-aconitine exert a paralyzing effect upon the perepheral, intra-muscular terminations of the motor nerves resembling *airarc*. The nerve trunks are not paralyzed. The respiration speedily declines and after a few minutes completely ceases. Blood dark violent. The heart finally ceases in diastole.

One-twelfth of a grain of aconitia will kill a good-sized rabbit, and we know of the following cases of death from its incautious use: A physician who was being treated for acute rheumatism, his wife administering so many drops of the strong tincture (Flemmings) in a tablespoonful of spiced syrup of rhubarb ; it was in the twilight and the two bottles were standing on the mantlepiece when she gave him his last dose ; as she thought she had given him a spoonful of the rhubarb, but unfortunately it was the aconite, and he died, almost instantly, in convulsions.   Another case occurred in Texas, where two drops were ordered and twenty were taken with fatal results.

You are well aware of the case of the late Dr. Lamson, who killed his patient by this agent in small doses.   In April, 1880, Dr. Meyer, of Wins-choten, died from a dose of about 3 or 4 milligrammes of aconitin nitrate, the preparation of Petit, of Paris, having been substituted for that of Fried-lander, which was intended to be used.

The aconitin nitrate of Petit was in hard white, crystals, soluble with difficulty in cold water.   That of Friedlander was a hard, gum-like mass, grayish white in color and easily soluble in cold water.   The chemists, Hui-zinga and Plugge, who examined the body of Dr. Meyer, were unable to prove the presence of aconite conclusively, either by chemical re-agents or by the physiological tests on pigeons.

The preparation of Petit is weaker than that of Duquesnel.   That of Petit's was at least 8 times stronger than that of Mercks, and 20 or 30 times stronger than that of Friedlander's ; therefore, no pharmacist should dispense this powerful agent except from a physician's prescription.

CURES BY FAITH.

At the present day, as in days of yore, credulity, or a belief in the marvelous, is part of poor human nature's misfortunes, and if there is a mystery and an improbability about *a cure* of a disease, the gullible public will swallow the most absurd treatment. You are constantly being informed, or seeing published in the newspapers, of this or that individual having been cured of some deadly malady either by miraculous interference, as the laying on of hands or by persistent prayer.   Now, we physicians know that there are certain forms of disease, such as chronic rheumatism, chorea, or St. Vitus' dance, hysterial forms of deafness, blindness and paralysis, that the power of the will can cure the patient ; and we have all witnessed the powerful influence of the strong-minded physician or layman over that of feeble-minded, delicate, nervous or impressible person, who say to them, "Get up and walk ; throw away that crutch ; get out of that bed ; open your eyes, or unstop your ears."   This will, with the aid of some important antispasmodic medicine, piece of metal or apparatus, we have at times worked what would have been at other times pronounced impossible, or almost miraculous, cures.   Let me relate one case reported by the fun-loving physician and poet, Dr. Oliver Wendell Holmes, as a fit conclusion to my long, dry lecture.

On the church records of the revered old Indian apostle and pastor, at Roxbury, John Eliot, is found this entry, under date of 1632 : " Mary Chase, wife of William Chase, had a paralitik humor wh. fell into her backbone, so that she could not stir her body, but as she was lifted, and filled her with great torture, & caused her back to goe out of joynt, and bunch out from ye beginning to the end ; of wh. infirmity she lay 4 years & a half great part of the time a sad spectàcle of misery.   But it pleased God to raise her again, and she bore children after it."

I have submitted this case professionally to Dr. Holmes.   As your proclivities will lead you to prefer the Doctor's account of it to the apostle's, I will read it to you as the close of my speech :

"296 BEACON STREET, June 3d, 1881.

"MY DEAR DR. ELLIS.—A consultation without seeing the patient is like a murder trial without the *corpus delicti* being in evidence. You remember the story of Mr. Jeremiah Mason and the witness who had had a vision in which the Angel Gabriel informed him of some important facts; 'Subpœna the Angel Gabriel.' So I should say, carry us to the bedside of Mary Chase. But she has been under green bedclothes so long that I am afraid she would be hard to wake up.

"We must guess as well as we can under the circumstanecs. The question is whether she had angular curvature, lateral curvature, or no curvature at all. If the first, angular curvature, you must consult such authorities as Bryant, De Witt, and the rest. If you are not satisfied with these modern writers all I have to say is, as I have said before when asked whom to consult in such cases—go to *Pott*, to Percival Pott, the famous surgeon of the last century, from whom this affection has received the name by which it is still well known, of 'Pott's Disease;' For if a doctor has the luck to find out a new malady it is tied to his name like a tin kettle to a dog's tail, and he goes clattering down the highway of fame to posterity, with his Æolian attachment following at his heels.

"As for lateral curvature, if that had existed, it seems as if the Apostle, Eliot, would have said she bulged sideway, or something like that, instead of saying the backbone bunched out from beginning to end. Besides I doubt if lateral curvature is apt to cause paralysis; crooked backs are everywhere, as tailors and dressmakers know, and nobody expects to be palsied because one shoulder is higher than the other—as Alexander the Great's was, and Alexander Pope's also.

"I doubt whether Mary Chase had any real curvature at all. Her case looks to me like one of those *mimoses*, as Marshall Hall called certain forms of hysteria which imitate different diseases, among the rest paralysis. The body of an hysteric patient takes on all sorts of more serious affections. As for mental and moral manifestations, an hysteric girl will lie so that sapphira would blush for her, and she could give lessons to a professional pickpocket in the art of stealing. Hysteria might well be described as possession,—possession by seven devils, except that this number is quite insufficient to account for all pranks played by the subject of this extraordinary malady. I do not want to say anything against Mary Chase, but I suspect that getting nervous, and tired, and hysteric, she got into bed, which she found rather agreeable after too much house work, and perhaps too much going to meeting, liked it better and better; curled herself up in a bunch, which made her look as if her back was really distorted, found she was cosseted, posseted, and prayed over, and made much of, and so lay quiet until a false paralysis caught hold of her legs and held her there. If some one had 'hollered fire!' it is not unlikely that she would have jumped out of bed, as many other such paralytics have done under such circumstances. She could have moved, probably enough, if any one could have made her believe she had the power of doing it. *Possumus quia posse videmur.* She had played *possum* so long that at last it became *non possum.*

"Yours very truly,

"O. W. HOLMES, M. D."

REMARKS

Made by Prof. Jos. P. Remington, at same meeting, on the New Pharmacopœia.

Mr. CHAIRMAN:—I have been very much interested in the paper of Dr. Turnbull, and while he was reading it I thought I would make a few notes, in order that some doubtful points might be cleared up.

The United States Pharmacopœia of 1880 is probably destined to receive more criticism than any other Pharmacopœia that has ever been issued. There have been more radical changes made in the New Pharmacopœia than in any other. Some of these the Committee are responsible for, but the majority of the changes they are not responsible for, they having been ordered and directed by the convention; which body was made up of physicians and pharmacists of this country, some of the best physicians of the United States being members.

The points which have been made ground for adverse criticism by the most distinguished pharmacist in this country at the present time, Dr. Squibb, are themselves open to a great deal of criticism. Dr. Squibb published in a paper called the *Ephemeris*, a criticism on the change in the strength of the opium preparations. Many medical and pharmaceutical journals have copied this criticism without comment, and have adopted his views without looking further into the matter and publishing the whole state of the case.

As this is the most important that has been touched upon, I will endeavor to give an explanation. The Pharmacopœia of 1870 directed powdered opium to have the strength of *not less* than ten per cent. of morphine. It will thus be seen that it might contain thirty per cent. and yet be Pharmacopœia opium. Now, the facts are that opium has been coming in the market within the last six or seven years of far better quality than ten per cent. when assayed as powdered opium. Many of the preparations of opium have been made from commercial opium yielding fifteen per cent. of morphine, and the New Pharmacopœia of 1880 has not set a standard for opium higher than what is warranted by many actual assays that have been made of good commercial opium.

The statement that Dr. Squibb makes in the *Ephemeris* that a pound of laudanum of the Pharmacopœia of 1880 represents as much opium as a pound and a half of the Pharmacopœia of 1870, only applies to the laudanum of Dr. Squibb, and it does not apply to the laudanum in general use. Dr. Squibb assayed his laudanum, U. S. P., 1870, and limited the strength so that it should contain only four grains of morphine in the fluid ounce, whilst many samples of laudanum dispensed as U. S. P., 1870, from some of the best stores contained 6 grains of morphine in the fluid ounce.

Now, here is the error which many of the journals have made. They have accepted the views of Dr. Squibb upon the subject, as applicable to the laudanum usually dispensed in drug stores, when the facts are that they are only applicable to the opium preparations made by Dr. Squibb, and when we come to the laudanum most largely used throughout the country, I do not think it will be found to conform with either the Pharmacopœia of 1870 or the Pharmacopœia of 1880.

With regard to one of the other points which was touched upon, pyrophosphate of iron, I would say that the amount of iron has not been very materially changed. The preparation is only made in a different way. Citrate of iron is used and pyrophosphate of sodium, and the reaction which results gives pyrophosphate of iron, which is rendered soluble by citrate of sodium. The sodium salt having been selected because it is far more satisfactory than the ammonium salt, as the old preparation was readily decomposed, losing ammonia. Now, we have a staple preparation and one which will remain in a staple condition for a longer time than the one in the Pharmacopœia of 1870.

Now, as to the medicated waters, I think that there has been a mistake made in the use of the absorbent cotton, in place of the old method of the use of carbonate of magnesium. There is a good theoretical reason for the change, however. It is this. Carbonate of magnesium has been shown to be soluble in water. Medicated waters, made with carbonate of magnesium, always retain a certain amount of the carbonate of magnesium. In prescriptions containing salts of some of the alkaloids dissolved in a medicated water the result very often is a very slight precipitation of the alkaloid through decomposition. This you will find to be the case, because the alkaloids are almost always insoluble in water, but the greater practical convenience of the use of carbonate of magnesium, or some other insoluble powder, and the saving in time by its use, are greater advantages which should not be overlooked. There is, however, more to be said in favor of the cotton method. If, after adding oil to the cotton, and picking it apart, a plug of raw cotton be first put into the funnel, and then the cotton which has been picked apart be put upon the top and the water poured upon it, I think it will be found in very many cases that a great deal of the difficulty will be avoided.

With regard to the dropping of infusion of senna, it will be found that, the compound infusion of senna has been introduced instead, as black draught in the Pharmacopœia. The fluid extract of spigelia and senna as a mixture is no longer officinal. The fluid extract of spigelia is officinal, however, and so is the fluid extract of senna. The oil of coriander is also officinal, so that it is very easy for the physician to prescribe the right quantities, and get the mixture as desired.

Now, in regard to the abstracts, I would say a few words about this class. There has been a good deal of misapprehension. In the first place, in regard to the name. If they had been introduced as powdered extracts into the Pharmacopœia, being made of a definite and different strength, there would be constant confusion, and physicians would prescribe one for the other, and pharmacists would dispense one for the other continually, and the result would be endless confusion. In introducing an entirely new class of preparations which bear a definite relation to the drug, it seemed eminently proper that they should be introduced under a new name. As to the etymology of the word "abstract," if it be looked up, and, I would say, that it has been very carefully looked up by lexicographers, it will be found that it more accurately defines these preparations than the word "extract" defines the extract.

Now, in regard to the preparation of abstracts, I would say a few words. A greater part of the adverse criticism comes from those who have made but hasty examinations of the subject, and sufficient exposure to heat and air has not been allowed to see whether they would stand or not, and here has been the greatest error into which the critics have fallen.

They have also been condemned because some of them are not strong enough. To criticise abstracts because they are not strong enough is just as wise as it would be to criticise fluid extracts, because some of that class of preparations are not strong enough. Who will doubt that the fluid extract of aconite root cannot be made stronger than a gramme in a cubic centimetre? No one, I think. I have no doubt that some of my fellow pharmacists have been keeping on hand fluid extracts double the strength of the officinal fluid extract. For instance, the fluid extract of aconite ; and yet it would be bad pharmacy or theory to *change the strength of the class*, because some of them can be made stronger. Any one can see that there is no trouble in making an abstract stronger, but the point must not be overlooked that they bear a definite relation to the drug and a definite relation to the fluid extracts, just as fluid extracts bear a definite relation to the drug ; and the aim of the committee was not to get each one as strong as it could be made, any more than it was the aim to make each fluid extract as strong as it could be made. Physicians and pharmacists in using and making them can now have a class of standardized solid concentrated preparations.

Now, the difference in yield of extracts from drugs is very variable. For instance, under the old Pharmacopœia, the yield of extract of Bella-donna varied from twenty to thirty per cent. The yield depends largely upon the character of the menstruum. If the menstruum is alcohol, a smaller yield is obtained, but the extract is proportionately stronger, for it contains a larger amount of the alkaloids. Now, in the class of abstracts, the men-struum in each case is alcohol, and the amount of inert extracted matter is reduced to a minimum. The concentrated fluid extract is incorporated with sugar of milk, and in some cases Dr. Squibb's suggestion of a point in manipulation may be taken advantage of where the fluid extract can be put upon a dinner-plate and the alcohol evaporated off at a low tempera-ture. But care must be taken not to have the heat too high and thus dis-associate the alkaloids as they exist in their natural state and injure the product. It will be found, I think, upon a careful trial that where the abstracts have been tried carefully therapeutically that they will be about equal in strength to the extracts themselves, although they do not vary as much, and they are theoretically not so strong.

The point made by Dr. Squibb in his paper, the *Ephemeris*, that they are not well adapted to be made on the large scale by the manufacturing chemist, is one which is undoubtedly well taken. They are not adapted to the work of the manufacturing pharmacists, and they are not intended to be made by them, but by the pharmacist behind the counter. He is the proper man to make the abstracts, and in fact all his preparations. The making of abstracts might be an expensive operation to the manufacturing pharmacist, because on a large scale he cannot save the alcohol very well. But what difference does it make to a pharmacist who wants to make an abstract on a scale adapted to his wants. He takes the alcoholic fluid extract which he has made himself and puts it in an evaporating dish, drives off the alcohol, adds sugar of milk to it, and he has made his abstract.

With regard to the citrate of bismuth and ammonium, I would say that this preparation is used all over the United States, and it is principally employed in making "liquor bismuth," by dissolving the salt in water after adding to it a trace of water of ammonia, which renders it soluble. Then it is very readily used, and it is the best way of making this solution of bismuth.

As to the introduction of new remedies, I would say that a great many were introduced into the Pharmacopœia, which, personally, I did not vote for and I am certain a great many physicians will perfectly agree with Dr. Turn-bull and others on this subject ; but, Mr. President, the United States Pharma-copœia is intended for the whole United States. The fact may be that here in Philadelphia we may not use certain drugs and preparations, but it must not be forgotten that in some sections of the country such drugs or preparations are used, and in order that the book may have a wider scope, that it might be more national in its character, when representations were made to the Committee that such and such a drug was used in that locality it was introduced. We have one illustration of a preparation which, I think, should have been in the Pharmacopœia before this, and yet it is very rarely used in our section, and I have very little personal knowledge of it, although it is quite largely used in the States of New York, Connecticut, Massachusetts, and throughout the other New England States. I allude to Tully's powder. The Pulvis Morphinæ Compositus of the Pharmacopœia. It is occasionally used here in Philadelphia, but in Hartford, New Haven, and particularly in Connecticut and in the immediate neighborhood of Dr. Tully's former residence, and in some of the Western States it is frequently used. As it was introduced by Dr. Tully some years ago, physicians have prescribed it and gone to the Western country and there continued to prescribe it. I certainly agree with Dr. Turnbull that it is very questionable to attach the name of a doctor to a disease. I remember the story of the tin pan and the dog's tail, and I also certainly think it is a bad plan to give the name of a doctor to a medicine. There is, however, the correct English name in the Pharmacopœia for this preparation, the compound powder of morphine, under which name it should be used and prescribed, or under its correct officinal name.

With regard to the putting of doses into the Pharmacopœia and the introduction of therapeutical matters, the subject was introduced in the Pharmacopœial Convention which met at Washington, and the pharmacists, I think, were largely in favor of putting the doses into the Pharmacopœia. But it was voted down, principally by the physicians in the convention, the argument used was that it would encourage counter prescribing which was indulged in by the pharmacists, so the doses were not introduced into the Pharmacopœia. Another strong argument which was used against the introduction of the doses was that the dose of a drug or preparation is properly an indefinite quantity. It is very difficult to set a minimum or a maximum dose, and the Pharmacopœia is a national authority; by introducing doses into the book, it would very frequently be brought into court in the trials of various cases, and it would then be subjected to the interested criticisms of sharp lawyers. The authority of the book would suffer, and, besides, the experience of our British brethren, on the other side of the water, where doses have been introduced into the British Pharmacopœia, is decidedly against it.

Remarks of Louis Genois, Ph. G., Class 1881, Dr. A. W. Miller and others, at same meeting:

I did not know that I should be called upon to speak, and therefore have not prepared myself to say anything on this subject, and would say that I am not yet familiar with the New Pharmacopœia, although I have written a short article on some of the changes in it; I deprecated the dropping of a few old-time preparations such as the solution of sulphate of morphia, Deshler's salve, etc., which physicians had been accustomed to prescribe for years past, and the properties of which they know perfectly well.

There are some innovations which the average pharmacist will consider hardly advantageous. Taking it as a whole, however, the book is far superior to the older ones; in fact, it compares favorably with any of the European standards, and on that account, if on no other, I think we have sufficient reason to congratulate the Committee of Revision on the result of their labor.

I was not aware of the authorship of the abstracts until this moment, nor had I considered them a good class of preparations, but since hearing Prof. Remington speak about them I admit that they *seem* to fill a want that might have been felt.

The subject of doses is one of importance ; since the book was intended to supply, to a considerable extent, information usually found in a dispensatory, the introduction of approximate doses would have been of great assistance to the pharmacist under existing circumstances. We must refer to comparatively old books for doses : Yet as some one has remarked, the book might be brought into court and its correctness questioned. I am sure as it stands now there can be nothing of the kind done.

Dr. Miller :

In reference to the derivation of the word "abstracta," I would say that the word "abstracta" and the word "extracta" are both from the same root, "*traho, trahere ;* to draw, to draw out from." One is drawn out and the other is drawn from, so that the meaning amounts to very nearly the same thing.

Another rather interesting point struck me when the paper was being read, and that was in relation to the diversity in use in regard to the pronunciation of pharmaceutical Latin. I notice this in reference to the pronunciation of "conium." We all are pretty well satisfied that we pronounce it just as it suits our convenience. It would be very desirable if we would adopt some authority on the subject. If some one would get up a medical pronouncing dictionary it would be of service ; the pronunciation would then be uniform.

Louis Genois :

I know you are an authority on the Latin language, and I would like to know the correct term for the Compound Syrup of Hypophosphites ; is it Syrupus Hypophosphitis, or is it Hypophosphorum ? Should it be in the plural ?

Dr. Miller :

I think Hypophosphitum is correct.

Mr. Genois :

Then it belongs to the third declension ?

Dr. Miller :

Yes, it belongs to the third declension, and not to the second. The termination is *um* in the third declension, and *orum* in the second declension, so that I think that that is correct.

I would say, in reference to the Latin of the New Pharmacopœia, that I believe that I have found it all correct so far.

Are there any further remarks on this very interesting subject?

A Member :

I would ask in reference to the termination of the Latin name, "Syrupi Tolutani."

Dr. Miller :

"Tolutanus" is an adjective, and agrees with the ·noun, "Syrupus," being in the masculine gender.

There is another point, rather characteristic with regard to the best mode of preparing the articles. I would say that many of the articles mentioned by the last speaker have been employed for fully two thousand years. I would say that he was right in his figures, and that Prof. Duemichen has deciphered some hieroglyphics in a town in Upper Egypt, where he found those hieroglyphics and pictures, which proved that some of the articles which we are now using every day almost had been employed fully seventeen centuries before the present era, making nearly double the length of time quoted by our last speaker. Some of the articles—ivory, myrrh, olibanum and precious stones—are represented as being carried from Arabia into Egypt, showing their use for double the length of time given by the last speaker; so that we may give more credit for the length of time than is given by our fellow-alumnus, Dr. Turnbull.

SPIRITUS VINI GALLICI.

By Adolph W. Miller, Ph. G., M. D.   Read at the 5th Social Meeting, February 13th, 1883.

The U. S. Pharmacopœia of 1880 has retained French brandy as one of its officinal drugs. It is described as being an alcoholic liquid obtained by the distillation of fermented grapes, and it is directed to be at least four years old. The conscientious pharmacist, who is always disposed to obey implicitly the behests of his standard authority, will no doubt be sorely distressed by a recent announcement of the American consul at La Rochelle, in the wine-producing district of France. This official document announces that French brandies are very generally falsified, and that large amounts of these sophisticated liquors are exported to this country. It is even asserted that the word "Brandy," as applied to a spirit produced by the fermentation of grapes, is now a misnomer, as by far the greater portion of the alcohol of this liquid is derived from grain, potatoes, or, worst of all, from the refuse of the beet sugar refineries. It seems to be fairly impossible to purchase pure Cognac, as the proprietor of every little vineyard has become a distiller and manipulator. He has learned to compound liquors so skilfully that he can readily imitate any special flavor or vintage that may be called for. Potato spirits and beet alcohols, the most deleterious and obnoxious of all the varieties of alcoholic beverages, are sent from Germany into France in vast quantities to be consumed in this novel industry. They are flavored, colored and branded or labeled to suit the fastidious tastes of American connoisseurs. They are eagerly bought up here on the assumption that, coming direct from the Custom House, or out of bond, they have not been tampered with.
   Unfortunately but too many of our physicians promote this hallucination by giving the most stringent orders to their patients, when these are in need of an alcoholic stimulant, to purchase none but genuine imported Cognacs, even though it command ten-fold the price of an absolutely pure spirit of American production. Many consumers have undoubtedly been led into intemperance by the absurd notion which prevails in the popular mind, that if brandy is only pure, genuine, imported from *La Belle France* (and very high priced), it will not be productive of any evil consequences.
   Truly, this imperative command to procure an article affording so exorbitant a profit to every one engaged in its manufacture and sale is a cruel

injustice on the part of the physician towards his poor, phthisical patient, whom it is perhaps necessary to support for many months on alcohol.   Under the best of circumstances, what is there to be gained by the use of French brandy ?   The Pharmacopœia advises us that it contains from 46 to 55 per cent. by volume of alcohol, the remainder being almost entirely water.   It states that when 100 C. C. are slowly evaporarated, the last portions volatilized should have an agreeable odor, free from harshness, showing the absence of fusel oil from grain or potato spirit.   The agreeable odor referred to is due to the fusel oil produced during the fermentation of the wine and consists of pelargonic, œnanthic, butyric, acetic and other ethers.   The residue, when dried at 212° F., should not weigh more than $\frac{1}{4}$ of one per cent., demonstrating the absence of an undue amount of solids.   The residue should have no sweet or distinctly spicy taste, thus proving that neither sugar, glycerin, or spices have been added, though it is rather difficult to conceive what possible harm these might be productive of.   We are further informed by the same authority that the residue must be entirely soluble in water, and that this aqueous solution is colored light green by ferric chloride on account of the traces of oak tannin dissolved from the staves composing the casks.   Possibly this homœopathic proportion of tannic and gallic acids causes some practitioners to prefer brandy in those cases where a slight astringent effect seems desirable.   If, however, it is the intention to make use of this re-action as a test of purity, it fails conspicuously in accomplishing its objects, as artificial brandy almost invariably contains a small proportion of tincture of white oak bark, which will certainly produce the same color changes.   The Pharmacopœia evidently does not object to a small amount of acetic acid in brandy, as it prescribes the amount of caustic soda which is to produce a distinctly alkaline re-action.

Would it not be infinitely better for the physicians to abandon this expensive, meretricious imported liquor, each specimen of which differs from every other not only in alcoholic strength, but also in the proportion of every one of its component parts, being uniform only in one fact of perpetual adulteration, for a pure standard domestic preparation of almost chemical purity, definite alcoholic strength, which is readily obtainable at a comparatively moderate price ?   We possess such an article in that which is commercially known as rectified spirit, French spirit, sweet liquor or cologne spirit, though this latter term is frequently also used to indicate a highly purified ninety-five per cent. alcohol, while the former are generally reserved for pure fifty per cent. spirit.   This is produced by carefully percolating grain whisky, the so-called high wines of the distillers, through large tanks containing granulated charcoal.   Every particle of coloring and flavoring materials, all the fusel oils, amylic and other higher alcohols are thus removed, and the spirit is rendered perfectly clean and sweet.   The main consumers of this rectified spirit are the compounders of liquors, who use the article to prepare cordials, wines, gins, brandies, and the like by the addition of suitable flavoring and coloring substances.   In order to imitate these successfully it is absolutely essential that the basis must be entirely devoid of any inherent flavor of its own, in other words, it must be chemically pure fifty per cent. ethylic alcohol.   We have, therefore, in rectified spirit a strictly pure alcoholic stimulant, free from most of the objections which can be urged against other forms.   It is to be regretted that this article was not incorporated into the New Pharmacopœia in place of the new forms which have there found recognition.   In prescribing, it might be well to designate this preparation by the title of *spiritus dulcis*, in order to avoid confusion with the term *spiritus vini rectificatus*, which is often applied to alcohol.   A still more distinctive, though rather more cumbersome title, would be *spiritus frumenti dulcis*, which could hardly be confused with any other.

REMARKS

On the above paper by various members:

Mr. Chas. Bullock, Ph. G.,

Stated that the climate of California had been proved to be well adapted for raising grapes and for the manufacture of wine.

Dr. Miller,

Stated that he saw no reason to doubt the purity of the California wine, and said its use had grown into great favor on account of its superior make. He further stated that as there was some time left yet, and he would be glad to hear from any one who felt disposed to further discuss the subject of the New Pharmacopœia, and particularly the class of spirits, and called upon Prof. Remington, stating that the professor seemed to be well acquainted with the subject.

Prof. Remington replied as follows:

I do not know how Dr. Miller could have found out that fact, unless he has been with me; but I suppose I may be allowed to criticise Dr. Miller on his own ground. He used a word a few moments ago, which is very commonly mispronounced. I refer to the word "centimetre." Dr. Miller gave the French pronunciation to the first syllable and the English to the last. Now, I think it is well recognized that we should either use all English or all French. *It is about as bad as mixing spirits.*

I would just add a word or two of criticism on tannin in the description of the spiritus vini gallici. This is a test which enables one to determine the true from the fictitious article. As has been said, a trace of tannin should be there; that the tannin that is in it is of no medicinal value at all, but it is a test of the identity of the articles, showing that it has been imported in casks.

In reference to rectified spirit, I think that the objection that there would be about it would be the liability of conflict with the rectified spirit of the British Pharmacopœia, which has the same name. The English name is "rectified spirit," and the Latin name is "spiritus rectificatus." I thought that Dr. Miller was going to touch upon the general class of the spirits in the Pharmacopœia. A criticism, and a just criticism, made upon the general class in the New Pharmacopœia, that many of the tests for strength have been to a great extent arbitrary, is a very true criticism. Now, I am glad that I have had an opportunity of saying in a general way why the changes in the strength have been made ·in the preparations in the Pharmacopœia. It was to secure some degree of uniformity in the tinctures, medicated waters, wines, infusions and decoctions, etc. The preparations have been brought usually to a definite strength, with one or two exceptions, where a dangerous result might ensue if the strength was altered. It comes very hard at first to reconcile the changes, but the Committee took the ground, that if there had to be a complete change in the alphabetical arrangement of the book, and in many other subjects, by the direction of the convention, other changes might be introduced, and it would be better to make them all at once.

In reference to medicated wines and the officinal menstruum for medicated wines, I would say that the old names, sherry wine and port wine, have been dropped from the Pharmacopœia entirely, and the two wines that have been introduced are the white wine and the red wine—vinum album and vinum rubrum. Prof. Parsons analyzed a great many samples of the prominent American wines which were used in this country. He established by the analysis of these wines, in comparison with the analysis of foreign wines the fact that the American wines were superior in purity to the old wines which had previously been used. Therefore, red wine and white wine were introduced, allowing the use of any pure wine, whether it is American or foreign. I think the test applied to define the amount of alcohol was that it shall contain at least 12 per cent. of alcohol. This test 'is very simple, and very easily made. It is no trouble to ascertain the amount of alcohol in the wine, and if the amount of alcohol is more than 12 per cent, it indicates a stronger wine than is directed by the Pharmacopœia. The difference in the amount of alcohol generally varies between 12 and 16 per cent. To make stronger white wine, one part of alcohol is to be added to 7 parts of this wine which has previously been tested, and we have no more trouble about securing a desirable menstruum. Medicated wines will not be preserved if they have not a certain percentage of alcohol.

Now, by the use of the alcoholmetric test, pharmacists are used to applying it themselves, and become informed as to the condition of the wines. In order to do this and to determine the value of the wine, you have only to weigh a definite volume, evaporate it down to one-third, then make up to the original volume with water, weigh and divide the first weight by the second, and it gives you a quotient, which must be carried out to four decimal places. This gives at once the percentage. of alcohol in the wine, by referring to the table.

Dr. Miller:

In reference to Prof. Remington's remarks, I would state as he has corrected the pronunciation of the word "centimetre," that he is right. It should be all French or all English. I should be glad to hear from any one else concerning the spirits or wines.

Dr. Turnbull:

I would say one word in regard to American wines. Some time ago I noticed an article on this subject, which stated that it was impossible to procure an American wine that could be recommended to our patients. I am very glad to find that there are wines of American make, especially those from St. Louis and those from New York. Those which are called valley wines, that are exceedingly nice, indeed. I find that upon making strict investigation in reference to this subject, that a pure wine or champagne should have at least a percentage of 17 per cent. of alcohol. They must have this percentage of alcohol so as to keep. If we could get a wine such as we have in Germany or Italy, or in the south of France, almost free from spirit, it could be more largely indulged in. In that country the laborer is as free with his wine as with his food. It is a wine that has the smallest percentage of alcohol. Scarcely enough to say that there is any. I have been told that in this country the wine must have about 17 per cent. of alcohol in order to keep it. I hope that this wine will take the place of a great deal of the miserable brandy and whiskey which has been spoken about this afternoon. As has been seen, they produce a trouble with the kidneys and intestines, and the largest amount of difficulty at the present day is the acute inflammation of the kidneys, frequently amounting to Bright's disease of the kidneys.

Obituaries.

PHILADELPHIA, March 14, 1883.

To the President, Officers and Members of the Alumni Association of the Philadelphia College of Pharmacy.

GENTLEMEN :

It becomes the sad duty of your Committee on Deceased Members to report that since our last annual gathering six members of the Association have been taken from us, and from their spheres of earthly labor, by the relentless hand of death.

SIMON WOLF was born March 2, 1861, in Harrisburg, Pa., in which city he resided at the time of his death. He received his education in the public schools of that city, and in March, 1878, entered the drug business with Mr. O. J. Hillegass. After remaining with him about one year and a half he engaged with Dr. W. Gross & Son, wholesale and retail druggists, with whom he remained up to the time of entering the College of Pharmacy. During the interim between the junior and senior courses he was in the employ of Mr. Herr, Twelfth and Jefferson streets, Philadelphia.

While in attendance upon his last course at College, Mr. Wolf's health became seriously impaired, and immediately after his return home he was prostrated with an attack of typhoid pneumonia. His recovery from this was followed by ulceration of the throat, which resulted in his sudden and unexpected death on the 28th of May, 1882.

Mr. Wolf was but a young man, having barely attained his majority, and was just about entering upon what would undoubtedly have proved a successful business career. Of the Hebrew faith, he possessed the characteristic business energy and ability of that people. He was widely and favorably known in his native city, and while at College made many friends who will hear of his death with sorrow. Being an only son, the bereavement was deeply felt by the family.

Mr. Wolf became a member of the Alumni Association at its last annual meeting, March 13, 1882, immediately succeeding his graduation.

B. FRANKLIN SHUGARD died at Georgetown, Colorado, May 28, 1882, in the forty-first year of his age. The deceased was a son of William A. Shugard, a highly respected resident of White Marsh, Montgomery County, Pa. He served an apprenticeship of two years, from 1859 to 1861, with David L. Stackhouse, when he relinquished the drug business for a time. In 1866 he entered the store of Jas. G. Wells, N. E. cor. Ninth and Spring Garden streets, this city, for a period of five years, and graduated at the Philadelphia College of Pharmacy in the spring of 1868. He continued in the employ of Mr. Wells, whom he served with fidelity, until about two years before his death, when, being threatened with pulmonary trouble, he sought to recover his health by visiting Colorado. The climate of Colorado had a beneficial effect for a time, and he returned to Philadelphia, but not having entirely recovered, he again visited Colorado, where he died as above stated. The deceased was a conscientious, upright man, possessed of great urbanity of manner, which won the respect of all persons with whom he came in contact.

Mr. Shugard joined the Alumni Association March 16, 1868, and continued in active membership up to the time of his death.

Dr. HIRAM GOLD was born on the 5th of November, 1834, at Belfast, Pa., about eight miles from Easton. He was brought up on a farm, attended school at Belfast, and subsequently taught school at the same place. In the year 1859 or 1860 he entered the drug business at Easton, where he remained about eighteen months. Subsequently he came to Philadelphia and entered Dr. DeLacy's store, at Fourth and South streets, where he remained until he graduated in 1864 at the Philadelphia College of Pharmacy. He then studied medicine under his former employer, and graduated at the Jefferson Medical College in the year 1867. The Doctor died on Wednesday, July 12, 1882, of peritonitis, after an illness of three days, leaving a widow and six children to mourn the loss of a devoted husband and parent.

Dr. Gold became a member of the Alumni Association at its organization, July 15, 1864, and was its first Secretary, serving until March, 1865, when he declined a re-election, but continued in active membership until the time of his death.

CHARLES WILLIAM ELKINS was born June 23, 1857, in the city of Philadelphia. He attended the public schools of this city, and graduated from the senior class of the H. W. Halliwell Grammar School. On the 5th of February, 1877, he entered into the employ of Mr. Lewis F. Segrest, at 838 East Cumberland street, as an apprentice, after having previously served in that capacity for about one year, and graduated from the Philadelphia College of Pharmacy March 16, 1880. His thesis on Aralia Spinosa was published in the August number of the *American Journal of Pharmacy*. After graduation the deceased continued in the employ of Mr. Segrest, as assistant, until a short time before his death, which occurred November 1, 1882, as the result of pulmonary consumption, and just one week after the death of a brother, who had been stricken by the same disease. Mr. Elkins was a proficient pharmacist, careful and attentive to his duties, exemplary in character, and quiet and unobtrusive in disposition; nevertheless his sterling worth was appreciated by all who knew him. He became a member of the Alumni Association November 16, 1881, and by his death the profession has lost a valuable member.

JAMES AUGUSTUS MASTON was born in Alexandria, Va., July 16th, 1854, and was a son of John and Mary A. Maston. He received his early education in the public schools of Alexandria, Va. At an early age he removed with his parents to Philadelphia, Pa. Desiring to learn the drug business, he first entered the wholesale store of Oberholtzer & Co., and remained with them for a short time, when he engaged in the store of John R. Stevenson, Twelfth and Callowhill streets, remaining with Dr. S. about two years. He was then employed by Dr. P. J. L. Carberry, whose store was then located at Sixth and Bainbridge streets. While in the latter store he attended the Philadelphia College of Pharmacy, and graduated in March, 1875. After his graduation he clerked in two or three stores in the city, the last one being W. F. Simes & Son's, Eleventh and Market streets. He then procured the position of apothecary at the Episcopal Hospital, at Front street and Lehigh avenue, where he remained until the time of his decease, which occurred on Saturday, September 16th, 1882, at the Episcopal Hospital, of that fatal disease, consumption, aged twenty-nine years. In early life he was bereft of his parents, which left him to rely entirely upon his own resources for his pharmaceutical education, which only those who have passed through the same trial can sympathize.

He was of a lively and generous disposition, and a great favorite with those with whom he was acquainted. He was also energetic and ambitious, which was fully shown during the last four months of his life, for when wasted by disease and suffering intensely he still remained at his chosen position, notwithstanding a loving sister offered him the care and attention of a good home, and died at the post of duty. He connected himself with the Alumni Association August 4th, 1875, and continued in active membership until he was called away. During his last illness he was confirmed and connected himself with the Episcopal Church, in the chapel at the hospital. He was interred at Fernwood Cemetery, Delaware County, Pa., on Wednesday, September 20th, 1882.

PRATT R. HOAGLÀND, of the Class of 1868, recently departed this life. He became a member of the Alumni Association, March 18, 1868, but no particulars of his death have as yet been received by the Committee.

WILLIAM ELLIS, graduate of Class 1834, died in Philadelphia, October 13, 1881, aged 68 years. He was born at Muncy, Lycoming Co , Pa., in 1813, and at the age of seventeen went to Philadelphia to learn the drug business with his uncle, the late Charles Ellis (for many years President of our College), after his graduation he spent several years in a New York establishment to perfect his knowledge of the wholesale drug business, and on his return to Philadelphia he was associated in the old drug house as a partner, which was carried on by his uncle and himself as Charles Ellis & Co., at the old stand, No. 56 Chestnut street; subsequently with the addition of E. T. Ellis on Market street until 1863, at which time a dissolution of the the firm ensued, when he entered into business on his own account, and in 1874 he retired. Mr. Ellis was well known to the profession throughout the United States ; was of a genial disposition and pleasing address, well posted in his avocation as a wholesale druggist and manufacturing chemist. The latter years of his life were enfeebled by illness. Four children survive him. Mr. Ellis became a member of the Alumni Association at its organization by the resolution making all graduates of the College members who graduated previous to 1850.

Also the following, but no particulars have been received :—

GEORGE W. PATRICK, M. D., of the Class of 1846, died at Terre Haute, Indiana, in the year 1874. Dr. Patrick became a member of the Association by resolution, the same as Mr. Ellis.

WILLIAM J. WATSON, Class 1853, died at Brooklyn, N. Y., in 1872, aged 40 years. Joined the Association in January, 1866.

MORTIMER H. EAYRE, Class 1868. Joined the Association, March 16th, 1868.

WM. W. MOORHEAD.
ALONZO ROBBINS, } *Committee.*
FREDERICK B. POWER,

INTRODUCTORY LECTURE

TO THE

Course of 1882 and 1883,

AT THE OPENING OF THE

Sixty-Second Session of the Philadelphia College of Pharmacy,

DELIVERED

MONDAY EVENING, OCTOBER 2d, 1882,

BY

JOSEPH P. REMINGTON, Ph. G.,

Professor of Theory and Practice of Pharmacy.

Students of the Philadelphia College of Pharmacy:

GENTLEMEN :—It becomes my duty this evening to formally open the Sixty-second Annual Course of Lectures in the Philadelphia College of Pharmacy. The labors upon which we are all about to enter are such as should at once engage our most serious attention; for he who has either actively or indirectly acquired the habit of underrating their importance, and of regarding a pharmaceutical education as an easily-attained accomplishment, must have this mischievous idea speedily dispelled, and he must be forced to acknowledge the height, the width, the depth, and the comprehensive grasp of the science of pharmacy. The very great importance of your adopting a sound view of this subject has influenced me, in selecting the theme for your consideration this evening; whilst the time set apart for treating the various technical and scientific subjects in our curriculum is so short that an opportunity could not be spared, the present occasion seemed to be well suited for the purpose. In choosing the subject for your attention, I have unhesitatingly selected one which, I am sure, cannot fail to command your earnest attention, even though it may be presented to you in a manner more forcible than elegant, and the absence of rhetorical flourishes and beautifully-turned sentences will doubtless be painfully apparent. It is hardly necessary to say that the services of the ocean cable will not be called into requisition to transmit an abstract of this address to Europe, nor has a request been sent to the agent of the Associated Press to send a representative here; no, not even a reporter of the daily press has been invited. My remarks shall be addressed to you individually. The questions that I wish to bring before you are these: Is the ultimate object of a college course a successful *education*, or merely a successful *examination?* What is the aim of your Alma Mater in this direction? These questions at once lay bare the objects and policy of an institution professing to teach Pharmacy; and, without further preface, the facts bearing on the subject will be brought before you. It is now somewhat more than half a century since an earnest band of men, the founders of the Philadelphia College of Pharmacy, assembled in Carpenters' Hall, that historic spot, where gathered, in 1787, the "convention of wise and far-seeing statesmen which framed the Constitution of the United States of America." The need of educating their apprentices was the impelling motive which brought these Fathers in Pharmacy to the council chamber, and it was unanimously resolved that a School of Pharmacy should be erected, in which lectures, designed especially for the use of druggists and apothecaries, should be delivered.

It would occupy too much of your time, although it would doubtless interest you to hear of the early struggle of this pioneer in pharmaceutical education in America. The College, of course, was soon in debt, many who started in well with the new enterprise gradually became engrossed in their own private affairs and allowed the burden of sustaining the institution to rest upon the shoulders of a few, but these "few" had hearts of oak; to them belongs the real honor of founding the school. Wisdom, foresight, and sound common sense were their distinguishing characteristics. The first requisite for graduation was then, as it is yet, four years practical experience in the drug and apothecary business, then came the examination, and I may be pardoned if I quote a few passages from the address published in 1829 of one of the first presidents of the College, Daniel B. Smith, upon this subject of the examinations at that time. "Those who have already passed their examination, may be disposed to smile at the contrast between the trial to which they have been subjected, and the severe ordeal of the Prussian Code. It is true that we require as yet no proof of skill in analytic chemistry, but the questions of the examiners extend to all the branches of chemistry, pharmacy and natural history which are taught in the lectures, as well as to the more practical details of the business of an apothecary. To answer these questions with the promptness and accuracy that have in most cases been done, implies an acquaintance with the theory and practice of our art highly creditable to the candidates, and when contrasted with the state of things but a few years past, full of promise for the future." More than half a century has passed since these words were uttered, and it is for us to-night to inquire how far this promise for the future has been fulfilled. The examinations from this time until the year 1871 were altogether oral (the recognition of certain number of specimens being also required); there are good grounds for believing that an oral examination is one of the best means yet devised for judging of a candidate's ability to practice Pharmacy, yet the great increase in the size of the classes, coupled with the necessity for more thorough sifting of the applicants, compelled the Committee of Examination to adopt written examinations, and these have now been in use for about ten years. The advantages of written examinations are obvious; with the increase in the number of candidates it became desirable to grade their ability and this cannot be done in an oral examination. If sufficient time is given to a student of a retiring disposition who is naturally slow of speech, to write down his answers, he certainly has an opportunity to show that he knows the answer in a written examination, when he would probably fail, if required to give his answer by word of mouth.

In addition, orthography and chirography can both be considered in a written examination, and these are, certainly, pharmaceutical accomplishments, for the apothecary is expected to be a better writer than the physician, and I need hardly add the "expectations are usually realized." But if written examinations are *exclusively depended upon* as tests of fitness, there is a great danger of ruining the value of the College diploma, yet if one system must be used to the exclusion of the other, there can be no question that the written examination is the most impartial, accurate and satisfactory. The greatest evil that menaces both systems of examination, is what has been aptly termed the " gospel of cram." It is not confined to our own country. Our English pharmaceutical brethren are suffering probably to a greater extent than we are from this terrible scourge.

Prof. Attfield, of London, is battling valiantly in Great Britain against it, and the serious aspect of English pharmacy there, at present, should cause lively apprehension on our part, lest we permit the vicious system to get beyond our control here. The passage of the Pharmacy Act in Great Britain in 1868, which was believed by all to be a great boon, has proved to be a serious drawback to sound pharmaceutical education, and in a manner which was entirely unforeseen. The act mentioned, requires all who expect to practice pharmacy to pass one of two examinations, termed minor and major, the successful passage of the first conferring the title of " Chemist and Druggist," and that of the more difficult, the major, that of " Pharmaceutical Chemist." The examinations under the act are to be conducted by boards of examiners, stationed in certain cities, and these Boards are authorized to grant the necessary licenses to the successful candidates. Soon after the passage of the act private schools were established in various parts of Great Britain, whose object was to prepare students for these public examinations. Competition soon developed the energies of the rival schools, and it was not long before the pharmaceutical journals teemed with advertisements of the advantages of this and that school. Private instructors, who guaranteed success at the examination, soon became prominent; and finally amongst the most flourishing are some who are so convenient and accommodating as to furnish students at a distance with the necessary amount of stuffing *by mail* to guarantee success before the examiners. This pernicious system has so thoroughly fastened itself upon the practice of pharmacy in Great Britain, that one of the finest schools of pharmacy in the world, having for its instructors such brilliant men as Redwood, Bentley and Attfield, situated in the great city of London, with a population of ——— millions, is carrying on a languishing existence, not from want of ability or effort on the part of the faculty, but for want of students. This school really furnishes to its graduates a pharmaceutical education, and because it does, it suffers, whilst the schools and tutors that do not waste the time of the students by giving any information outside of that which by long experience they know will not be required by the boards of examiners, are in a wonderfully flourishing condition. The examining boards in the various States of our own country have it in their power to seriously injure the progress of pharmacy in our country in the future, if they permit their examinations to run into grooves, which can be readily measured by the professional coachers. Little danger need be apprehended at present. except in certain localities, because of the difference in the requirements of the laws in the various States, and sufficient time has hardly elapsed for an organization of the professionals to get into successful working order. Yet it is a danger which must always be guarded against, and it behooves every friend of sound pharmaceutical education to be ever on the alert. The chief bulwark of safety after all, however, is the progressive and rational element in the science of pharmacy itself, which is happily very active in America at present. When I see before me, as I do to-night, four hundred young men gathered in this hall from all parts of our country, probably nearly all voluntarily subjecting themselves to the inconveniences of breaking their home ties and usually lucrative positions, and incurring often heavy expenses hundreds of miles away from home for the purpose of attending lectures here, when they could easily satisfy the requirements of the law by passing the State Board's examination at home and forego these sacrifices, I say there can be but one reason for it, they believe that this institution aims to give them an *education* as well as an *examination*.

It is but fair for you to expect on our part some statement of what we have done, are doing, and expect yet to do to further the cause of *education*, and I desire to plainly draw the line here between an *examination education* and a *pharmaceutical education*. *Punch* has so aptly described the first that I am sure I cannot equal him and although his education and aëration has been quoted twice recently in public, it is good enough to be heard again : "So it seems that a disappointed mother's two sons were educated at the private school as soda-water bottles are aërated in a soda-water manufactory. The minds of the former were charged with learning by a process like that of pumping carbonic acid gas into the latter. The gas is retained in the bottles whilst it continues corked down, but escapes on the removal of pressure ; so, if the then boyish minds are left open, the learning, when set free from forcible compression, seems to go off in youthful effervescence. How glorious is the result of that system of cram by which our youth at an early age are enabled to pass the examinations which, at maturer years, they prove incapable of undergoing without being crammed all over again." A sound education is on the other hand one which serves the possessor well all through life ; the facts which the student has acquired are not evanescent, they are permanently stored away on the shelves of the mental knowledge case, like precious manuscript, ready to be brought forth and consulted as needed in his daily professional life.

What steps have been taken by the Philadelphia College of Pharmacy to protect their graduates from the evil results of cramming ? I know you are interested in the answer to this question. The Faculty and Committee of Examination have ever been alive to the danger of permitting the examinations from becoming mere matters of parrot-like memory and form. Some questions can hardly be framed which do not give an advantage to the candidate possessing a good memory, but it is possible to ask questions which require answers that compel the use of the student's own language, and he is compelled to fall back on his own knowledge of the subject. Two students were dolefully discussing last spring the prospects of getting easy questions at the final examination ; one said, " I feel pretty solid on Professor ——'s examination. I have been all over his questions from the beginning since they were printed in the Journal, and I know them all." The other said, " Well, suppose you have, if that is all you know, you will be sure to be left. I have gone over them all myself, and every year they are different ; he takes you on a different tack every year."

Here then, gentlemen, is one, great safeguard ; the student who expects to creep through, after cutting lectures, wasting precious time, and then at the eleventh hour cramming on the " previous questions," will be sure to fail. The principle of not only changing the questions but changing their character every year, as well as that of marking *with a higher value* those answers which show the exercise of reasoning and perceptive faculties on the part of the student has been in use by every one of the Professors of this institution ever since I have been connected with it, and I have no doubt the habit has extended back since the founding of the school. One of the plans of preventing the diploma from being captured by these sappers and miners, is that of requiring a certificate, testifying that the applicant has served an apprenticeship of four years with a person qualified to conduct the drug and apothecary business. This has been a requirement since the founding of the College, and yet it has been urged by some so-called friends of pharmaceutical education that this is an unnecessary hardship, that the examination should be the sole test of fitness for entrance into the ranks of the profession. "If a brilliant young man, even without practical experience, can acquire enough knowledge in two months to pass an examination which has required the laborious efforts of an industrious plodder three years to master, he should be eligible to examination, and is entitled to as much credit or even more than he who has acquired his knowledge slowly." But, stop a moment! What kind of an examination are they required to undergo. Is it one of the high-pressure *ad captandum* sort, so prevalent in many of our institutions of learning? For the questions are often framed on the same general model by the professor, year after year, and special stress is laid upon some high-sounding theories which look profound and technical on paper, and the coachers knowing beforehand, from a diligent study of the professor's methods, just where to lead the student into the paths of pleasantness and peace, quickly shear the examination of its terrors for him, and the brilliant young man stands before the world with a diploma in his hand, which certifies that he is competent to practice his profession and he claims the patronage of a too-confiding public, when in truth he is utterly ignorant of the first principles of Pharmacy. There never has been yet, and probably never will be, devised an examination in Pharmacy or any other science which will show *thoroughly all that a candidate knows and all that he does not know*. It is only when surrounded by safeguards and conducted by experienced and intelligent committees that examinations are valuable, and usually, the longer the examination the better, not only for the college but for the candidate.

The Faculty and Board of Trustees of this College have long recognized the importance not only of thorough practical training, but of the necessity of inaugurating some plan which would enable the Examining Committee to form a judgment of a candidate's ability to perform properly his daily professional duties. It was not, however, until 1877, that a plan was adopted which is now recognized as one of the distinguishing features in our examinations. The examination in pharmaceutical manipulations was used here five years ago, for the first time in this country, as a test of fitness for the Degree in Pharmacy, and, so far as I am aware, it still remains to be an exclusive feature in this school. The adoption of this innovation was a sad blow to the aspirations of those students who merely study for the examination. The midnight oil did not avail here, whole chapters of works on practical pharmacy might be digested and assimilated into their mental pabulum, and memorized *verbatim et literatim*, and yet neither tongue, pen nor sword availed an iota here, for the *pestle* was mightier than all combined. The conscientious labor of the daily toiler behind the counter was recognized henceforth, and, we trust, forever. He who was compelled by stern necessity to earn with his own hands his pharmaceutical education was not now compelled to stand aside and see his more wealthy companion reap *all* the honors of the college course; the patient attention to practical professional duties, which before was regarded as a positive factor in pulling down his examination record, by depriving him of the golden opportunity of study, now became valuable.

The attributes of neatness, accuracy, dispatch and finish in the discharge of his daily labors were eagerly sought, as a means of helping to retrieve his record. In 1878, but one year after the inauguration of this feature, the effects of this practical examination were so apparent that the Committee of Examination determined to extend their scope. In 1877, out of about one hundred emulsions (one of the classes of liquid mixtures) prepared by the candidates, *but ten were adjudged perfect;* in 1878, a similar preparation having been purposely selected for the next class, out of over one hundred mixtures *but ten were worthless*, and it cannot be said that the class knew what they were expected to prepare beforehand, for the majority felt sure that they would *not* get an emulsion again; because they had it only the year before. It can thus be seen that the examination of 1877 was turned to the excellent practical account of stimulating the interest and arousing an emulation in a branch before utterly neglected, and regarded by the student as indirectly useless to him in his examination, but far transcending in importance the passing of an examination. The possession of the diploma of the Philadelphia College of Pharmacy is now a guarantee of the possession of manipulative skill in pharmacy. But it must not be supposed that the grade of scholarship has been lowered, or the standard one whit debased, to admit this new comer. Midnight oil is more valuable than it was before. The other departments are expanding and growing. We have now a separate Chair of Analytical Chemistry, and this year, we are to have a new departure in the method of teaching this branch; for the first time in the history of the College class instruction in analytical chemistry is offered. The introduction of volumetric tests into the New Pharmacopœia requires on the part of the graduate in pharmacy a knowledge of volumetric analysis, at least so far as to the detection of impurities and the recognition of official chemicals. Our Professor in Analytical Chemistry is admirably equipped for giving this instruction, and it only remains for you to avail yourselves of the excellent opportunities afforded for obtaining a knowledge of qualitative and volumetric analysis. The system of reviewing the lectures, as conducted by the corps of assistant professors, although inaugurated but one year ago, has proved a complete success. In the regular course of lectures delivered by the professors many facts are mentioned which are not absorbed by the student, even though he be reasonably attentive. The habit of the human mind is usually to concern itself but slightly about matters that do not appeal at once for acceptance, and important facts are in this way entirely lost. Facts are often obscurely grasped, and the attentive student is sure that he comprehends a statement fully whilst the lecturer is dealing with it, only to find that, when it comes to his turn to restate it, the clearness vanishes, and he is in a fog. The great value of hearing a statement or fact reiterated has been long recognized; the practice serves to fix the fact in the mind; it stores it on the shelf, and it is usually there permanently. Every effort should be made in this system to clinch the facts soon after they are presented at the lecture; and no truth is more palpable than this: *If a student thoroughly understands a subject, he can explain it.* His inability must be accepted as proof that he has not fully mastered it.

I cannot close this address to you without referring to the praiseworthy efforts now being made by a committee of the Alumni Association to establish a class in microscopy. The microscope is justly regarded by all who keep abreast of improved methods in Pharmacy, as one of the most important additions to our means of detecting adulterations and recognition of fine distinctions in articles of materia medica, and I take pleasure in informing you incidentally that it has just been announced that George W. Hayes, a graduate of last year's class, has been awarded the prize of $100 offered by Allaire, Woodward & Co., of Peoria, Ill., for the best microscopical essay on powdered drugs; this prize was open to universal competition and its reception by one of our graduates is an honor to the recipient and the College. Our senior professor has for many years advocated the use of it, and I know that few forward movements would please him better than the establishment of a class in practical microscopy. The cost of equipment has been the most serious drawback to its successful working in the past, yet it should not be now. It will be but a few years before it will be as common for an educated pharmacist to add a microscope to his outfit as a prescription scale,

and it is impossible to grasp the intricacies of botanical microscopic structure without understanding the practical use of this instrument. But why
not begin now? Suppose twenty-five members of this large class make an
arrangement with a maker of a good, moderate-sized instrument (the Acme
stand would answer all requirements) to furnish them each with an instrument, the cost of each one, with all necessary accessories, would probably
then be not more than thirty-five dollars—and I cannot help adding here,
what most practical microscopists have long known, that the best microscopical work has been done with the low-priced achromatic instrument, and
that after all, it is not the microscope that does the work so much as the microscopist. Gentlemen, will you start it? One more subject and I shall
conclude. I have endeavored to show you that this Institution is irrevoca-
bly committed against superficial methods of instruction, and the Board of
Trustees have, by recent action on their part, shown their faith by their
works by offering to all an opportunity to extend the time for receiving instruction in this Institution without increasing the expense to the student.
As it is a new feature I shall bring it before you by quoting the regulations
as adopted by the Board.

MODIFIED OR PARTIAL EXAMINATIONS.

"The enlarged scope of instruction in all the branches taught in this
College, the increased demands at the Junior and at the final examination,
and the limited time afforded for home study to many of those who, while attending the College, are at the same time obtaining their practical instruction
at the store, have for a number of years past induced an annually increasing number of students to attend two, and even three, courses of lectures
in the Senior Class before applying for the examination. A similar course
has been followed by a number of Junior students, and it is evident that
many prefer, before graduating, to extend their studies over a period of
three or four years, remembering that knowledge is to be acquired for the
sake of thorough information, and of its practical application in life, and
not merely for the purpose of passing the examinations. Such will doubtless find it to their advantage to pass either the Junior or Senior examinations, or both, at two different periods, whereby they would be enabled to
extend over a longer time their studies in those branches in which a greater
perfection seems desirable. To carry out these views, the following plans
for passing the various examinations are offered :—

MODIFIED JUNIOR EXAMINATION.

"A student having attended one full course of lectures in the Junior
Class, may, at the end of this course, select of the parts into which the
Junior examination is divided (Botany, Pharmacy, Chemistry, Committee,)
any number, not less than two, in which he may desire to be examined,
notice of said selection to be given in writing to the Dean of the Faculty on
or before February 1st. If he pass in all the branches selected by him,
the results will be placed to his credit, and after attending another Junior
course, he may in like manner make application to come forward in the
remaining parts of the examination, and if he pass also in these, he will be
entitled to join the Senior Class. If at the first partial examination he
should fail in any one branch selected, he will be re-examined in this
branch also at the end of his second year as Junior.

"The student who takes out all his Junior tickets, and then elects to
divide his examination in this way, may attend the second year, as well as
the first, on these tickets."

MODIFIED SENIOR EXAMINATION.

"A Senior student having attended at least two full courses of lectures
may, at the end of the Senior course, select of the parts into which the

Senior examination is divided (Materia Medica, Pharmacy, Chemistry, Committee, Specimens, and Practical Examination,) three, in which he may desire to be examined, notice of said selection to be given in writing to the Dean of the Faculty on or before February 1st. If he pass in the three branches selected by him, the results will be placed to his credit ; and, after attending another course of lectures within the next two years, he may in like manner make application for examination in the remaining branches, and if he thus complete his examination in accordance with the rules of the College, he will be recommended to the Board of Trustees for the degree of Graduate in Pharmacy.

" This distribution of the Senior examination over two years, does not involve any extra expense in the way of tickets, as one complete set of Senior tickets only is required.

" The examination fee must be handed in with the application for the first part, and the thesis with the application for the second part of the Senior examination.

" A student applying for the final examination in all branches and failing to pass, will be credited with all those branches in which he had attained the grade of ' satisfactory ' or ' very satisfactory,' and in these he will not be required to undergo another examination. As just explained, the adoption of either one or more of these plans does not entail any additional expense upon the student, and either one of the Professors, on being consulted by the student, will be pleased to give his advice as to the best course to be pursued by one desiring to embrace the above plan or any portion thereof."

In conclusion, gentlemen, I feel as if almost an apology were needed for so grossly violating the proprieties usually observed in presenting introductory addresses. I have failed to quote a single line of poetry, and my promise to avoid rhetorical flourishes has been, as you see, literally carried out; but, gentlemen, I can say that I have honestly tried to realize my responsibilities, and, in bringing before you such practical matters, I felt that they would have more interest for you in the outset of your careers than fine words.

Before me are four hundred earnest, trusting, living souls. You have chosen us for your guides in one of the highest and noblest vocations that can absorb the efforts of man; and I say to you here to-night that the Faculty of the Philadelphia College of Pharmacy will see to it that, as long as you are under the sheltering care of your Alma Mater, you shall never look in vain for a guide or a friend.

After the close of Prof. Remington's Introductory, Profs. Maisch, Sadtler and Dr. Miller were called upon, and responded as follows :

Prof. Maisch :

GENTLEMEN :—After the eloquent address of my colleague, Prof. Remington, it would seem entirely unnecessary for me to say anything this evening. I heartily concur with every syllable he has uttered, and I wish you to feel, from the very beginning of your course, that our sole aim is your education. In the beginning of the lectures of both the Junior and Senior Courses, I shall, perhaps, have more to say, especially on the line which will be followed in my branch and to-morrow evening I shall have the pleasure of opening the Junior Course, and hope to see you here.

Prof. Sadtler :

GENTLEMEN :—This has been a day of introductory lectures. There have been delivered in Philadelphia to-day introductory addresses in the

Medical Department of the University of Pennsylvania, in the Jefferson Medical College, in the Hahnemann College, in the Pennsylvania College of Dental Surgery, in the Women's Medical College, and last, but not least, in the Philadelphia College of Pharmacy. If we were to take all these introductory lectures and endeavor to boil them down into a single sentence, I believe they would read: "Use wisely the advantages that are offered to you now, for these several years of study will have a controlling influence on your after life." For this we, who have reached years of maturity, have realized. The Philadelphia College of Pharmacy is the only College that has to uphold the dignity of the study of pharmacy, therefore there is a double responsibility resting upon us, and we must see that the results of our studies do not suffer in comparison with those attained by any other college.

Dr. A. W. Miller:

GENTLEMEN:—You have already heard so many words of wisdom, I will not presume to add anything further to the knowledge you have derived. I am, however, reminded by the papers I see distributed, that there is still another subject which has not been mentioned. I now refer to the claims of the Alumni Association. For several years this Association has instituted a series of social meetings which have been very well attended. There are there presented matters of current interest, and subjects of importance are offered for discussion, and you are in every way urged to bring forward original matter for the criticism of your instructors. I would therefore earnestly recommend that you attend these meetings ; also the Pharmaceutical Meetings of the College. At the latter you will have the additional advantage of turning the tables on your instructors. The professors will be there, and you will be able to quiz them on any subject not perfectly clear to you. You should embrace this opportunity of asking questions and becoming familiar on all points that have hitherto been obscure.

The following deaths of graduates of the Philadelphia College of Pharmacy have been reported since our last report was issued :—

George W. Patrick, M. D., Class 1846, died at Terre Haute, Ind., in 1874.
William Ellis, Class 1834, died in Philadelphia, October, 1881.
David Patrick Miller, Class 1878, died at his home in Virginia, in 1881.
Joseph H. Crawford, Class 1872, died in March, 1882.
Frederick Stryker Boisnot, Class 1876, died in New York, January 31st, 1882.
B. F. Shugard, Class 1868, died May 28th, 1882.
Simon Wolf, Class 1882, died May 29th, 1882.
George W. Gray, Class 1878, died June 22d, 1882.
John A. Lins, Class 1881, died July 19th, 1882.
Dr. Hiram Gold, Class 1864, died July 12th, 1882.
James A. Maston, Class 1875, died September 16th, 1882.
George W. Levering, Class 1877, died September 30th, 1882.
Charles William Elkins, Class 1880, died November 1st, 1882.
John Friedrich Stolz, Class 1874, died January 9th, 1883.
Stephen Liversidge Talbot, Class 1880, died in Providence, R. I., Jan. 15th, '83.
Jacob Francis Orsell, Jr., Class 1878, died 1883.
Joseph Halbert Kernan, Class 1878, died 1883.
George Edward Witsil, Class 1879, died in Philadelphia, January 1st, 1883.
Daniel B. Smith, the first President of the Philadelphia College of Pharmacy,
     died at his residence in Germantown, March 29th, 1883, aged 91 years.
Edward Peat, M. D., died at Delphos, O., April 19, 1883, of acute consumption, aged 28 years.

VALEDICTORY ADDRESS

BY

PROF. JOHN M. MAISCH, PHAR. D.,

DELIVERED AT THE

Sixty-Second Annual Commencement of the Philadelphia College of Pharmacy

Held at the Academy of Music,

Friday Evening, March 16th, 1883.

My Friends:

The present occasion forms a conspicuous milestone in the life of each one of you. The ceremonies through which we have in part gone and which will yet be performed this evening, attract many by the excellent music which they expect to hear, or by the floral displays and other surroundings. But the large majority of the audience which fills this spacious edifice to-night, is composed of your personal and professional friends, who rejoice in your success and by their presence desire to testify to their appreciation of your victory, and to cheer you right at the threshold of your professional career. To you it marks the close of a period of probation and study which has borne ripe fruits amidst labor and anxiety. With a 'dim and vague conception of the duties devolving upon the pharmacist, you have entered upon your apprenticeship and your first entrance, doubtless, created a well-excusable bewilderment when you noticed the thousand and one articles of all shades of color, liquid and solid, in irregular lumps, of well-defined shape or in impalpable powder, which should henceforth be the material to become familiar with, and that ultimately under your hands should be worked up in such a manner as to be used for the cure or for the prevention of the numerous physical ailments of the human race. Perhaps you felt serious distrust as to the possibility of ever acquiring the requisite knowledge for the safe handling of all those drugs and preparations, many of which you were told were among the most active and destructive agents known. But after you had gradually become familiar with the more humble but no less important duties of your calling, such as the cleaning of mortars, graduates, evaporating dishes, balances, and other utensils and apparatus, you began to be initiated into a certain familiarity with vegetable drugs and with chemicals by comminuting them with the aid of the drug mill or the mortar, by acting upon them with various solvents and treating them in other ways. The awe which you had at first felt gradually diminished, and finally vanished, being replaced by the confidence in your ability to master that, which had been mastered by others before and around you. It was the alphabet of your pharmaceutical experience which you had at last conquered, and when you began your pharmaceutical spelling lessons by consulting works of reference that were at your command, you soon began to learn

that each manipulation performed by you had to adapt itself to certain
peculiarities of the material in hand and to the object in view; that each
process was depending for its success not solely upon mechanical skill, but
likewise upon precautions inherent to the physical and chemical laws involved.   The well defined crystals of compounds scarcely varying in shape,
began to teach a history reaching outside of the shop and laboratory, em-
bracing the elements which enter into composition, their sources, properties
and affinities.   The infusion or tincture, syrup or extract, obtained by the
work of your hands, suggested thoughts·as to the origin, the commercial
history, and the properties of the crude material which your labor converted into preparations in which the medical properties should be preserved
without alteration.

It was by such and similar considerations that you were led to seek
instructions which, in the nature of our pursuit, cannot properly be expected
to be obtained solely behind the counter.   Your ambition was aroused to
read pharmacy under the guidance of others, to enter and pass through a
college, whose aims are the supplementing of the experience of the shop
with the teachings of science, based upon the facts and laws upon which
the existence and development of the products and the phenomena of
nature depend.   You found new avenues of thought opening themselves,
requiring further exertions in various directions, until at the end of several
years of study a thorough examination furnished the proof, that in the
opinion of the Board of Trustees and of the Faculty of the Philadelphia
College of Pharmacy, you could safely be entrusted with the responsible
duties which await you in the future.   You know, and I sincerely trust, you
appreciate it now, if you did not in the early part of your college career,
that the aim of your teachers was the *training*, but not the *drilling*, of your
minds, or as my honored colleague so aptly expressed it at the beginning of
the last course, that education and knowledge was the object in view, and
not merely the fitting you for passing the examinations that were surely in
waiting for you.

The accomplishment of these purposes is now a fixed fact, acknowledged by the public bestowal of the diplomas of this College, which, with
these commencement exercises, closes its sixty-second annual course of
instruction.   Your days of pupilage have passed, and you may now enter
the arena of business life without further requiring that special guidance
that had been accorded to you in the past.   To be sure you understand full
well that your studies are not ended; on the contrary they may be said
to now commence in reality; but as compared with former years, with this
difference, that henceforth you will have to depend in a greater measure upon
your own resources.   Your eyes have been trained to see, your minds have
been educated to perceive cause and effect, your hands have been taught
dexterity and skill.   It will rest with you now to apply these attainments in
the proper manner, not merely for your own advantage, but primarily for
the benefit of the public, the sick and the healthy, who may have occasion
to require your services.

It is scarcely necessary for me now to tell you that in your dealings
with the public the most scrupulous care and honesty are paramount in
importance.   If these are virtues in all ordinary business transactions, they
become sacred duties in pharmacy, and, without them, no one can be a true
pharmacist.   The health, maybe the life, of those dealing with you, depends
upon them.   Shun adulterations, and spoiled, as well as inferior drugs.
They constitute an evil from which pharmacy suffers no less than the public.
Its existence cannot·be, and is not denied; yet I am fully convinced that its
extent is far less than sensational reports occasionally make it appear; and

who could deny that during the past half century the American drug
. market has materially improved in the quality of the supply? The evil is
not a new one inaugurated in late years. It has existed as long as there
were men whose cupidity was stronger than their sense of justness, and it
will, doubtless, continue as long as there may be men with conceptions of
business principles so vague that they expect to purchase gold for the
money value of dross. The inculcation of ethical precepts generally will
lessen the demand for goods cheaper than their presumed value, and will
diminish the introduction of others under pretentious names, which are
chosen for the purpose of deception. On the other hand, the mastering of
all the details pertaining to an avocation, and their active and prudent
execution, will lessen the chances of being cheated by those whose conscience may be wide and whose morality blunted by their eagerness for
gain. There are no other moral principles required for transacting a pharmaceutical business than are necessary for any other business. Unwavering
integrity, that remains uninfluenced by visions of gold along the road of
questionable or deceitful practices, is the only foundation for success that
is worthy of the name. It is so in every pursuit, and more particularly in
that of pharmacy where, as a matter of necessity, it must be combined with
constant vigilance in all directions so as to secure all possible safeguards.

Soon after its organization the Philadelphia College of Pharmacy
turned its attention to this matter, and in the code of ethics adopted many
years ago expressed the views of its members in the following language:
"As the apothecary should be able to distinguish between good and bad
drugs, in most cases, and as the substitution of a weaker inert drug for an
active one may, negatively, be productive of serious consequences, we
hold that the sale of impure drugs or medicines, from motives of competition or desire of gain, when pure articles of the same kind may be
obtained, is *highly culpable*, and that it is the duty of every honest apothecary or druggist to expose all such fraudulent acts as may come to his
knowledge. But in reference to those drugs which cannot be obtained in a
state of purity, we should, as occasion offers, keep physicians informed of
their quality, that they may be governed accordingly."

Sickness has been known as long as mankind is in existence. While
in a low state of culture, man regarded and, among the uncivilized nations
of the present time, still regards disease as visitations of evil spirits, or as
an unknown or concealed power or force, producing a more or less disastrous effect. The search for specifics against such influences was then a
natural outgrowth of deficient knowledge, and the discoverer of such a supposed or reputed specific kept its nature and mode of preparation strictly
secret. Even after the dawn of modern medical science, during the last
century, many celebrated physicians refused to divulge their modes of
treatment to their friends. The hosts of remedies of those times—many
of them the most revolting and disgusting nature—have been properly
doomed to oblivion; nearly all the secret preparations then in use have
been buried deep enough to prevent their resurrection at any time in the
future, and the few which have survived have come to us in a materially
modified and, more especially, simplified condition. The chemical compounds then known and medicinally employed have been perfected in
composition and mode of preparation, and the crude drugs of those times
have been reduced in number, those only being now employed the useful-
ness of which has been tested in the course of time. A few of the really
valuable crude drugs which were formerly secretly employed acquired a
historic fame in consequence of the money consideration paid for the
divulging of the secret. The now universally employed cinchona bark,

after it had been introduced into Europe for nearly forty years, was used as a secret remedy, by means of which an English physician, Robert Talbor, acquired fame and honors at the courts of England and France, and obtained a round sum of money from Louis XIV. for his secret. This occurred a little over two hundred years ago, and a few years afterwards the same king paid the sum of 1000 louis d'ors to another physician, John Helvetius, for the remedy which had been successfully employed by the latter in dysentery; the drug, ipecacuanha root, is still regarded as a most valuable remedy. Scarcely more than one hundred years ago two parties sold the secret of the use of male fern as a remedy against tapeworm—the one to Frederick the Great, of Prussia, for 200 thalers (about $150); the other to Louis XVI., of France, for 18,000 francs.

With the gradual advance of medical science, and the recognition of the fact that disease is either a functional or structural disorder or derangement, secrecy of treatment has ceased, and at the present time no physician of note or respectability will probably be found who would hesitate to impart to the members of his profession his experience with certain remedies or with the treatment of the various diseases; the secret of success in the practice of medicine does not lie in the use of the remedy as much as it does in using the remedy for a proper cause and at the proper time.

Medicine is a liberal profession, and its offspring, pharmacy, is not less so. The secret practices of by-gone days have no claim to existence in our present age, and wherever secrecy of composition is maintained, as a rule, success is due to commercial enterprise, rather than to any inherent superiority. As far as it lay in their province, all reputable colleges of pharmacy have discountenanced secret remedies as baneful to the welfare of the public and to the interests of pharmacy and medicine. The code of ethics of this College treats of this subject in the following manner: "As the practice of pharmacy can become uniform only by an open and candid intercourse being kept up between apothecaries, which will lead them to discountenance the use of secret formulas, and promote the general use and knowledge of good practice; and, as this College considers that any discovery which is useful in alleviating human suffering, or in restoring the diseased to health, should be made public for the good of humanity and the general advancement of the healing art, no member of this College should originate or prepare a medicine the composition of which is concealed from other members, or from regular physicians. Whilst the College does not at present feel authorized to require its members to abandon the sale of secret or quack medicines, it earnestly recommends the propriety of discouraging their employment, when called upon for an opinion as to their merits." My friends, substitute in this declaration for "members" the word "graduates," and you will find in it a precept for your professional deportment both honorable and just.

Another step against secrecy was taken by the American Pharmaceutical Association in 1878, when rules were formulated for the exclusion from the annual exhibitions of all medicines in the composition or preparation of which secrecy is maintained or the names of which are legally monopolized. These rules have since been adopted by most State pharmaceutical associations for their guidance also. It is evident from all this that the claims of pharmacy to the distinction of a liberal profession are being maintained by the enlightened pharmacists of our country, and from this view your instruction was conducted in every department. Whatever secret could be unravelled by your teachers, no pains were spared in the attempt, and we now look upon you as being wedded to the cause in which you have been trained.

But, Graduates of the Class of 1883, time admonishes me to be brief. This is most likely the last occasion on which we all will be assembled together. From all sections of this continent you came here for the noble purpose of studying; that purpose being now accomplished, to-morrow will see many of you on the way to your homes from which you have been separated for months or years. The hours you have spent together at College, in the lecture halls or laboratory, or in your private chamber, will henceforth live in your memory only, and we trust they may be not merely memories of hard labor, but likewise recollections of unalloyed joys, which, after the lapse of many years, may still afford you genuine pleasure. Now the hour of parting has arrived, and I am privileged to offer you on behalf of the Faculty and of the Trustees and Members of the Philadelphia College of Pharmacy, the sincere congratulations to your success and the best wishes for an honorable and successful professional career. Your Alma Mater will rejoice on learning of the fulfillment of these wishes, for she claims you now as a part of that corps of able pharmacists who were sent forth from her halls, and of whom she has good reason to be proud. To one and all of you I bid *farewell* and *God speed*.

PROCTER PRIZE.

The "Procter Prize," consisting of a gold medal and certificate, will be annually awarded to the most meritorious Graduate in Pharmacy; *provided*, that, in accordance with the will of the late Prof. Wm. Procter, Jr., such a reward is, in the opinion of the Board of Trustees, deserved.

The Committee on Examinations and the Professors shall, previous to the Annual Commencement, specially report upon the most meritorious student of the graduating class, as determined from the regular examination, or from other proofs in addition thereto, and, if deemed worthy of distinction, the Procter Prize shall be awarded to him by the Board of Trustees.

The student to whom this prize shall be awarded must have obtained the highest general average of the class, passed a "very satisfactory" examination in all of the branches, and in the recognition of specimens, and must have presented a meritorious thesis.

The Procter Medal has been presented to the following :—

Joseph LeRoy Webber, of Springfield, Mass. Class of 1876.
Olaf Martin Oleson, of Fort Dodge, Iowa. Class of 1877.
George Havens Colton, of Springfield, Mass. Class of 1880.
Louis Genois, New Orleans, La. } Class of 1881.
Wm. Earl Jenks, Philadelphia, Pa. } Class of 1881.
Virgil Coblentz, Springfield, Ohio. } Class of 1882.
Jonas Gerhard Clemmer, Philadelphia, Pa. } Class of 1882.
Wm. Frederick Jungkunz, Freeport, Ill. } Class of 1883.
Wm. Edwin Saunders, London, Ont., Canada. } Class of 1883.

10

Commencement Exercises.

The Sixty-second Annual Commencement of the Philadelphia College of Pharmacy was held as usual, at the American Academy of Music, on Friday evening, March 16th, 1883.

The large building was well filled with an audience largely composed of ladies.

The exercises commenced with the performance of several choice pieces by the Germania Orchestra, and promptly at eight o'clock the members of the Graduating Class entered from the rear of the stage, under the marshalship of Wm. C. Bakes, Ph. G., of the Class of 1855, and occupied the front seats in the parquet centre. After the Class were seated the Members of the Faculty, Officers, Trustees, Members of the College and of the Alumni Association took seats upon the stage.

After all had been seated and quiet had been restored, Prof. Joseph P. Remington stepped forward and announced to the audience that we had assembled together to participate in the ceremonies attending the Sixty-second Commencement of the Philadelphia College of Pharmacy. He stated that the Graduates of the College now numbered more than 1000, the present Graduating Class being the largest that had ever left its halls, numbering 153 members (see list of Class), and for the first time in the history of the College a *lady* would receive the diploma, she being the first female graduate.

He then called the roll of the Class, and as their names were called they came forward upon the stage and the degree of Graduate in Pharmacy (Ph. G.) was then conferred upon them by the President of the College, Dillwyn Parrish, Ph. G., of the Class of 1830. Prof. Remington then announced that two Procter gold medals would be awarded, one to Wm. F. Jungkunz, of Freeport, Ill., and one to Wm. E. Saunders of London, Ont. (Canada), on behalf of the Board of Trustees, by First Vice-President Charles Bullock, Ph. G. Mr. Bullock then presented the gold medals to each of the gentlemen, with appropriate remarks, after which each one responded with remarks suited to the occasion, thanking the Board of Trustees for the high honor conferred upon them.

The following gentlemen were also announced as worthy of honorable mention, with the general grade "Distinguished:" Howard D. Dietrich, Jos. W. England, Wm. W. Light, Chas. F. Randolph, and Flor. Joseph Schmidt, and with the general grade 'of "Meritorious," Robt. C. Browning, Milton Campbell, John Peter Frey, Owen B. Hannon, Daniel R. Jones, Frank G. Kerr, Louis C. Leonhard and Gustav Scherling.

The Chemical Prize (a Troemner analytical balance) for the best analytical work, was then awarded to John Peter Frey, of Union City, Indiana, by Prof. Sadtler, with appropriate remarks, and honorable mention was made of John H. M. Clinch, Mimms Wm. Coleman, Chas. F. G. Helm, Jr., and Wm. F. Jungkunz.

Mr. Wm. J. Jenks, Ph G., Secretary of the College, presented the H. C. Lea prize one hundred dollars, for the best thesis to Joseph W. England, of Philadelphia, Pa., with honorable mention of Mathew V. Cheatham, Howard D. Dietrich, Wm. C. Franciscus, Wm. B. Gleim, Wm. W. Light, Wm. E. Saunders and Reinhard J. Weber. The prize offered as the Prof. J. M. Maisch Prize, by Mr. J. H. Redsecker, of Lebanon, Pa., twenty dollars in gold, for the best examination of drugs by means of the microscope was presented by the Chairman of the Committee on Instruction, Charles Bullock, to Wm. F. Jungkunz, of Illinois, with honorable mention of Wm. E. Saunders, John Peter Frey, Wm. W. Light, Chas. F. G. Helm, Jr., Jos. W. England, Fred'k R. Eilinger, Harry H. Deakyne and Howard D. Dietrich.

The valedictory address was then delivered by Prof. John M. Maisch, Phar. D. (See page 141).

After this "Home, Sweet Home," was well rendered by the orchestra to the delight of the audience, and at its conclusion the Committee of the Alumni Association, consisting of Wm. C. Bakes Dr. A. W. Miller, H. P. Thorn, George W. Schimminger, Alfred Mullhaupt, the Secretary, and others, distributed the various presents, consisting of floral tributes, books, canes, umbrellas, etc., of which there was an abundance left or sent by the friends of the new graduates, and at a late hour, amid the sweet strains of the finale of the orchestra, the exercises of the Sixty-second Annual Commencement of the Philadelphia College of Pharmacy for the Class of 1882 and 1883 came to a close and the large audience, together with the graduates and friends of the College, dispersed to their various places of abode, many of them never to meet again this side of eternity.

THE PROFESSORS' ANNUAL BANQUET,

Thursday evening, March 15th, 1883, will long be remembered by the Graduating Class of 1883, as well as the Professors and

Members of the Board of Trustees, who assembled at the Museum Hall of the College in response to an invitation extended by the Professors, and partook of a sumptuous repast. The tables, of which there were four in number, were well loaded with the good things, and to which those present did ample justice. After all present had satisfied the inner man Prof. Maisch, who presided and sat at the head of the table, called upon his fellow-professors and members of the Board of Trustees, who responded and made brief addresses. Prof. Maisch then called upon Howard D. Dietrich, a member of the Graduating Class, who presented Prof. Samuel P. Sadtler, on behalf of the Class, with a comfortable easy chair, as follows :

HONORED PROFESSOR :—I have the pleasure of representing our Zeta Phi Society this evening, in one of those pleasant little affairs which help to make life sweet.

To you, as well as to each of our very able corps of professors, the past college term has no doubt been a long, tedious and tiresome one ; and, perhaps, upon more occasions than one have your instructions and labors in our behalf been received in a manner which certainly did not tend to lighten them. But, notwithstanding this, there has never been a doubt in our minds but that all was being done for our success that it was possible for you to do. This I say with due respect for and appreciation of the labors of each of your worthy colleagues.

The desire of each of us being that our appreciation be manifested in a manner more substantial than words, and having well considered the fact that after the arduous duties of the winter, you can certainly enjoy a good rest, and especially so if there is an easy place to take it in, we have selected for this purpose an easy chair. In it are combined utility, durability, beauty and comfort. It is offered with the best wishes of each member of the Society, and we fear not but that it will be accepted, not for its real intrinsic value, but merely as a slight token indicating the high esteem in which you are held by us.

Our selection of the chair, which is an *easy* one, is not that we think that it bears any comparison whatever to our recent examination in Chemistry. Nevertheless, all of us who have passed through that ordeal safely are certainly glad we can tender you at least this much ease and comfort, and hope you will enjoy it long and often during the brief vacation before you, believing your thoughts will occasionally revert to the members of the Zeta Phi Society of the Class of '83.

Prof. Sadtler responded in a few brief remarks thanking the Class for the gift.

Charles Henry Baker then arose and presented Mr. Thos. S. Wiegand, the Actuary, with a handsome book case, with the following remarks :

MR. WIEGAND :—The time will soon come when all of us will be compelled to say to you Farewell. We all deeply feel this, and notwithstanding our pleasant associations with the Professors and the College, our closer association with you has been such as we will more deeply feel the parting words with you—"Good-bye."

For the last two winters our intercourse and associations with you have been more than agreeable ; your actions have been such as to warrant the warmest feeling of friendship between the students and yourself; as you have been in former years, we recognize you at the present—the student's friend. It is unnecessary for me to detail your many kind acts and deeds, your ever-willing replies, and your encouraging words. · All of us acknowledge your kindness, and to show our appreciation of the same, allow me, in behalf of the Zeta Phi Society, to present this book case as a token of our unlimited amount of respect for you.

As years roll by and classes come and go, it would be perfectly natural for you to forget us individually, but we sincerely hope you never will forget us as a class, and at any time you may have occasion to compare one class with another, our wish is that we will compare favorably. Do not look at this token of respect in its value of dollars and cents, but rather consider the feeling it represents, the respect, friendship and love it bears from us. Accept it then with the best wishes of the Zeta Phi Society of the Class of '82–'83.

Mr. Wiegand responded with a few happy remarks, thanking the Graduating Class for the valuable gift, and would always hold the Class of 1882–'83 in grateful remembrance.

This closed the programme, and the participants in the festivities separated for their various places of abode, well pleased with the evening's enjoyment.

NAMES OF THOSE WHO HAVE HELD PROFESSORSHIPS IN THIS COLLEGE (all deceased).

GERARD TROOST, M. D., Professor of Chemistry from 1821 to 1822.

SAMUEL JACKSON, M. D., Professor of Materia Medica from 1821 to 1827.

BENJAMIN ELLIS, M. D., Professor of Materia Medica from 1827 to 1831.

GEORGE B. WOOD, M. D., Professor of Chemistry from 1822 to 1831, when he was elected to the chair of Materia Medica made vacant by the death of Dr. Ellis, and continued till 1835.

FRANKLIN BACHE, M. D., Professor of Chemistry from 1831 to 1841.

R. EGGLESFIELD GRIFFITH, M. D., Professor of Materia Medica from 1835 to 1836.

WILLIAM R. FISHER, Professor of Chemistry from 1841 to 1842.

JOSEPH CARSON, M. D., Professor of Materia Medica from 1836 to 1850.

WILLIAM PROCTER, JR., Professor of Theory and Practice of Pharmacy from 1846 to 1866, and from 1872 to 1874.

ROBERT P. THOMAS, M. D., Professor of Materia Medica from 1850 to 1864.

EDWARD PARRISH, Professor of Materia Medica from 1864 to 1866, and Professor of Pharmacy from 1866 to 1872.

ROBERT BRIDGES, M. D., Professor of Chemistry from 1842 to 1879, and Emeritus Professor of Chemistry from 1879 to 1882.

ZETA PHI ALPHA,

The Social Organization of the Philadelphia College of Pharmacy.

PROCEEDINGS OF THE ANNUAL MEETING.

Held in the Society Room, March 15th, 1883.

The Fourth Annual Meeting of the Zeta Phi Alpha Chapter of the P. C. P. was held this day, President French in the chair. Members present, Fellows Krewson, Gatchell, Parker, Warrington, C. C. Meyer, H. A. Newbold, G. R. Ross, McClintock, Weidemann, Zeller, Matthes, Beetem, Potts, Scholl, Matthews, Power, W. C. Mayer, J. D. Taylor, Sayre, Biddle and Procter. The minutes of the last annual meeting were read and approved. The minutes of the Executive Council for the last year were read, and after correction approved. Fellow Krewson moved to transpose the order of business, so that the Chapter might proceed with the election of candidates for fellowship. Carried.

The applications of Robert England, '46; Mimms W. Coleman, '83; W. W. Light, '83; and Henry G. Kalmbach, '83' were received, and referred to a committee consisting of Fellows Parker, Warrington and C. C. Meyer, who reported favorably in each case. M. W. Coleman was then balloted for, and Fellow Gatchell having been appointed teller, reported a unanimous election. Fellow Krewson moved that the remaining candidates be balloted for collectively. Agreed to, and a ballot being taken the teller reported the unanimous election of the applicants. Initiation of candidates being next in order, the President appointed Fellow C. C. Meyer, Doorkeeper; Fellows Newbold, Jones and Gatchell, Conductors, and Fellows Potts and Beetem, Masters of Ceremonies. Messrs. Light, Coleman and Kalmbach being on hand, the ceremony of initiation proceeded with much zeal and numerous variations of the programme, until they were finally admitted into the Arcana of the Fraternity. The Committee on Ritual reported progress. Fellow Warrington moved that the Committee be continued. Carried.

Committee on Banquet reported progress, without any idea of the time of the conclusion of Mr. Shuster's suit against them. A motion to continue the Committee was carried.

There being no unfinished business the President's address was now delivered and was ordered to be spread in full upon the minutes. (See President's Address, page 152.)

The Secretary's report not being available for reading, Fellow Wm. E. Krewson moved that it be spread upon the minutes. Carried. (See Secretary's Report, page 153.)

Under the head of new business an amendment· to Article III, Chapter 7, of the By-Laws, as offered by Fellows Krewson and Potts at the last meeting of the Executive Council, was considered, and after discussion, on motion of the Secretary, was adopted, It reads as follows: "They shall hold their regular stated meetings on the third Thursday of every February, and on the first Thursday of every June, September and December."

The report of the Treasurer having been presented, it was referred to an Auditing Committee, consisting of Fellows Parker, Meyer, and Warrington, who reported it correct and moved its adoption. It will be found on page 154.

Nominations to fill three vacancies in the Executive Council to serve three years, being in order, the following names were presented:—

> Fellows F. B. Power,
> W. A. Ball,
> T. L. Buckman,
> E. W. Gatchell,
> W. C. Mayer,
> D. W. Ross.

On motion, the nominations were declared closed, and an election was proceeded with. Fellow Weidemann being appointed teller announced the choice of. Fellows Power, Ross and Buckman, they being the three receiving the highest number of votes.

Fellow Krewson moved "that a committee of three be appointed to devise some means for enlarging the membership of the Chapter." Carried, and appointment of Committee reserved by the President.

Mr. Robert England being in waiting, the Initiation Committee, previously appointed, proceeded with great solemnity to admit him to full membership. Fellow Jones with much difficulty restrained the powerful efforts of the candidate, who, no stranger to such ceremonies, evidently expected and was prepared for the worst; he, however, passed the ordeal with flying colors.

There being no further business the Chapter, on motion, adjourned.

WALLACE PROCTER,
Secretary.

The following is the list of the officers of the Zeta Phi Alpha for 1882–1883:

President—Howard B. French, '71' cor. Fourth and Callowhill Streets.
First Vice-President—Albert P. Brown, '62, Camden, N. J.
Second Vice-President—Wm. E. Krewson, '69, N. E. cor. Eighth Street and Montgomery Avenue.
Treasurer—C. W. Hancock, '57' West Philadelphia, Pa.
Secretary—Wallace Procter, '72' No. 900 Lombard Street.
Chaplain—Rev. James C. Craven, '69' No. 608 N. Forty-fourth St., West Philadelphia, Pa.

Executive Council—
    Edward C. Jones, '64' Media, Pa.   ⎫
    Chas. W. Warrington, '76' Philadelphia, Pa.   ⎬ 1 year.
    Chas. J. Biddle, '74' West Philadelphia, Pa.   ⎭
    Jos. L. Lemberger, '54, Lebanon, Pa.   ⎫
    Jas. A. Parker, '73' Philadelphia, Pa.   ⎬ 2 years.
    Thos. H. Potts,. '71, Philadelphia.   ⎭
    F. B. Power, '74, Philadelphia, Pa.   ⎫
    D. W. Ross, '77' Philadelphia', Pa.   ⎬ 3 years.
    Thos. L. Buckman, '74' Chestnut Hill, Philadelphia, Pa. ⎭

    N. B.--Applications for membership can be procured from any of the
above-named gentlemen composing the officers of the Council, and their
certificate of membership will be sent to them by mail.
    Applicants for membership will please forward the initiation fee ($2.00),
giving full name, age, class, degrees taken and address, all plainly written,
to the Secretary, or to any member of the above list of officers.

PHILADELPHIA, March 15th, 1883.

*To the Officers and Fellows of the Zeta Phi Alpha of the Philadelphia
    College of Pharmacy :*

    DEAR FELLOWS:—With to-day terminates another year of the existence
of our Chapter. In reviewing the events of the past year, I have to draw
your attention to the first triennial reunion, held just one year ago, in the
museum of this College. The event was one long to be remembered by
those who participated in it as guests, and also by your Committee, who
have been compelled to defend themselves in the courts, from what they
felt was an unjust overcharge and imposition on the part of the caterer, W.
H. Shuster, they had employed to serve the banquet. The case is still in
the courts, and from present appearances will be continued for some
months to come. I regret that our Association should have been involved
in a lawsuit at this early.stage of its existence; but the case was so unjust
that your Committee felt warranted in retaining attorneys for their defence,
which action has since been indorsed by your Executive Council. The
money received from the sale of the banquet tickets has been deposited by
the Chairman of the Committee in a trust and safe deposit company.
The cost of defence will be paid by the Committee, so that the Association
will be at no expense.
    As yet, no ritual has been adopted, but I am in hopes that by the next
annual meeting you will have one regularly established. As the Committee
appointed at your meeting a year ago has reported progress at the meetings
of the Executive Council, and it is but reasonable to suppose that with
another year's deliberations they will be ready to make their final report.
    The Association has not received as many graduates to fellowship
during the past year as it had during the preceding years of its existence. The number admitted to fellowship this year was but sixteen (16),
while last year there were twenty-two (22) admitted. This is but a small
percentage of the graduates annually turned out by our College, and I feel
that by far the larger portion of them should become members of the Zeta
Phi Alpha, if the proper means was devised to interest them in our Association; and to this end I would suggest that a Committee be appointed at
this meeting to devise means of increasing our membership, with instruc-.
tions to report to your Executive Council at their next regular meeting, June

7th. In this connection I would urge upon all the fellows of this Chapter to take an active part in securing the application of eligible graduates for fellowship. Many of you have friends who would gladly make application, did they know that it forms a social bond of fellowship between the graduates of our Alma Mater, and renews and perpetuates the pleasant associations formed during our Collegiate course. I therefore ask that each member use his influence in the best interest of our Chapter.

The most interesting event of the past year was the organizing of the Zeta Phi Society, by the Committee appointed on September 7th, 1882, at a meeting of the Executive Council, who were ably assisted by a number of the fellows of this Chapter, among whom deserving of especial mention and the thanks of our Association was Dr. A. W. Miller, who for an hour entertained the class with humorous recitations, while the tellers were recording their ballots for officers.

The meeting was of the most pleasant character, and the friendly feeling manifested by the Class can best be explained in the words of my predecessor; they seemed to "realize that we proposed no antagonism to them or their works, no monopoly of their pleasures, privileges or plans, but simply and freely proffered friendly help, with a view to the prosperity of a fraternity that they must realize is a close one as children to the same Alma Mater," and with this feeling they accepted the Constitution and By-Laws which this Chapter had adopted for their use.

Their action was very gratifying to your Committee, as it promised a friendly and united action during the course, and, I trust, to-day to have the pleasure of welcoming many of them as fellows of the Zeta Phi Alpha.

The Zeta Phi Society sent a communication to the Executive Council, asking their approval to a change in their By-Laws. The change being immaterial, it was approved by your Council and returned to them.

In conclusion, I wish to acknowledge the kindly assistance of my co-officers and the members of the Executive Council, who have, at all times, shown an active interest in the welfare of the Zeta Phi Alpha.

Respectfully submitted,

HOWARD B. FRENCH.

REPORT OF THE SECRETARY.

PHILADELPHIA, March 15, 1883.

To the Officers and Fellows of the Zeta Phi Alpha:

FELLOWS:—Your Secretary would respectfully report that since your last Annual Meeting your Executive Council has held four stated and two adjourned meetings, at but one of which no quorum was present. The attendance of its members was as follows: Present, Fellows French and Brown, four times; Fellows Parker, Warrington and Krewson, three times; Fellows Lemberger, Moorhead, Potts and Hancock, twice, and Fellows Biddle, Jones, Buckman and Craven, once, each; Fellow Ball not at all, and the Secretary at five meetings. At these meetings was transacted the routine business, as will be shown by their minutes. Six candidates for fellowship were elected, and four of them initiated in due form. Our total membership, as shown by signatures to the Constitution, is one hundred and seventy-nine.

WALLACE PROCTER,
Secretary.

REPORT OF THE TREASURER.

PHILADELPHIA, March 15, 1883.

To the President, Vice-Presidents, Officers, and Fellows of the Zeta Phi Alpha :

GENTLEMEN :—As directed by the Constitution and the practice of former years, I herewith present a report of my transactions during the past year. All the bills of which I am cognizant have been paid, and there is a balance in the treasury of $11.70. The membership during the past year has increased in greater ratio than any preceding one, though not as much as we desire and expect, and I trust that greater interest may be manifested by the Fellows generally, and our Graduates, that your Treasurer may have the pleasure of presenting a much larger balance a year hence. Thanking his brother officers and the Fellows for the pleasant intercourse of the past year, I respectfully submit this report.

RECEIPTS.

1882, Cash Balance at last report,	. . . . . .	$40 00
" for initiations, .	. . . .	36 00
1883, " "	. . . .	10 00
Total,	. . . . . .	$86 00

DISBURSEMENTS.

1882, March 29,	By Cash,	Ware & Bro., Application Blanks, .	$4 50
June 8,	"	T. H. Potts, Postage, . . .	5 27
9,	"	E. Morgan, Printing, ...	6 25
9,	"	W. H. Hoskins, Envelopes, . . .	90
9,	"	C. A. Bush, Filling Certificates, . .	6 30
9,	"	Stuart & Bro., Record Book, . .	50
9,	"	Chas. Cook, Carpenter Work, . . .	9 83
July 31,	"	W. E. Krewson, Sec'y of Alumni Association, for Closets, . . .	20 00
Sept. 7,	"	Ward & Barnitz, Printing, . . .	1 75
1883, March 14,	"	E. C. Jones, Treasurer of Alumni Association, printing Annual Report, .	16 50
14,	"	Horstman & Sons, Ballot-box, . .	2 50
		Total, ...	$74 30
		Balance to new account, . . .	$11 70

C. W. HANCOCK,
Treasurer.

PHILADELPHIA, March 15, 1883.

The undersigned committee having examined the books and vouchers of the Treasurer find the same to be correct.

JAMES A. PARKER, }
C. CARROLL MEYER, } *Committee.*
C. W. WARRINGTON, }

LIST OF DECEASED ACTIVE MEMBERS OF THE ALUMNI ASSOCIATION, AS FAR AS KNOWN.

Patrick, Geo. W., M. D.,	1846	Hoagland, Pratt R.,	1868
Selfridge, Mathew M.,	1852	Shropshire, Jas. B.,	1868
Watson, Wm. J.,	1853	Simes, Samuel F.,	1868
Barr, Thomas H.,	1854	Shugard, Benj. F.,	1868
Leamy, James C.,	1855	Bowman, Henry K.,	1869
Bringhurst, Ferris,	1857	Davis, Aaron R.,	1869
Heydenreich, Victor F.,	1858	Fritchey, James G.,	1869
Seegar, Roland,	1859	Kolp, Christopher H.,	1869
Rhodes, Elam, M. D.,	1861	Hannaman, John B.,	1870
Fisher, Theophilus, M. D.,	1862	Stretch, Charles F.,	1870
Mullen, Wesley W.,	1862	Bolton, Charles F.,	1871
Rohrer, Earl Penn,	1863	Alvarez Miguel, Y. Ortis,	1873
Jones, Samuel T.,	1864	Schnabel, Charles,	1873
Gold, Hiram, M. D.,	1864	Jacobs, George Harris,	1874
Keen, Francis,	1865	Brown, Frank Pierce,	1875
Rubencam, Chas. E.,	1865	Maston, Jas. A.,	1875
Wendel, Frederick W.,	1865	Koehler, Walter W.,	1877
Barnitz, Frank M.,	1866	Hendricks, Elwood G.,	1878
Shoemaker, Chas.,	1866	Peat, Edward, M. D.,	1878
Corbridge, John E., Jr.,	1868	Elkins, Chas. Wm.,	1880
Eayre, Mortimer H.,	1868	Wolf, Simon E.,	1882

List of Students who took the Quizzes under the auspices of the Alumni Association, Session of 1882–83.

SENIORS.

Apple, Milton S., Hellertown, Pa.
Armbrecht, Wm. Chas., Wheeling, West Va.
Arnold, Chas. Fred'k, Fort Dodge, Iowa.

Baker, Chas. Henry, Trenton, N. J.
Ballentine, Allen De Bow, Phila., Pa.
Barr, Wm. Henry, Milwaukee, Wis.
Boorse, Henry Augustus, Norristown, Pa.
Booth, Fred'k Smith, Phila, Pa.
Brown, Jos. Henry, Morris, Ill.
Browning, Robt. C., Indianapolis, Ind.
Butler, Geo. White, Bryn Mawr, Pa.

Campbell, Milton, Easton, Md.
Cox, Geo. Washington, Phila., Pa
Cuskaden, Albert Duglass, Phila., Pa.

Dare, John Henry, Bridgeton, N. J.
Davis, Wm. Henson, Germantown, Pa.
Deakyne, Harry Hartup, Smyrna, Del.
Dietrich, Howard Dickson, Harrisburg, Pa.
Dundore, Milton Jacob, Reading, Pa.

England, Jos. Winters, Phila., Pa.

Fasig, Harry Buckley, Columbia, Pa.
Fell, Edgar Burnside, Wilmington, Del.
Finck, Robert F., Phila., Pa.
Frangkiser, John Fred'k, Loudonville, Ohio.
Fries, Chas. Jos. Valentine, Reading, Pa.

Gregg, Henry Hamilton, New Lisbon, Ohio.

Hahn, Gustav, Sheboygan, Wis.
Hannon, Owen Burdette, Greene, N. Y.
Harris, Frank Pierce, Hamburg, Pa.
Harrison, Jas. Oliver, St. Michael's, Md.
Hillan, John Michael, St. Clair, Pa.
Horsey, John Marshall, Charleston, S. C.

Jones, Daniel R., Milwaukee, Wis.
Johnson, Theo. Milton, Huntington, Ind.

Kalmbach, Henry Geo., Phila., Pa.
Kempfer, Emil Frank, Racine, Wis.
Kerr, Frank Gault, Marshall, Mo.
Kerr, Richard F., Phila., Pa.
Kindig, Rudolph, Switzerland.
Krider, Jas. Delaplaine, Chester, Pa.

MacNair, Whitmel Horne, Tarboro', N. C.
McCreight, Robert, Phila., Pa.
Maddock, Wm. Worrell, Atlantic City, N. J.
Miller, Harold Baughman, Carlisle, Pa.
Miller, Turner Ashby, Danville, Va.

Neuhart, Laurence Aug., Caldwell, Ohio.

O'Brien, Christopher, Conshohocken, Pa.
Ott, Chas. Wm., Phila., Pa.

Randolph, Chas. Fitz, Altoona, Pa.
Reeser, John Wesley, Sunbury, Pa.
Rickey, Chas. Frank, Mt. Sterling, Ill.
Roedel, Wm. Ruthrauff, Lebanon, Pa.
Roehrig, Geo. Fred'k, Pottsville, Pa.
Ruth, Wm. Augustus, Alliance, Ohio.

Salot, Geo. Washington, Dubuque, Iowa.
Scherling, Gustav, Dubuque, Iowa.
Schmidt, Flor. Jos., Evansville, Ind.
Scheffler, Jas. Samuel, Chapmansville, Pa.
Sellers, Albert Tobias, Pottstown, Pa.
Smith, Chas. Michael, Lebanon, Pa.
Smith, Stephen Douglass, Birdsboro, Pa.

Trusler, Chas. Lawrence, Indianapolis, Ind.

Walter, Wm. Henry, Phila., Pa
Weber, Geo. Washington, Millville, N. J.
Weber, Reinhard Julius, Ashland, Pa.
Werst, Allen Leidig, Hellertown, Pa.
Willard, Theo. Newton, Shamokin, Pa.

JUNIORS.

Anderson, Henry Warren, Bath, Me.
Ball, John Price, Phila., Pa.
Clayton, Abraham Theophilus, Phila., Pa.
Hoffman, Ephraim Zeigler, Maytown, Pa.
Knight, Howard, Edgewood, Pa
Moore, Christian, Ardmore, Pa.
Parker, Jas. Pleasant, Springfield, Mo.
Petrie, Edward Sing, Oswego, N. Y.

Pierce, Wm. C., Wilmington, Del.
Ryan, Frank Gibbs, Elmira, N. Y.
Sher, Fred'k Paul, Phila., Pa.
*Taylor, Jas. Grant, Ottumwa, Iowa.
Thompson, Geo. Edward, Henry Clay, Del.
Ward, John Martin Broomall, Chester, Pa.
Wickham, Anthony Smith, Wheeling, W. Va.

LIST OF CLASS WHO TOOK COURSE IN MICROSCOPY.

Hancock, Chas. W., Ph. G., W. Phila., Pa.
Boring, Edwin M., Ph. G., Phila., Pa.
Armbrecht, Wm. Charles, Wheeling, West Va.
Barr, Jr., Wm. Henry, Milwaukee, Wis.
Baker, Chas. Henry, Trenton, N. J.
Browning, Robt. Craighead, Indianapolis, Ind.

Boynton, Willis Carlton, Auburn, Me.
Jones, Daniel R., Milwaukee, Wis.
Parker, James Pleasant, Springfield, Mo.
Randolph, Chas. Fitz, Altoona, Pa.
Ruth, Wm. Augustus, Alliance, Ohio.
Saunders, Wm. Edwin, London, Ont. (Can.)

* Died in February, during the course of lectures.

GRADUATING CLASS,

Sixty-Second Session,

PHILADELPHIA COLLEGE OF PHARMACY,

1882—1883·

NAME.	PLACE.	SUBJECT OF THESIS.
Allen, E. Floyd	Espyville, Pa	*Oleum Gossypii Seminum.*
Andrews, Charles Howard	Binghampton, N. Y	*Elaterium.*
Apple, Milton Shimer	Helletown, Pa	*Glechoma.*
Armbrecht, William Charles	Wheeling, W. Va	*Essentials of a Pharmacist.* [ure.
Arnold, Charles Frederick	Fort Dodge, Iowa	*Parts by Weight and Parts by Meas-*
Bagge, Edward Everett	Camden, N. J	*Chimaphila Umbellata.*
Baker, Charles Henry	Trenton, N. J	*Toxicology.*
Ballentine, Allen D. B	Philadelphia, Pa	*Coccus Cacti.*
Balmer, John Henry	Elizabethtown, Pa	*Xanthoxylon.*
Barr, William Henry, Jr	Milwaukee, Wis	*Inœsthetics.*
Baumgardner, Charles Benjamin	Altoona, Pa	*Pills and Excipients.*
Bellis, William Henry	Flemington, N. J	*Heat in Percolation.*
Benjamin, Samuel Newman	Deckertown, N J	*Iris Versicolor.*
Bolton, Stephen Conklin	Watertown, N. Y	*Boroglyceride.*
Boorse, Henry Augustus	Norristown, Pa	*Pill Excipients.*
Booth, Frederick Smith	Philadelphia, Pa	*Oleum Morrhuæ.*
Boyd, Evan Garrett	New Castle, Del	*Rhus Toxicodendron.*
Brown, Joseph Henry	Morris, Ill	*Salicylic Acid.*
Browning, Robert Craighead	Indianapolis, Ind	*Spiritus Ætheris Nitrosi.*
Bruenchenheim, Byron Edwin	Milwaukeé, Wis	*Cambogia.*
Butler, George White	Bryn Mawr, Pa	*Pepsin.*
Campbell, Milton	Easton, Md	*Improved Syrup of Wild Cherry.*
Cheatham, Mathew Venable	Clarksville, Tex	*Xanthium Strumarium.*
Clinch, John Houston McIntosh	Waynesville, Ga	*Ceanothus Americanus.*
Cline, Walter Howard	Atlantic City, N. J	*Plants and Minerals.*
Cole, Edward Nelson	Toledo, Ohio	*Glycerin.*
Coleman, Mimms William	Selma, Ala	*Tinctura Ferri Chloridi.*
Cook, John William	Hagerstown, Md	*Extractum Cannabias Indicæ.*
Craig, Clark Rankin	Chambersburg, Pa	*Commercial Arsenic.*
Cuskaden, Albert Douglass	Philadelphia, Pa	*Emulsions.*
Cozens, Nathan Alexis	Woodbury, N. J	*Alcohol.*
Daly, John	Belvidere, N. J	*Oleum Picus Liquidæ.*
Dare, John Henry	Bridgeton, N. J	*The Pharmacist.*
Davis, Harry Irvin	Hollidaysburg, Pa	*Water.*
Davis, William Henson	Germantown, Pa	*Cinchona.*
Deakyne, Harry Harttup	Smyrna, Del	*Boric Acid.*
Dietrich, Howard Dickson	Harrisburg, Pa	*Hydrargyri Chloridum Mite.*
Duffey, Roger William	Hillsborough, Md	*Alcohol.*
Dundor, Milton Jacob	Reading, Pa	*Citrine Ointment.*
Eilinger, Frederick Rudolph	Rochester. N. Y	*Emulsions with Acacia.*
England, Joseph Winters	Philadelphia, Pa	*Cheken.*
Esenwein, John Riley	Reading, Pa	*Syrupus Theobromæ.*
Fasig, Harry Buckley	Columbia, Pa	*Absorbent Cotton.* [dum.
Fell, Edgar Burnside	Wilmington, Del	*Extractum Pruni Virginianæ Flui-*
Fleming, Frank Byerly	Philadelphia, Pa	*Tinctura Vanillæ.*
Flemming, Daniel William	Shippensburg, Pa	*Balsamum Peruvianum.*
Franciscus, William Charles	Lock Haven, Pa	*Analysis of Liquor Potasii Arsenitis.*
Frangkiser, John Frederick	Loudonville, Ohio	*Hamamelis Virginica.*

NAME.	PLACE.	SUBJECT OF THESIS.
Frey, John Peter	Union City, Ind	*Canella Alba.*
Frey, John William	Philadelphia, Pa	*Acetic Acid.*
Fries, Charles Joseph Valentine	Reading, Pa	*Chemistry of Volatile Oils.*
Gleim, William Bomgardner	Lebanon, Pa	*Trifolium Pratense.*
Good, Harvey Jonas Tilghman	Allentown, Pa	*Emulsions with Gelatin.*
Gray, Harry Tilford	Bloomington, Ill	*Sugars.*
Gregg, Henry Hamilton, Jr	New Lisbon, Ohio	*Nitric Acid*
Guest, Samuel Stratton	Camden, N. J	*Gelatin.*
Hahn, Gustave	Sheboygan, Wis	*Hops.*
Hallowell, Charles Wesley	Philadelphia, Pa	*Cascara Sagrada.*
Hanigan, William T	Pottstown, Pa	*Growth of Pharmacy.*
Hannon, Owen Burdette	Greene, N. Y	*Gaylussacia Resinosa.*
Harris, Frank Pierce	Hamburg, Pa	*Rhamnus Purshiana.*
Harrison, James Oliver	St. Michael's, Md	*Crystallography.*
Hayhurst, Susan	Philadelphia, Pa	*Pharmaceutic Manipulations.*
Haynes, Thomas Jerdone	Milford, Del	*Pills.* [*Potassium.*
Heisler, John Clement	Mifflinburg, Pa	*Separation of Iodide from Bromide of*
Helm, Charles Frederick Gustav	Philadelphia, Pa	*Citrate of Magnesium.*
Horsey, John Marshall	Charleston, S. C	*Fluid Extract of Wild Cherry.*
Jones, Daniel R	Milwaukee, Wis	*Commercial Pepsin.*
Jones, Henry Morford	Winchester, Ky	*Chemistry.*
Jones, James Miles	Reading, Pa	*Comptonia Aspenifolia.*
Johnson, Theodore Milton	Huntington, Ind	*Pills and Excipients.*
Jungkunz, William Frederick	Freeport, Ill	*Granatum.*
Kalmbach, Henry George	Philadelphia, Pa	*Aconite and its Alkaloids.*
Kempfer, Emil Frank	Racine, Wis	*Cubeba.*
Ker, Heber, Jr	Staunton, Va	*Mineral Acids.*
Kerr, Frank Gault	Marshall, Mo	*Carbonic Acid Water.*
Kerr, William D'Olier	Philadelphia, Pa	*Pharmaceutic Etiquette.*
Keys, John Cathcart	Philadelphia, Pa	*Laws Relating to Drops.*
Kindig, Rudolph	Switzerland	*Eriodictyon Californicum.*
Kirk, James Edgar	Dover, Del	*Syrupus Sennæ.*
Kline, Horace Thompson	Philadelphia, Pa	*Practical Hints.*
Klingler, John Harrison, Jr	Dover, Del	*Chemical Salts.*
Krider, James Delaplaine	Chester, Pa	*Calabar Bean.*
Lacy, William Reif	Reading, Pa	*Glycyrrhizæ Radix*
Lehman, Frederick Charles	Philadelphia, Pa	*Efflorescence of Salts.*
Leonhard, Louis Charles	Dayton, Ohio	*Podophyllum Peltatum.*
Light, William Wirt	Oregon, Ill	*Opuntia Vulgaris.*
MacNair, Whitmel Horne	Tarboro, N. C	*Viburnum Prunifolium.*
McCreight, Robert	Philadelphia, Pa	*Alkaloids.*
Maddock, William Worrell	Chester, Pa	*Pilulæ.*
Marshall, Thomas Chew	Pittsburg, Pa	*Ergot and its Preparations.*
Michel, Bernard	Dubuque, Iowa	*Commercial Liquid Malt.*
Miekley, Ewald Gustav Fred	Davenport, Iowa	*Pharmacy.*
Miller, Harold Baughman	Carlisle, Pa	*Pulvis Effervescens Compositus.*
Miller, Turner Ashby	Danville, Va	*Tincture of Opium.*
Millikin, Thomas Newman, Jr	Wilmington, Del	*Sodio-Citrate of Bismuth.*
Moffét, James, Jr	Philadelphia, Pa	*Hamamelis Virginica.*
Moll, Horace	Barto, Pa	*Syrupus Pruni Virginianæ.*
Murray, Malcolm	Philadelphia, Pa	*Humulus.*
Neuhart, Lawrence Augustus	Caldwell, Ohio	*Cimicifuga.*
Norcross, Alfred Black	Trenton, N. J	*Miscibility of Powders.*
O'Brien, Christopher	Conshohocken, Pa	*New and Old Pharmacopœias.*
Ogden, John	Salem, N. J	*Glyceryl Borate.*
Ott, Charles William	Philadelphia, Pa	*Mitchella Repens.*
Parish, Thomas Pleasant	Martinsville, Va	*Cinchona Flava.*
Phillips, I. Spencer	Philadelphia, Pa	*Viburnum Prunifolium.*
Quick, Jacques Voorhees	Flemington, N. J	*Syrup.*
Ralston, George Foster	Harrisburg, Pa	*Preparations of Quebracho.*
Randolph, Charles Fitz	Altoona, Pa	*Examination of Sugar for Glucose.*
Rapp, Benedict Nicholas	Trenton, N. J	*Phosphorus.*
Reed, Charles Sumner	Atlantic City, N. J	*Salicornia.*
Reeser, John Wesley	Sunbury, Pa	*Camphor.*
Reichard, Charles Wolf	Wilkesbarrre, Pa	*Unguentum Hydrargyri Nitratis.*
Richardson, Harrie Knox	Trenton, N. J	*Oleum Erigerontis.*
Rickey, Charles Frank	Mt. Sterling, Ill	*Our Ph. G's.*
Roedel, William Ruthrauff	Lebanon, Pa	*Efflorescence of Salts.*
Roehrig, George Frederick	Pottsville, Pa	*Unguentum Hydrargyri Nitratis.*
Rohrman, Frank Randall	Philadelphia, Pa	*Characteristics of Pharmacy.*
Ruth, William Augustus	Alliance, Ohio	*Queen of the Meadow.*
Salot, George Washington	Dubuque, Iowa	*Dispensing Medicines.*
Saunders, William Edwin	London, Ontario, Can	*Insects Injurious to Drugs.*
Scherling, Gustav	Dubuque, Iowa	*Cosmoline.*
Schindler, Charles	Toledo, Ohio	*Confections.*

NAME.	PLACE.	SUBJECT OF THESIS.
Scheffler, James Samuel	Chapmansville, Pa.	*Glycerin.*
Schramm, Daniel, Jr.	Philadelphia, Pa.	*Choral.*
Schmidt, Flor. Joseph.	Evansville, Ind.	*Specific Gravity.*
Seeler, Andrew Jackson	Philadelphia, Pa.	*Viburnum.*
Sellers, Albert Tobias	Pottstown, Pa.	*Manipulations.*
Simpson, Robert.	Doylestown, Pa.	*Creasote.*
Smith, Charles Michael	Lebanon, Pa.	*Ipecacuanha.*
Smith, Stephen Douglass	Birdsboro, Pa.	*The Drug Apprentice.*
Souder, Lewis Reed	Atlantic City, N. J.	*Successful Pharmacy.*
Spence, William Bayne	Philadelphia, Pa.	*Manufacture of Olein.*
Steacy, Frank Hernlie	Columbia, Pa.	*Jacaranda Caroba.*
Stoner, James Buchanan	East Berlin, Pa.	*Cinchona.*
Streeter, Nehemiah Dunham	Clinton, N. J.	*Preparation of Syrups.*
Tatzel, Anton Swaberter	Philadelphia, Pa.	*Advantages of the Metric System.*
Titus, Samuel Henry	Pennington, N. J.	*Proprietary Medicines.*
Tod, Alva Forman	Camden, N. J.	*Sulphuric Acid.*
Trusler, Charles Lawrence	Indianapolis, Ind.	*Principle in Quillaia Bark.*
Walker, George Allen	Trenton, N. J.	*Adulterations.*
Walter, William Henry	Philadelphia, Pa.	*Digitalis Purpurea.*
Weber, George Washington	Millville, N. J.	*Boric Acid.*
Weber, Morris Ellsworth	West Chester, Pa.	*Glycerin.*
Weber, Reinhard Julius	Ashland, Pa	*Luffa Egyptiaca.*
Weir, John Wesley, Jr.	Wilmington, Del.	*Base for Ointments.*
Werst, Allen Leidig	Hellertown, Pa.	*Sulphur.*
Wilcox, William	St. Clair, Pa.	*Syrups.*
Willard, Theophilus Newton	Shamokin, Pa.	*Diffusibility of Powders.*
Williamson, James	Jacksonville, Ill	*Pharmacopœia.*
Wittig, Charles	Philadelphia, Pa.	*Malt Preparations.*
Zacherle, Otto Frank	Philadelphia, Pa.	*Unguentum Hydrargyri Nitratis.*
Zoeller, Joseph Philip	Pittsburg, Pa.	*Glycerin and its Tests.*

Alabama	1	Ohio	7
Delaware	8	Pennsylvania	75
Georgia	1	South Carolina	1
Illinois	6	Texas	1
Indiana	5	Virginia	3
Iowa	5	West Virginia	1
Kentucky	1	Wisconsin	5
Maryland	4	Canada	1
Missouri	1	Switzerland	1
New Jersey	21		
New York	4	Total	153
North Carolina	1		

List of those who have acted as President of the Association since its organization :—

Wm. C. Bakes,	1864–65	Rich'd V. Mattison, M. D.,	1877–78
Thos. S. Wiegand,	1865–72	Albert P. Brown,	1878–79
Chas. L. Eberle,	1872–73	Wm. E. Krewson,	1879–80
Clemmons Parrish,	1873–74	Hugh Campbell,	1880–81
Wm. McIntire,	1874–75	Henry Trimble,	1881–82
Adolph W. Miller, M. D.,	1875–76	Thos. H. Potts,	1882–83
Geo. W. Kennedy,	1876–77	Lucius E. Sayre,	1883–84

Address of John A. Witmer, Corresponding Secretary, S. E. cor. Eleventh and Master streets, Philadelphia, which was omitted in the List of Officers on title page.

ACTIVE MEMBERS BY RESOLUTION.

The following resolution appeared in the minutes of the First Annual Meeting of the Alumni Association :—

"*Resolved*, That all graduates of the Philadelphia College of Pharmacy, previous to 1850, be admitted as members of the Association, and that they be entitled to all the rights and privileges of members."

The following list of names comprises those who were made active members of the Association by the above resolution :

· DECEASED MEMBERS IN ITALIC.

1826.
Chas. H. Dingee.
William Sharp.
Chas. McCormick, address unknown.

1827.
Alexander Dawson, address unknown.

1828.
Geo. D. Coggeshall, address unknown.
John H. Dingee.
Chas. Hathwell.

1829.
John C. Allen, 335 S. 5th St., Phila., Pa.
Jos. H. Brooks.
Robeson Moore.
Chas. E. Pleasants.
Franklin R. Smith.
Joseph Scattergood.
Wm. R. Fisher.

1830.
Edward Brooks, address unknown.
Chas. D. Hendry,   "
Dillwyn Parrish, 1017 Cherry St., Phila., Pa.
Isaac Jones Smith.

1832.
Richard M. Reeve.
John Bringhurst.

1833.
Samuel W. Brown, address unknown.
Wm. P. Hansford,   "
Edward Hopper, 323 Walnut St., Phila., Pa.
Thos. J. Husband, N. W. cor. 3d and Spruce Sts., Phila., Pa.
Thos. H. Powers.
Samuel Simes, 2033 Chestnut St., Phila., Pa.
Jos. C. Turnpenny, 813 Spruce St., Phila., Pa.
Watson J. Welding.

1834.
Wm. B. Chapman.
Aug. J. H. Duhamel.
Wm. Ellis.
Alfred Guillou, address unknown.
Stephen Procter.
Ambrose Smith, 1311 Arch St., ad. unknown.
Samuel Thompson.
John H. Tilghman, address unknown.
David Trimble,   "
Joseph Trimble,   "

1835.
James Cockburn, Jr., address unknown.
Jonathan Evans, Jr. .
James Hopkins, 2018 Spruce St., Phila., Pa.
Wm. R. Kitchen.
Clement J. Lee, address unknown.
Isaac J. Martin,   "
A. J. Olmstead,   "
Richard Price,   "
Charles S. Shreve.   "

1836.
Henry C. Blair.
John W. Simes, Jr., S. E. cor. 22d and Market Sts , Phila., Pa.
Jos. M. Turner.

1837.
John Goodyear, N.W. cor. 17th and Pine Sts., Phila., Pa.
Wm. L. Hasbrook, address unknown.
Benj. F. Hœckley, 462 N. 4th St., Phila.
Thos. R. F. Mitchell, address unknown.
Gustavus Ober,   "
Wm. Procter, Jr. (Professor.)
James Elliot, address unknown.
Robert J. Kennedy, address unknown.

1838.

Henry Brooks, address unknown,
Thos. W. Harris,   "
Wm. E. Knight, S. E. cor. 10th and Locust
   Sts., Phila., Pa.
Claudius B. Linn, 13 S. Front St., Phila., Pa.
Robert B. Potts.
Richard Rushton.
Dickinson A. Woodruff, address unknown.
Henry W. Worthington.
Chas. W. Simons, address unknown.

1839.

Thos. Haines, address unknown.
Thos. C. Hopkins, address unknown.
Walter Shinn.

1840.

Wm. H. Corie, address unknown.
John W. Douglas, Chambersburg, Pa.
Albert S. Letchworth, 534 N. 4th St., Phila.,
   Pa.
Benj. F. Ritter.

1841.

J. Crawford Dawes, 36th St. and Gray's Ferry
   Road, Phila., Pa.
Caleb H. Needles, S. W. cor. 12th and Race
   Sts., Phila., Pa.

1842.

Peter Babb, address unknown.
Wm. G. Baker, address unknown.
Wm. J. Carter.
Adolph P. Grotjan.
Edward Parrish (Professor).
Wm. J. Jenks, 461 Marshall St., Phila., Pa.
Wm. H. Schively, 121 Harvey St., German-
   town, Pa.
Laurence Turnbull, M. D., 1502 Walnut St.,
   Phila., Pa.
Samuel Wetherell, address unknown.

1843.

Caverly Boyer, address unknown.
Edward Donnelly, address unknown.
Daniel S. Jones, N. W. cor. 12th and Spruce
   Sts., Phila., Pa.
Joshua S. Jones, address unknown.
Andrew McKim, address-unknown.

1844.

Robt. C. Brodie, S. W. cor. 20th and Callow-
   hill Sts., Phila., Pa.
Robt. Colton Davis, S. E. cor. 16th and Vine
   Sts., Phila., Pa.
Thos. Estlack, 1826 Market St., Phila., Pa.
Thos. S. Wiegand, 3742 Market St., Phila., Pa.
Jacob L. Smith, 1034 Green St., Phila., Pa.
Alfred B. Taylor, 31 S. 11th St., Phila., Pa.
Geo. H. Mitchell, address unknown.
Wm. St. Clair Nichols, address unknown.
Silas H. Wentz.

1845.

Thos. Leidy, address unknown.
Joseph A. McMakin.
Wm. H. Needles, Walnut Lane, cor. Green
   St., Germantown, Pa.
Wm. B. Webb, S. W. cor. 10th and Spring
   Garden Sts., Phila., Pa.
Caleb R. Keeney, N. W. cor. 16th and Arch
   Sts., Phila., Pa.

1846.

Jacob L. Baker, address unknown.
John Dickson.
Robt. England, S. W. cor. 10th and Catharine
   Sts., Phila., Pa.
Hiram C. Lee, address unknown.
Geo. W. Patrick, M. D.
Robt. M. Patterson.
Thos. J. Scott, care B. F. Bruce, Lexington,
   Ky.
Benjamin R. Smith, 4717 Germantown Ave,
   Phila., Pa.
Chas. F. Stoever, address unknown.
Peter T. Wright,   "
John A. Whartenby.

1847.

Chas. Bullock, 528 Arch St., Phila., Pa.
James H. Crew, address unknown.
Evan T. Ellis, 145 S. Front St., Phila., Pa.
T. Curtis C. Hughes.
Samuel Lenher.
John R. Lewis, address unknown.
G. Graves Louden, address unknown.
Chas. S. Rush, address unknown.
Alfred K. Scholl.
Alfred Lafayette Taylor.
N. Spencer Thomas, Elmira, N. Y.

1848.

John R. Andrews, address unknown.
Samuel M. Bines, 114 S. 4th St., Phila., Pa.
Chas. M. Cornell, address unknown.
Franklin C. Hill, Princeton College, Prince-
   ton, N. J.
James Laws, Jr., M. D., 1936 Spruce St.,
   Phila., Pa.
Chas. A. Santos, Norfolk, Va.
John A. Springer, address unknown.
Edmund Pollitt,   "
Geo. T. Wiggan,   "
Chas. M. Wilkins, Philadelphia, Pa.

1849.

Chas. H. Bache.
Samuel L. Costill, address unknown.
Chas. Hartzell,   "
Samuel Hastings,   "
Wm. W. D. Livermore.
T. Morris Perot, 1810 Pine St., Phila., Pa.
Isaac W. Stokes, Medford, N. J.
Avery Tobey, address unknown.
Edmund A. Crenshaw, 528 Arch St, Phila,
   Pa.
Oscar Steel, address unknown.

Total, 146.

11

List of Active Members

OF THE

ALUMNI ASSOCIATION

OF THE

Philadelphia College of Pharmacy.

1830

Parrish, Dillwyn, 1017 Cherry St., Phila., Pa.

1841.

' Needles, Caleb H.. S. W. cor. Twelfth and Race Sts., Phila., Pa.

1842.

Jenks, Wm, J., 160 N. Third St., Phila., Pa.

1844.

Brodie, Rob't C., S. W. cor. Twentieth and Callowhill Sts., Phila., Pa.
Davis, Robert Colton, S. W. cor. Sixteenth and Vine Sts., Phila., Pa.
Wiegand, Thos. S., 3742 Market St.,Phila., Pa

1845.

Keeney, Caleb R., N. W. cor. Sixteenth and Arch Sts., Philadelphia, Pa.

1849.

Crenshaw, Edmund A., 528 Arch St., Pa.

1850.

Bunting, Samuel S., N. E. cor. Tenth and Spruce Sts., Phila., Pa.

1851.

Stratton, James, Bordentown, N. J.

1853.

Gutekunst, Fred'k, 712 Arch St , Phila., Pa.
Sheaff, John F., 114 S. Fourth St., Phila , Pa.

1854.

Bower, Henry, cor. Gray's Ferry Road and Twenty-ninth St., Phila., Pa.
Lemberger, Jos. L., Lebanon, Pa.
Miller, William J., 224 N. Third St., Phila.

1855.

Armstrong, Jas. A., M D , Camden, N. J.
Bakes, Wm. C., Ocean Grove, N. J.
Bancroft, Jos. W., 424 Franklin St., Phila., Pa.
Bannvart, Chas. J., Treasury Department, Washington, D C.
Griffith, J. Clarkson, 134 Stanton Ave., Chicago, Ill.
Lawall, Edmond, Allentown, Pa.
Rittenhouse, Henry N., 214–220 N. Twenty-second St., Phila., Pa.
Robbins, Alonzo, S. E. cor Eleventh and Vine Sts., Phila , Pa.

1856.

Evans, Jr , Wm., 252 S. Front St., Phila., Pa.
Warner, Wm. R., 1228 Market St., Phila., Pa.

1857.

Blinkhorn, George, S. E. cor. Tenth and Chestnut Sts., Phila., Pa
Campbell, Samuel, 1412 Walnut St , Phila.,Pa.
Hancock, Chas. W , 3425 Spring Garden St., Phila., Pa.
Hughes, C Collin, S W. cor Eighth and Race Sts., Ph la., Pa.
Mercein, James R., 41 Montgomery ave., Jersey City, N. J.
Massenburg, T. L , Macon, Georgia.

1858.

Fox, Peter P., N. E. cor. Twenty-third and Spruce Sts., Phila., Pa.

1859.

Coombe, Thomas R., Delanco, N. J.
Dodson, Chas. G., N. E. cor. Fifth and Chestnut Sts., Phila., Pa.
Eberle, Chas. L., cor. Mill and Main Sts., Germantown, Pa.
Geyer, Henry T., No. 20 S. Delaware Ave., Phila., Pa.
Jefferson, Chas. L., Zoological Garden, Thirty-fifth and Girard Ave.
Richards, Geo. K., N. W. cor. Tenth and Market Sts., Phila., Pa

1860.

Bolton, Joseph P., Germantown, Pa.
Boyd, John W., address unknown.
Franklin, Thomas H., N. E. cor. Twenty-fifth and Jefferson Sts.
Gegan, J. J, 812 S. Second St., Phila., Pa.
Newman, Geo. A., 380 Myrtle St., Brooklyn, N. Y.
Parrish, Wm. G., M. D., 477 Hudson St., New York City.
Vogelbach, Herman A., Melrose, Alachua Co., Florida.

1861

Abernethy, J. Maxwell, 188 Newark Ave., Jersey City, N. J.
Brown, Frederick, Jr., N. E. cor. Fifth and Chestnut Sts., Phila., Pa.
*Githens, Wm. H. H., M. D., 2033 Spruce St., Phila., Pa.
Heydenreich, Emil, 169 Atlantic Ave., Brooklyn, N. Y.
Stover, J. Melancthon, Chester, Pa.

1862.

Brown, Albert P., Camden, N. J.
Blithe, Henry, 3212 Market St., Phila., Pa.
Chipman, Edward D., Unionville, Orange Co., Va.
Diehl, C. Louis, (Prof.,) cor. Third and Broadway, Louisville, Ky.
Dobbins, Edward T., 1808 S. Rittenhouse Square, Phila., Pa.
Jacobs, Henry H., 622 Race St., Phila., Pa.
Leslie, Henry W., Parker City, Pa.
Miller, Adolph W., M. D., N. W. cor. Third and Callowhill Sts., Phila., Pa.
Naulty, Wm. H., 53 Cedar St., N. Y.
Peck, Henry T., M. D., Coulter House, Germantown, Pa.
Senneff, Jacob, address unknown.
Shoemaker, Richard M., N E. cor. Fourth and Race Sts., Phila., Pa.
Smedley, Bennett L., S. E. cor. Twenty-first and Vine Sts., Phila., Pa.
Witmer, David L., cor. Fifth and Germantown Ave., Phila , Pa.

1863.

Eldridge, Geo. W., S. W. cor. Seventh and Thompson Sts., Phila., Pa.
Fox, Daniel S., 323 Franklin St., Reading, Pa.
Hambright, Geo. M., 584 State St., Chicago, Ill.
Kirkbride, Joseph C., St. Louis, Mo.
McIntyre, Wm., 2229 Frankford Ave., Phila., Pa.
Mellor, Alfred, 214-220 N. 22d St., Phila., Pa.
Murray, Talbot C., 296 Delaware Ave., Washington, D. C.

Ruan, James, 1328 Otis St., Phila , Pa
Tomlinson, Edwin, M. D., Gloucester City, N. J.
Tilge, F. A., 25 N. Sixth St., Phila., Pa.

1864.

Buehler, Ed. H., Room 6, Portland Block, Chicago, Ill.
Croft, Henry C., Park Ave. and Madison St , Baltimore, Md.
Ebert, Albert E. (Prof.), Peoria Sugar Refinery, Peoria, Ill.
Jeannot, G. E., Louisville, Ky.
Jones, Edward C., S. E. cor. Fifteenth and Market Sts., Phila., Pa.
McCollin, S. Mason, M. D., 1128 Arch St., Phila., Pa.
Moore, Joseph E., 154 Newark Ave , Jersey City, N. J.
Morris, Henry B., address unknown.
Newton, Alfred W., 2530 N. Sixth Street, Philadelphia, Pa.
Simes, J. Henry C., M. D., 2033 Chestnut St., Philadelphia, Pa.

1865.

Blair, Andrew, S. W. cor. Eighth and Walnut Sts., Phila., Pa.
Blomer, Aug. P., M. D., N. W. cor. Moyamensing Ave. and Dickinson St., Philadelphia, Pa.
Ditman, Andrew J., 10 Astor House, N. Y.
Gross, Geo. A., 119 Market St., Harrisburg, Pa.
Heller, Marx M., 24 Orange St., Cleveland, O.
Hillery, J. F., address unknown.
Huber, Milton, Williamsport, Pa.
Kennedy, Chas. W., 447 Maria St., Phila., Pa.
Lindsay, John B., address unknown.
McElroy, Jas. B., Twenty-fourth and Alabama Ave., San Francisco, Cal.
Milner, Jas. P., M. D., N. E. cor. Sixth and Lombard Sts., Phila., Pa.
Moser, Americus H., Allentown, Pa.
Orth, Fred'k C., Holmesburg, Phila., Pa.
Preston, David, S. W. cor. Ninth and Lombard Sts., Phila., Pa.
Ranck, J. W., M. D., 3922 Germantown Ave., Phila., Pa.
Rinker, Wm. H., S. W. cor. Mervine and Norris Sts., Phila., Pa.
Smith, Wilson B., address unknown.
Vogelbach, Edmond, S. W. cor. Frankford Ave. and York St., Phila., Pa.
Walker, John T., M. D., N. W. cor. Second and Columbia Ave., Phila., Pa.
Wendel, H. Edward, S. E. Cor. Third and George Sts., Phila., Pa.
White, James T., cor Twenty-first and Pine Sts., Phila., Pa.

1866.

Allen, Wm. E., 2237 Mascher St., Phila., Pa.
Blair, Henry C., S. W. cor. Eighth and Walnut Sts., Phila., Pa.
Braddock, Isaac A., Haddonfield, N. J,
Campbell, Hugh, N. W. cor. Twenty-first and Locust Sts., Phila., Pa.
Kneeshaw, Wm. W., N. E. cor Twenty-first and Lombard Sts., Phila., Pa.
Laird, Wm. R., 250 Washington St., Jersey City, N J.
Lippincott, Robt. C., 717 N. Delaware Ave., Phila , Pa.
McPike, Wm. C., Atchison, Kansas.
Milleman, Philp, cor. Milwaukee Ave. and Division St., Chicago, Ill.

---

* Resigned.

Miliac, John A., S. E. cor. Tenth and Bainbridge Sts., Phila., Pa.
Newbold, Thos. M., S. E. cor. Forty-first and Chestnut Sts., Phila., Pa.
Newton, John S., M. D., 4106 Hutton St , West Phila., Pa.
Painter, Emlen, M. D. (Prof.), cor. Clay and Kearney Sts., San Francisco, Cal.
Remington, Jos P. (Prof.), N. E. cor. Thirteenth and Walnut Sts., Phila , Pa.
Riley, Chas. W., 1115 Race St., Phila. Pa.
Ross, Hugh H., N. W. cor. Thirteenth and Brown Sts., Phila., Pa.
Sayre, Lucius E., S. W. cor. Eighteenth and Market Sts., Phila., Pa.
Shoemaker, Allan, N. E. cor. Fourth and Race Sts., Phila., Pa.
Shoemaker, Jr., Benjamin, 1926 N. Seventeenth St., Phila., Pa.
Simson, Wm. H., Halifax, N. S. (care Brown Bro. & Co).
Souder, Jos. A., N. E. cor. Sixth and McKean Sts., Phila., Pa.
Strehl, Louis, Peoria, Ill.
Walker, Thos. A , S. E. cor. Fifteenth and Market Sts., Phila., Pa.

1867.

Allaire, Chas. B., 108 Main St., Peoria, Ill.
Bartram, Ernest, 1513 Vine St., Phila., Pa.
Borhek, Jr., J. T., Bethlehem, Pa.
Boring, Edwin M., N. E. cor. Tenth St. and Fairmount Ave., Phila., Pa.
Brown, Sam'l A., M. D., 12 Market St., New York City.
Brown, Thos. J., 233 S. Ninth St., Phila., Pa,
Buckman, Jas., S. E. cor. Eighth and Green Sts., Phila., Pa.,
Carberry, P. J. L., M. D., S. W. cor. Tenth and Green Sts., Phila., Pa.
Erwin Bertine S., Bethlehem, Pa.
Haig, Chas. R., N. W. cor. Nineteenth and Master Sts., Phila., Pa.
Harner, Jas. M., S. Fourth St., cor. Fifth St., Brooklyn, N. Y.
Himmelwright, F. E., M. D., 2002 N. Eighth St., Phila., Pa.
Hoffman, John V., 748 Madison Ave., Baltimore, Md.
Jones, Edward B., Mt. Holly, N. J.
Kurtz, Augustus M., San Francisco, Cal.
Little, Arthur H., address unknown.
Moore, Chas. C., 807 N. Broad St. ; or, 215 Market St., Phila., Pa.
Roche, Wm. F., S. E. cor. Fifteenth and South Sts., Phila., Pa.
Shivers, Chas. Jr., N. E. cor. Seventh and Spruce Sts., Phila., Pa.
Simes, Samuel, N. E. cor. Twenty-second and Market Sts., Phila., Pa.
Swaim, Geo. M., address unknown.
Vandegrift, Isaac P., 166 S. Fourth St., cor. Fifth Ave., Brooklyn, N. Y.
Webb, Sam'l W., 1706 Sydenham St., Phila., Pa.
Weichselbaum, J., Chatham Square, Savannah, Ga.
Weidemann, Charles A., M. D., 543 N. Twenty-second St., Phila., Pa.
Wike, Albert D., Marietta, Pa.

1868.

Beck, J. W., Lancaster, Ohio.
Boyd, Abraham, Tabor Block, Denver, Col., per. Wiswall, agt. Life Ins. Co.
Bradley, Thos. F., address unknown.
Bronson, Eugene C., "
Clark, A. B., Jr., 9 Main St., Galesburg, Ill.

Day, Robert L., Sommerville, N. J.
Dilks, S. Levin, N. E. cor. Sixth and Pine Sts., Philadelphia., Pa.
Elliott, Frederick G., 141-43 N. Fourth St., Phila., Pa.
England, Howard, 228 Newark Ave., Jersey City, N. J.
Estlack, Horace W., 1233 S. Seventeenth St., Phila., Pa.
Farr, Wm. L., Oxford, Ohio.
Foulke, James, M. D., 250 Washington St., Jersey City, N. J.
Fronheiser, Jas. J., Johnstown, Pa.
Harrop, Joseph, Leavenworth, Kansas.
Hecker, Jacob K., 1154 Wister St., Phila., Pa.
Jordan, Henry A., Bridgeton, N. J.
Klump, Chas. C., Allentown, Pa.
Karch, Joseph, Ninth and Cumberland Sts., Lebanon, Pa.
Kay, Samuel D., 224 Monticello St. ;. or, J. C. C. Hospital, Jersey City, N. J.
Lillard, Benjamin, 56 Lafayette Place, N. Y.
McInall, Jr., Edward, Wilmington, Del.
Mathews, Chas. C., Shippensburg, Pa.
Marshall, Robert T,. 1215 Market St., Phila., Pa.
Parrish, Clemmons, 27 Park Place, N. Y.
Raser, Wm. H., care Stillman & Fulton, 53. Cedar St., N. Y.
Rice, Wm. C., Jr., 702 N. Second St., Phila., Pa.
Seybert, Robert S., Hillsboro', Ohio.
Shoffner, John N., South Bethlehem, Pa.
Shaw, Jos. B., M. D., Del. Water Gap, Monroe Co., Pa.
Simon, Matthias, La Crosse, Wis.
Shryock, Allen, 1213 Green St., Phila., Pa.
Smith, Homer A., address unknown.
Stackhouse, George P., 2324 Christian St., Phila., Pa.
Steifel, Louis, 346 Dillwyn St., Phila. Pa.
Thomas, Frank W., Dayton, Ohio.
Wilson, Wm., 106 Broadway (or Pine St.), N. Y.

1869.

Bates, Louis A., 739 Sixth Ave., N. Y. City.
Bell, Jas. S., Memphis, Tenn.
Davis, Harry H., N. E. cor. Third and Kaighn's Point Ave., Camden, N. J.
Fruh, Carl D. S., 2321 Ridge Ave., Phila., Pa.
Husband, Thos., J., Jr., N. W. cor. Third and Spruce Sts., Phila , Pa.
Jones, D. Augustus, Vincentown, N. J.
Kelty, Clement, Salem, N. J.
Kennedy, Geo., W., 103 N. Centre St., Pottsville, Pa.
Krewson, Wm. E., N. E. cor. Eighth St. and Montgomery Ave., Phila., Pa.
Lamparter, Eugene, M. D., S. E. cor. Seventeenth and Reed Sts., Phila., Pa.
Merklein, Chas. H., M. D , address unknown.
Moorhead, Wm. W., M. D., S. W. cor. Broad and South Sts., Phila., Pa.
Penrose, Stephen F., cor. Main and Broad St., Quakertown, Pa.
Pfromm, Adam, 233 N. Second St., Phila., Pa.
Phelps, Fred k H., Jackson, Cal,
Reynolds, John J., Flemingsburg, Ky,
Robertson, Henry H., N. E. cor. Fifth and Chestnut Sts., Phila., Pa.
Sharp, Robt. P., M. D., Atglen, Chester Co., Pa.
Stein, Jacob H., 803 Penn St., Reading, Pa,
Taylor, Harry B., 1306 Girard Ave., Phila., Pa.
Treichler, L. Alpinus, cor. Main and Penn Sts., Germantown, Pa.
Unsicker, Charles B., Cincinnati, Ohio.
Ware, Samuel F., Cape May, N. J.

1870.

Chiles, Edward, Denver, Col.
Clark, Silas B., Townsend, Vt.
Connally, W. C., Atlanta, Ga.
Ehler, Wm. Rush, Eayrestown, N. J.
Hunter, Thos., M. D., S. W. cor. Fifteenth and Wharton Sts., Phila., Pa.
Hall, Jos. J., 41 Cedar St., Marshall, Tenn.
Hassenger, S. E. R., N. E. cor. Twenty-third and Fairmount Ave., Phila., Pa.
Herbert, Eugene, N. W. cor. Twelfth and Spruce Sts., Phila , Pa.
Kirkbride, Jos. J., M. D., 35 S. Nineteenth St., Phila., Pa
Lee, Chas. S., S. E. cor. Twenty-second and Christian Sts., Phila., Pa.
McLaughlin, John T., Peoria, Ill.
Newbold, Henry A , S. E. cor. Forty-first and Chestnut Sts., W. Phila., Pa.
Rau, Eugene A., Bethlehem, Pa.
Schell, Harry D., 626 N. Fifteenth St., Phila.
Segrest, Lewis F., N. W. cor. Cedar and Cumberland Sts., Phila., Pa.
Supplee, Jesse L., N. E. cor. Thirteenth and Green sts., Phila., Pa.
Tomassevick, Leopold, St. Jago, Cuba.
Williamson, J. L., Meadville, Pa.
Wilhelm, J. Alexander, York, Pa.
Wenrich, Alfred B., 16 N. Thirteenth St., Phila., Pa.

1871.

Anthony, Joseph, 529 Broad St., Richmond, Va.
Camm, Henry V., 81 Commerce St., Bridgeton, N. J.
Ewing, Wm. G., 38 Union St., Nashville, Tenn.
French, Howard B., 410 Callowhill St., Phila.
Gramm, Edgar C., 4439 Frankford Ave., Frankford, Phila., Pa.
Hoskinson, J. Thos., Jr., N. W. cor. Front and Norris Sts., Phila., Pa.
Huneker, John F., 33 N. Twelfth St., Phila.
Ink, Parker P., Washington, Iowa.
Iungman, Julius, New York City, N. Y.
Kadish, Chas. J., Chicago, Ill.
Kannal, Emmet, Kansselaer, Ind.
Lee, Emmor H., 410 Callowhill St., Phila., Pa.
Lehman, J. Ehrman, Camden, N J.
McKelway, Geo. I., 1410 Chestnut St., Phila.
Odenwelder, A. J., Easton, Pa.
Paxson, Elliot D., care Caswell, Hazzard & Co., New York City.
Potts, Thos. H., S. E. cor. Broad and Parrish Sts., Phila., Pa.
Raser, John B., 164 N. Eighth St., Reading.
Shaw, Louis, Cheyenne, W. T.
Sniteman, Chas. C., Neillsville, Wis.
Snyder, E. D., Toledo, Ohio.
Vernon, Geo. R., Clifton Heights, Delaware Co., Pa.
Weaver, John A., 210 Madison Ave., Easton, Pa.
Weber, Fred'k C., M. D., Silver Cliff, Col.
Weber, William, S. E. cor. Fifteenth and Thompson Sts., Phila., Pa.
Worthington, J. W., Moorestown, N. J.

1872.

Addington, Wm. B , 700 Olive St., St. Louis, Mo.
Bille, George, S. E. cor. Second and Thompson Sts., Phila., Pa.
Bolton, Alfred H., 742 Christian St., Phila.
Cave, Joseph, Handel Villa, Liverpool Road, Lancashire, Eng.

Dawson, John H., N. W. cor. Twenty-third and Valencia Sts., San Francisco, Cal.
Evans, Chas. B., Augusta, Ga. (care Sholes & Co.)
Fraser, Horatio, N., cor. Wabash Ave. and Sixteenth St., Chicago, Ill.
Matos, Louis A., 3935 Aspen St., West Phila.
McElhenie, Thos. D., 259 Ryerson St., Brooklyn, N. Y.
Mitchell, Chas. L., M. D., N. E. cor. Ninth and Race Sts., Phila., Pa.
Mutchler, Henry M., Junction, N. J.
Procter, Wallace, S. W. cor. Ninth and Lombard Sts., Phila., Pa.
Schiedt, Jacob A , 123 N. Seventh St., Phila.
Shrum, John H., Lancaster, Pa.
Thiebaud, Chas. O., Vevay, Ind.
Wiley, Joseph, 123 N. Seventh St., Phila., Pa.

1873.

Addis, S. D., M. D., address unknown.
Antill, Jos. V., N. W. cor. Fifth and Dauphin Sts., Phila., Pa.
Apple, Ammon A., N. E. cor. Second and Dauphin Sts., Phila., Pa.
Beck, J. Howard, M. D., Ocean Grove, N. J., (P. O. box, 66).
Bond, Monroe, M. D., 2500 N. Broad St., Phila., Pa.
Brakeley, Philip F., Philipsburg, N. J.
Bridger, Paul, 745 Spring Garden St., Phila.
Chiles, Richard T., Frankford, Ky.
Conlyn, Thos. A., Park Ave. and Madison St., Baltimore, Md.
Conrath, Adam, 630 Chestnut St., Milwaukee, Wis.
Cook, John E., S. W. cor. Seventeenth and Carpenter Sts., Phila., Pa.
Delker, William, N. E. cor. Seventh and Arch Sts., Phila., Pa.
Dubois, L. Stanley, P. O. box 101, Paducah, Ky.
Eberle, Herman T., care G. E. Eberle & Son, Watertown, Wis.
Flint, John Henry, Marysville, Yuba Co., Cal.
French, Arthur S , East Hampton, L. I., N.Y.
Gill, Wm. C., N. W. cor. Eleventh and Sommerville Sts., Phila., Pa.
Griggs, Allan G., Ottowa, Ill.
Gross, Edward Z., 119 Market St., Harrisburg, Pa.
Guth, Morris G., M. D., Mount Pleasant, Ia.
Harper, Frank M., 45 E. Main St., Madison, Ind.
Hohl, August, N. E. cor. Fourth and Girard Ave , Phila., Pa.
Hurt, James F., Broadway, Columbia, Md.
Jefferson, Edward, S. E. cor. Sixth and Bainbridge Sts., Phila., Pa.
Jones, J. Morris, Bethlehem, Pa.
Keasbey, Henry G., 328-34 N. Front St , Phila., Pa.
Kielhorn, Henry, cor. Ash St. and Christian Ave., Indianapolis, Ind.
Kille, Geo. Henry, N. W. cor. Tenth and Montgomery Ave., Phila., Pa.
Lange, Chas. R., address unknown.
Lerch, Wm. I., cor. Twenty-first and Vine Sts., Phila., Pa.
Magill, B. Morris, N. W. cor. Seventeenth and Columbia Ave., Phila., Pa.
Martin, Samuel W., Lewistown, Pa.
Martindale, Wm. N., 1504 Vine St., Phila., Pa.
Mattison, Richard V., M. D., 328-34 N. Front Phila., Pa.
McCrea, J. Howard, Norristown, Pa.
Meyer, C. Carroll, 1802 Callowhill St., Phila., Pa.

Parker, Jas. A., 1871 Frankford Ave., Phila ,
Pa.
Potts, David G., N. W. cor. Eighteenth and
Master Sts., Phila., Pa.
Radefeld, Frederick, 500 Lombard St., Phila.,
Pa.
Ritter, Eugene D., address unknown.
Schmidt, Henry, Newark, N. J.
Smith, A. E., Williamsburg, Va.
Stifel, Albert F., M. D., Twelfth St., Wheel-
ing, W. Va.
Stewart, A. B., Duncannon, Pa.
Stem, Wm. N., S. W. cor. Twentieth and
Callowhill Sts , Phila., Pa.
Truckenmiller, Geo. L., box 187, Petersburg,
Ill.
Wood, James P., 637 N. 7th St., Phila., Pa.
Willard, Jr., Roland, Haddonfield, N. J.
Zimmerman, Gustavus A., Johnstown, Pa.

1874.

Acker, Louis K., Franklin, Pa.
Allen, James Armstrong, address unknown.
Bakhaus, Edmund, Springfield, O.
Banks, Wm. Baker, S. E. cor. Nineteenth and
Shirley Sts., Phila., Pa.
Bantley, Bartholomew, Sixth and Spring Sts.,
Miiwaukee, Wis.
Biddle, Chas. J., 3348 Market St., W. Phila.,
Pa.
Bryan, Harry N , 821 S. Third St., Phila., Pa.
Dawson, Jr., Edward S., 13 S Salina St.,
Syracuse, N. Y.
Gleim, Francis H. E., Lebanon, Pa.
Hazlett, Edward E., M. D., Abilene, Dick-
inson Co., Kansas.
Hilton, Thos. C., Kittanning, Pa.
Henry, Geo. S., Lebanon, Pa.
Hunter, David, M. D , Atlantic City, N. J.
Jacoby, Aaron P., care C. Jacoby, South Beth-
lehem, Pa.
Johnson, Geo. H., Minneapolis, Minn.
Jummel, Frank R., 627 S. Warren St., Trenton,
N. J.
Keenan, Augustus H., 214 S. Main St., Wilkes-
barre, Pa.
Kingsbury, Howard, N. E. cor. Eleventh and
Walnut Sts., Phila., Pa.
Kruell, Fred'k John, M. D., 318 Milwaukee
Ave., cor. W Erie St., Chicago, Ill.
Latz, Fred'k Wm., Buffalo, N. Y.
Lescher, Geo. C., address unknown.
Lumb, Abraham L., 4783 Main St., Frankford,
Phila., Pa.
Mattern, Wm K , M D., cor. Tenth St. and
Germantown Ave., Phila., Pa.
Miles, John Joseph, Vicksburg, Miss.
Powers, Fred'k B., Ph.D., 145 N. Tenth St.,
Phila., Pa.
Rienhamer, Frederick, address unknown.
Stewart, Robert R., S. W. cor Thirteenth and
Fitzwater Sts., Phila., Pa.
Terrell, Thos. D., Columbia, Boone Co., Mo.
Tilton, Francis M , Haddonfield, N. J.
Walker, Samuel E , M. D., N. E. cor. Ninth
and Catharine Sts., Phila., Pa.
Wellcome, Henry S., 8 Snowhill, London, Eng.
Williams, John L., address unknown.

1875.

Bibby, Walter E., M. D , S. E. cor. York and
Tulip Sts., Phila , Pa
Beidler, Samuel McGill, 1229 N. Seventeenth
St., Phila., Pa.
Boisnot, Henry S., 1311 Broadway, cor. Thirty-
fourth St , New York City.

Braddock, Wm. H., S. E. cor. Third and Elm
Sts., Camden, N. J.
Clark, Louis G., Zanesville; O.
Conner, William, cor. Main St. and Chelten
Ave , Germantown, Phila , Pa.
Conrath, Frank, 296 Ninth St., Milwaukee, Wis.
Hartwig, Chas. F , Chicago, Ill.
Hopp, Lewis C., care A. Mayell & Co., Cleve-
land, O.
Jones, Howard G , N. W. cor. Twelfth and
and Spruce Sts., Phila., Pa.
Justice, Richard S., Fifth and Elm Sts., Cam-
den, N. J.
McRoberts, Wm. B., Stamford, Ky.
Means, Wm. B., M. D., Lebanon, Pa.
Messing, Jacob, Jr., 1009 East Grand St.,
Elizabeth, N. J.
Miller, Charles M , Mansfield, Ohio (St. James
Hotel Block).
Mitchell, Wm. S., 3501 Cottage Grove Ave.,
Chicago, Ill.
Patterson, James L., cor. Ridge Ave and
Twenty-second St., Phila , Pa.
Poley, Warren H., 5106 Germantown Ave.,
Phila., Pa.
Reimann, Louis P., M. D., N W. cor. Fifth
and Poplar Sts., Philadelphia, Pa.
Shamalia, Geo. M., Lambertville, N. J.
Taylor, Joseph Y., N. E. cor. Fifth and Reed
Sts., Phila., Pa.
Thorn, Henry P., Medford, N. J.
Voelcker, Rudolph F. G., 217 Market St., Gal-
veston, Texas.
Walch, Robert H., 3103 N. Broad St., Phila.

1876.

Baker, Walter T., N. W. cor. Nineteenth and
Oxford Sts., Phila., Pa.
Baur, Hugo F., 476 Milwaukee Ave., Chicago,
Ill.
Bley, Alphonso A W., S. W. cor. Huntingdon
and Jasper Sts., Phila., Pa.
Boerner, Emil L., Haas Block, Clinton St.,
Iowa City, Iowa.
Boileau, Wm. N. K., 4155 Main St., Frank-
ford, Phila., Pa.
Bowen, Daniel A., Bridgeton, N. J.
Burge. James Oscar, Bowling Green, Ky.
Dilg, Philip H , address unknown.
Emanuel. Louis, cor. Second and Grand Sts.,
Pittsburgh, Pa.
Fleming, Wm F , 28 Olive St., St. Louis, Mo.
Fry, Wilbur W., Wilkesbarre, Pa.
Gentsch, Daniel C , New Philadelphia, Ohio.
Griffith, Charles, Johnstown, Pa.
Groves, John D , M D., S E cor. Front and
Catharine Sts., Phila , Pa.
Keller, A Henry, Sutton, Clay Co., Neb.
Kœhler, Otto F., 19 Risington St., cor. Chrys-
tie, New York City.
Kœmple, Robert August, 1396 Second Ave.,
New York City
Kolp, Jacob L., 463 N. Tenth St , Phila. Pa.
Kram, George W., M. D , South Bethlehem,
Pa.
Lienthicum, Theodric, Helena, Ark.
Martin. John C., Fifth Ave. and Madison St.,
Chicago . Ill.
McFerren, Jeremiah D., N. E. cor. Eleventh
and Locust Sts., Phila., Pa.
Merritt, Joseph W., Woodbury, N. J.
Mitsch, Geo. Joseph, St. Paul, Minn.
Mœnkemœller, Chas., cor. Twenty-second
and Market St., Wheeling, W Va.
Murray, F, Marion, M. D., Lenni, Delaware
Co., Pa.
Railey, Irvin (care Logan Railey), Versailles,
Ky.

Risk, Clarence H., cor. Charles and Reed Sts., Baltimore, Md.

Ritter, John, 180 West Madison St., Chicago, Ill.

Schrœder, Henry, cor. Milwaukee and Chicago Aves., Chicago, Ill.

Sommers, Richard M., S. E. cor. Fifteenth and Oxford Sts., Phila, Pa.

Stewart, Frank E., M. D., 1110 Walnut St., Phila., Pa.

Taylor, Winfield S., 9 Peachtree St., Atlanta, Ga.

Taylor, Walter A., N. E. cor. Perry and Southard Sts., Trenton, N. J.

Toulson, Milbourne A., Chestertown, Md.

Trimble, Henry, N. W. cor. Fifth and Callowhill Sts., Phila., Pa.

Von Cotzhausen, Louis, N. E. cor. Twenty-fourth and Thompson Sts., Phila., Pa.

Von Wittkamp, H. L., Jr., 533 N. Thirty-sixth St., W. Phila., Pa.

Warrington, Chas. W., N. W. cor. Fifth and Callowhill Sts., Phila., Pa.

Webber, Joseph Leroy. cor. Main and State Sts., Springfield, Mass.

White, Hugh, address unknown.

Witmer, John A., S. E. cor. Eleventh and Master Sts., Phila , Pa.

1877.

Ball, Wm. A., 2001 N. College Ave., Phila.

Bissell Emery G., Main St., Waterville Onedia Co., N. Y.

Brennecke, Robert, Watertown, Wis.

Burroughs, Silas M., 8 Snow Hill, London, Eng.

Christman, Harry W., S. E. cor. Mervine and Norris Sts., Phila., Pa

Coxey, Joseph C., cor. Fifth and Mickel Sts., Camden, N. J.

Fisher, Henry, N. E. cor. Dauphin and Almond Sts., Phila., Pa.

Fulton, Joseph M., New London, Chester Co., Pa.

Landschutz, Peter, address unknown.

Martin, George, Jr., S. E. cor. Fifteenth and Oxford Sts , Phila., Pa.

Martin, John A., 967 N. Fifth St., cor. George, Phila., Pa.

Maulick, Wm. F., Marietta, Pa.

Moore, Frank, Cherry Hill, Cecil Co., Md.

Oleson, Olaf Martin, Market St., Fort Dodge, Iowa.

Parker, Fred. H., McIntyre Pharmacy, Eighth and Broadway, Auburn, N. Y.

Ross, David W., N. W. cor. Cumberland and Sepviva Sts., Phila., Pa.

Scheehle, Geo. P., Jr., N. W. cor. Fifteenth and Christian Sts., Phila., Pa.

Schwartz, Arthur, Trenton, N. J.

Smith, Albert H., cor. Main and Chelton ave., Germantown, Phila., Pa.

Stevenson, Richard G., N. W. cor. Sixth and Market Sts., Camden, N. J.

Trupp, Louis, S. w. cor. Fourth and Brown Sts., Phila., Pa.

Weiss, Louis, M. D., Del Norte, Col. (care Sheppard & Weiss.)

Wright, Geo. S R., 4502 Frankford Ave., Frankford, Phila., Pa.

Zacharias, Isadore, Columbus, Ga.

1878.

Albright, Franklin P., S. W. cor. Franklin and Berks St.. Phila., Pa.

Beetem, Jacob S., N. E. cor. Tenth and Spruce Sts., Phila., Pa.

Brunner, Norman I., cor Sixth and Arch Sts , Macon, Ga.

Bullock, Lawrence, M., M. D., Upland, Pa.

Button, Chas. E., 1558 Wabash Ave., Chicago, Ill.

Graybill, Peter, S. W. cor. Fourth and Scoll Sts., Covington, Ky.

Hall, Harry A., Danville, Ill.

Higgate, Wilford O., M. D., 4202 Lancaster Ave., West Phila., Pa.

Johnson, John G., Minneapolis, Minn.

Lilly, Chas. F., York, Pa.

Litz, Walter Kulp, 635 Broadway, N. Y.

Musser, Omar Henry, N. W. cor. Nineteenth and Arch Sts., Phila., Pa.

Noss, Henry, Norwich, Conn.

*Peat, Edward, M. D., Delphos, Ohio.

Podolski, Louis A., S. W. cor. Sixth and Poplar Sts., Phila., Pa.

Porter, Geo. C., Hollister, Cal.

Prall, D. Elwyn, 111 S. Jefferson Ave., East Saginaw, Mich.

Reinecke, Ernest Wm., South Side, Pittsburgh, Pa.

Shull, David F., 3928 Market St., West Phila., Pa.

Spenceley, C. E., N. E. cor. Seventh and Master Sts., Phila., Pa.

Strickler, Jacob, New Bloomfield, Perry Co., Pa.

Waterman, BenJ. C., N. W. cor. Thirty-ninth and Aspen Sts., West Phila., Pa.

Weis, William, 306 N. Ninth St., Reading, Pa.

1879.

Alleman, Emanuel A., Milton, Pa.

Castleton, Edward L. E., cor. Market and Tremont Sts., Galveston, Texas, care Massey, Caswell & Co.

Costelo, David, 1121 Broadway, N. Y.

Curran, John P., Jr., S. E. cor. Thirteenth and Jefferson Sts., Phila., Pa.

Day, Wm. G., care W. H. Schieffelin, New York City.

Drescher, August, cor. Bowery and Brill Sts., Newark, N. J.

Fahnestock, Levi, 76 Wood St., Pittsburgh, Pa.

Frederick, John H., 543 N. Twenty-second St., Phila., Pa.

Frey, Andrew G., Lancaster, Pa.

Fruh, Ernest, N. E. cor. Camac and Oxford Sts., Phila., Pa.

Jacobs, Joe, cor. College Ave. and Clayton St., Athens, Ga.

Jungman, Emil, S. W. cor. Fourth and Noble Sts., Phila., Pa.

Jones, Roland D., M. D., 2228 Green St., Phila., Pa.

Levi, Alex. B., 21 Sutter St., San Francisco, Cal.

Lock, John H., M. D., N. W. cor Cedar and Huntingdon Sts., Phila., Pa.

Ott, Emile, S.W. cor. Fifth and Lombard Sts., Phila , Pa.

Plumer, Wm. S., Jr. 2340 Olive St., St. Louis, Mo.

Raab, Ernest P., Highland, Ill.

Rudolph, John M., N. W. cor. Tenth and Mifflin Sts., Phila., Pa.

Rush, Warren B., Gallipolis, Ohio.

Siglinger, Chas. J., 527 S Halstead St., Phicago., Ill.

Simpson, Moses, S., 1414 N. Second St., Phila., Pa

Smith, Henry G., Allentown, Pa.

Troll, Conrad W., St. Clairville, Ohio.

Turner, Curtis W, 820 E. York St., Phila , Pa.

Vansant, Robert Hays, Trenton, N. J.

* Since Deceased.

Williams, Fred'k T., S. W. cor. Thirteenth and Wood Sts., Phila., Pa.

1880.

Bassett, Fenwick H., 4406 Frankford Ave., Phila., Pa.

Beale, Chas., Glassboro, N. J.

Colton, Geo. Havens, Springfield, Mass. (care H. & J. Brewer.)

Daniels, Adam C., Union Ave., S. Pueblo, Col.

Dockstader, Wm., C , Montclair, N. J.

Ferdinand, Geo. A., Dubuque, Iowa.

Frisby, Frank, Bismarck, Dakota.

Fruh, Gustav A., N. E. cor. Camac and Ox-Sts., Phila., Pa.

Garman, Franklin S., Lykens, Pa.

Hartzell, Alfred K., Allentown, Pa.

Hoell, Conrad G., M. D., 202 Federal St., Camden, N. J.

Hoffa, John Wilson, cor. Ridge Ave. and Cedar St., Harrisburg, Pa.

Kern, James P., 3825 Powelton Ave., West Phila, Pa.

Killingbeck, Wm. J , Camden, N. J.

Klemet, John, M. D., S. W. cor. Third and Columbia Ave., Phila., Pa.

Kohlerman, John Wm., S. W. cor. Seventh and Morris Sts., Phila., Pa.

Latan, Geo., cor. Brown and Buckeye Sts., Dayton, Ohio.

Luethe, Amandus J., Milwaukee, Wis.

Madison, Joseph S., Terre Haute, Ind.

Miller, Wm. Moses, Tarboro', Edgecombe Co., N. C.

Pechin, Wm. Jos., 608 N. Thirty-seventh St., West Phila., Pa.

Reynolds, John B., N. W. cor. Amber and Dauphin Sts., Phila., Pa.

Roberts, Chas. H., N. W. cor. Twentieth and Walnut Sts., Phila., Pa.

Ross, George R., Lebanon, Pa.

Schandein, Harry, 106 Market St., Phila., Pa.

Schimminger, Geo. W., 309-11 N. Third St., Phila., Pa.

Shelly, Jacob A., Mechanicsburg, Cumberland, Co., Pa.

Smedley, Harry L , D.D.S., M.D., Media, Pa.

Sombart, John E., M. D., Carthage, Jasper Co., Mo.

Stout, Chas. C., S. W. cor. Fourth and Poplar Sts., Phila., Pa.

Strunk, Samuel Wm., East Broad Street, Quakertown, Pa.

Zeller, Chas. F., N E. cor. Thirteenth and Walnut Sts., Phila., Pa.

1881.

Baur, Jacob, Terre Haute, Ind.

Beuter, John, Wheeling, W. Va.

Berube, Louis N., Osceola Mills, Clearfield Co., Pa.

Bernhard, Chas. H , Elgin, Ill.

Brakely, Philip F. H., Bordentown, N. J.

Bye, Charles A.,-4060 Chestnut St., West Phila., Pa.

Clabaugh, Alton, Altoona, Blair Co., Pa.

Clymer, Chas. W., 2140 N. 7th St., Phila., Pa.

Cramer, Walter, Milwaukee, Wis.

Cressler, David W., Atchison, Kas.

Culler, Fred'k W., Akron, Ohio.

Douglass, Serrill, Bristol, Bucks Co., Pa.

Eberly, Frank H., N. E. cor. Seventh and Spring Garden Sts., Phila., Pa.

English, Geo. H., 5033 Germantown Ave., Phila., Pa.

Genois, Louis, 1412 Walnut St., Phila., Pa.

Gerstacker, Michael, Cleveland, O.

Goebel, Jr , Geo., care J. E. Moore, 154 Newark Ave., Jersey City, N. J.

Gorgas, Geo. A., 800 Seventh St., N. West, Washington, D. C.

Gossling, Thomas R., 1602 Richmond St., Phila., Pa.

Gray, John F., Milton, Pa.

Gubbins, Chas. H., N. E. cor. Fifteenth and Race Sts., Phila., Pa.

Hæssig, Herman T., Cape May, N. J.

Hahn, John H., S. E. cor. Fourth and Court Sts., Williamsport, Pa.

Halloran, Frank M., Paducah, Ky.

Hamlin, Jr., Benj. B., Harrisburg, Pa.

Harper, Henry W., Fort Worth, Texas.

Hart, Joseph, 1614 N. Second St., Phila., Pa.

Hertsch, Bernhard A., 4010 Germantown Ave., Phila., Pa.

Hinchman, Walter L., 319 N. Third St., Phila., Pa.

Hunterson, Chas. B., Camden, N. J.

Ihrig, Theodore E., Pittsburgh, Pa.

Jacoby, John W., West Chester, Pa.

Jenks, Wm. E., 160 N. Third St., Phila., Pa.

Kelly, Irving W., Trenton, N. J.

Knowlton, Geo. H., 744 Elm St., Manchester, N. H.

Krauter, Chas. H., care Waldron & Covilland, Dallas, Oregon.

Kooker, J. Leedom, cor. Armat and Hancock Sts., Germantown, Pa.

Laschede, Peter W., 1322 Carson St., Pittsburgh, Pa.

Lawall, Edgar J., Catasauqua, Pa.

Linden, Washington E., 414 Prospect St., Cleveland, O.

Lœhle, John F., Reading, Pa.

Love, John Henry, 528 Arch St., Phila., Pa.

Luerssen, Frank, 423 Ninth St., Washington, D. C.

Manheimer, Edward A., 90 N. East St., Indianapolis, Ind.

Manz, Constanz, Lyons, Iowa.

Mayer, Wm. C., S. E. cor. Third and George Sts., Phila., Pa.

May, Chas. Henry, Piqua, Miami Co., O.

McClintock, Wm. C., Ardmore, Pa.

Mengle, Chas. W., 1410 Chestnut St., Phila., Pa.

Meyer, Frank B , Rensselaer, Ind.

Metzger, John B., Williamsport, Pa.

Miller, Samuel W., Jefferson College Hospital, Phila., Pa.

Moise, Jr., Benj. F., 17 Rutledge St., Charleston, S. C.

Morgan, Jas. H , Wilmington, Del.

Morgan, Frank E., N. E. cor. Sixteenth and Race Sts., Phila., Pa.

Nagle, Asher C., Bridge St., Wheeling, W. Va.

Otgen, Gustav A., Charleston, S. C.

Pape, Wm. F., Dayton, O.

Rehfuss, Emil G., 1316 S. Broad St., Phila., Pa.

Reed, David R., Asbury Park, N. J.

Reimann, George, Buffalo, N. Y.

Roland, Geo. W., Lewisburg, Union Co., Pa.

Rowe, Chas. E., cor. Lancaster Ave. and Forty-first St., Phila., Pa.

Scott, J. Harry, N. E. cor. Eighth and Montgomery Ave., Phila., Pa.

Smith, Edward W., Williamsport, Pa.

Speakman, Wm. E., Woodbury, N. J.

Spengler, John G., Dayton, O.

Strater, Henry H., 90 Erie St., Cleveland; O.

Swope, Jas. Wills, 1612 W. Ninth St., Kansas City, Mo

Tag, William, N. W. cor. Fifth and Poplar Sts., Phila., Pa.

Tyree, Josiah S., Staunton, Va.
Warner, Jr., Wm. R., 1228 Market St., Phila., Pa.
Warne, H. L., Whitewater, Wis.
Weiss, Christian, S. W. cor. Sixth and Girard Ave., Phila., Pa.
Wilson, Matthew J., 1863 N. Front St., Phila., Pa.

1882.

Acker, Chas. N., N. W. cor. Third and Spruce Sts., Phila., Pa.
Boger, Cyrus Maxwell, Jr., 3306 Market St., W. Phila., Pa.
Barkhuff, James Addison, Amsterdam, N. Y.
Bohn, Charles Henry, 2621 Girard Ave., Phila., Pa.
Clapp, Chambers Brown, Danville, Vermilion Co., Ill.
Clark, Jacob Miller (Haag's Block), Milton, Pa.
Clemmer, Jonas Gerhard, 2209 Franklin St. Phila., Pa.
Coblentz, Virgil, Springfield, O.
Corrie, Wm. M. G., 4516 Lancaster Ave., West Phila., Pa.
Dare, Chas. Wm., Troy, Bradford Co., Pa.
De Frehn, Chas. Wm., 3950 Lancaster Ave., W. Phila., Pa,
Edwards, Howard Mell, 35 W. Market St., West Chester, Pa.
Forney, Chas. McClellan, cor. Perry and Southard Sts., Trenton, N. J.
Geiger, Jacob Franklin D., Boyertown, Pa.
Gentry, Overton Harris, Independence, Mo.
Hayes, Robert G. H., Atlantic City, N. J.
Kohl, Emil John, Belleville, Ill.
Koser, Newton Alex., Oakland, Cal.
Kneedler, Harry Howard, S. E. cor. Fourth and Penn Sts., Reading, Pa.
Knouse, J. Hamilton, cor. North and Cowden Sts., Harrisburg, Pa.
Lambert, John Albert, 400 W. Michigan St., Indianapolis, Ind.
Lyman, David C., Paris, Ky.
Matthes, Franklin A., 24 N. Eighth St., Lebanon, Pa.
Matthews, W. Leaming, M. D., 2454 Christian St., Phila., Pa.
May, Wm. Henry, Egg Harbor City, N. J.
Mehl, Wm. Henry, 511 Miami St., Leavenworth, Kas.
Merriam, Evan B., 2140 Callowhill St., Phila., Pa.
Mullhaupt, Alfred, 1128 Arch St., Phila., Pa.
Nixon, Wm. G., Chambersburg, Pa.
Ott, George Leonard, West End Pharmacy, Wilmington, Del.
Power, Edward Samuel, M. D., 2231 Vine St., Phila., Pa.
Rambo, Ross, S. W. cor. Eighth and Race Sts., Phila., Pa.
Raser, Geo. Prentice, 309, 311 N. Third St., Phila., Pa.
Renz, Gustav Adolph, St. Paul, Minn
Reuting, Theodore Wm., 8 and 10 Diamond St., Titusville, Pa.
Reynolds, Wm. Davis, Mahanoy City, Pa.
Riggs, Chas. N., S. W. cor. Eighteenth and Chestnut Sts., Phila., Pa.
Roeschel, Wm. Ernest, Carthage, Mo.
Ross, Wm. Robinson, Lebanon, Pa.
Schambs, George M., Cleveland, Ohio.
Scheible, Fred'k Chas., 78 Gont St., Mobile, Ala.
Seitz, John Geo., 600 Woodland Ave., Cleveland, Ohio.

Sholl, Benjamin F., N. E. cor. Ninth and Race Sts., Phila., Pa.
Smith, Judson S., Tyrone, Pa.
Stahler, Eugene A., Bridgeport, Montgomery Co., Pa.
Steinhilber, Harry E., cor. Thirteenth and Jackson Sts., Omaha, Neb.
Thomas, Daniel Judson, Scranton, Pa.
Thomas, Oscar Ernest (care Wm. C. Fisher), 123 Richardson St., Columbia, S. C.
Thoms, Herman E., 76 Northeast St., Indianapolis, Ind.
Way, Julius, South Seaville, N. J.
Webster, Henry, Hannibal, Mo.
Woolley, Stephen D., Asbury Park, N. J.
Woolston, Clifford M., Morristown, N. J.

1883.

Apple, Milton Shimer, 2301 N. Second St. Phila., Pa.
Armbrecht, Wm Charles, Wheeling, W. Va.
Arnold, Charles Fred'k, Sioux City, Iowa.
Bagge, Edward Everett, S. E. cor. Broadway and Walnut Sts., Camden, N. J.
Baker, Charles Henry, 238 E. Hanover St., Trenton. N. J.
Ballentine, Allen D., 4516 Mulberry St., Frankford, Phila., Pa.,
Balmer, John Henry, 2815 Frankford Ave., Phila., Pa.
Barr, Wm. Henry, Jr. (care Drake Bro), Milwaukee, Wis.
Baumgardner, Chas. B., 1000 Seventh Ave., Altoona, Blair Co., Pa.
Benjamin, Samuel Neuman, Deckertown, N. J.
Bolton, Stephen Conklin, Watertown, N. Y.
Boorse, Henry Augustus, Norristown, Pa.
Booth, Fred'k Smith, 1037 Richmond St., Phila., Pa.
Boyd, Evan Garrett, New Castle, Del.
Brown, Jos. Henry, Morris, Grundy Co., Ill.
Browning, Robt. Craighead, Indianapolis, Ind.
Bruenchenheim, Byron Edwin, Milwaukee, Wis.
Butler, Geo. White, Bryn Mawr, Montgomery Co., Pa.
Campbell, Milton, 2041 Pine St., Phila., Pa.
Cheatham, Mathew Venable, Clarksville, Texas.
Coleman, Mimms Wm., Selma, Ala.
Craig, Clark Rankin, Chambersburg, Pa.
Cuskaden, Albert Douglass, Atlantic City, N. J.
Dare, John Henry, Bridgeton, N. J.
Davis, Harry Irvin, Hollidaysburg, Blair Co., Pa.
Davis, Wm. Henson, 4559 Main St., Germantown, Phila., Pa.
Deakyne, Harry Harttup, Atlantic City, N. J.
Dietrich, Howard Dickson, 1101 N. Third St., Harrisburg, Pa.
Dundor, Milton Jacob, 254 S Ninth St., Reading, Pa.
England, Joseph Winters, 800 S. Tenth St., Phila., Pa.
Fasig, Harry Buckley, Columbia, Lancaster Co., Pa.
Fell, Edgar Burnside, cor. Sixth and Market Sts., Wilmington, Del.
Fleming, Frank Byerly, Shippensburg, Pa.
Franciscus, Wm. Chas., Lock Haven, Pa.
Frangkiser, John Fred'k, Loudonville, O.
Frey, John Peter, Union City, Ind.
Fries, Chas. Jos. Valentine, Reading, Pa.
Good, Harvey Jonas Tilghman, 917 Turner St., Allentown, Pa.
Gregg, Jr., Henry Hamilton, New Lisbon, O.

Guest, Samuel Stratton, 528 Arch St., Phila , Pa.

Hahn, Gustave, Ridge Ave. and Master St., Phila., Pa.

Hannon, Owen Burdette, Shamokin, Northumberland Co., Pa.

Harris, Frank Pierce, Hamburg, Berks Co , Pa.

Harrison, Jas. Oliver, cor. Aisquith and Holland Sts., Baltimore, Md.

Hayhurst, Susan, M. D., Woman's Hospital, North College Ave. and Twenty-second St., Phila., Pa.

Horsey, John Marshall, N. W. cor. King and Radcliffe Sts., Charleston, S. C.

Jones, Daniel R., 170 Wisconsin St., Milwaukee, Wis.

Jones, James Miles, Reading, Pa.

Johnson, Theodore Milton, Huntington, Ind.

Jungkunz, Wm. Fred'k, Freeport, Ill.

Kalmbach, Henry Geo., 2819 Frankford Ave., Phila., Pa.

Kempfer, Emil Frank, care Louis Krouse, S. W. cor. Fifth and Green Sts., Phila., Pa.

Kerr, Frank Gault, Marshall, Mo.

Kindig, Rudolph, cor. Frankford and Girard Aves., Phila., Pa.

Krider, James Delaplaine, 1400 Walnut St , Phila., Pa.

Lehman, Fred'k Charles, 1246 Poplar St., Phila., Pa.

Leonhard, Louis Chas., Dayton, O.

Light, Wm. Wirt, Oregon, Ill.

MacNair, Whitmel Horne, 1900 Green Street, Philadelphia, Pa.

McCreight, Robt., 821 Sergeant St., Phila., Pa.

Maddock, Wm. Worrell, P. O. box 215, Chester, Pa.

Miller, Harold Baughman, Memphis, Tenn.

Miller, Turner Ashby, Danville, Va.

Neuhart, Lawrence Augustus, care Orr, Brown & Price, Columbus, O.

Norcross, Alfred Black, Trenton, N. J.

O'Brien, Christopher, Conshohocken, Pa.

Ott, Charles William, cor. Lawrence and Dauphin Sts., Phila., Pa.

Quick, Jaques Voorhees, Flemington, N. J.

Randolph, Chas. Fitz, Altoona, Pa.

Reeser, John Wesley, cor. Thirteenth and Morris Sts., Phila., Pa.

Rickey, Chas. Frank, Mount Sterling, Ill.

Roedel, Wm Ruthrauff, 119 Market St., Harrisburg, Pa.

Roehrig, Geo. Fred'k, Pottsville, Pa.

Ruth, Wm. Augustus, Alliance, O.

Salot, Geo. Washington, care- J. A. Mackimmer, 723 Fort St., West, Detroit, Mich.

Scherling, Gustav, box 408, Sioux City, Iowa.

Scheffler, Jas. Samuel, cor. Second and Hamilton Sts , Allentown, Pa.

Schramm, Jr., Daniel, 1428 Stiles St., Phila., Pa.

Schmidt, Flor. Joseph, Evansville, Ind.

Seeler, Andrew Jackson, 1121 Shackamaxon St., Phila , Pa.

Sellers, Albert Tobias, 1635 N. Twentieth St., Phila , Pa

Smith, Chas. Michael, S. E. cor. Eleventh and Master Sts., Phila., Pa.

Smith, Stephen Douglass, Birdsboro', Pa.

Steacy, Frank Hernlie, care Gail & Bleckie, Palmer House, Chicago, Ill.

Trusler, Chas. Lawrence, 190 Fort Wayne St., Indianapolis, Ind.

Walter, Wm. Henry, 2339 N. Fifth St., Phila., Pa

Weber, Geo. Washington, Millville, N. J.

Weber, Reinhard Julius, N. E. cor. Sixth and Washington Ave., Phila , Pa.

Werst, Allen Leidig, 2458 N. Second St., Phila., Pa.

Willard, Theophilus Newton, Loysville, Perry Co., Pa.

1830	1	1858	1	1871	26
1841	1	1859	6	1872	16
1842	1	1860	7	1873	49
1844	3	1861	4	1874	32
1845	1	1862	14	1875	24
1849	1	1863	10	1876	42
1850	1	1864	10	1877	24
1851	1	1865	21	1878	23
1853	2	1866	23	1879	27
1854	3	1867	26	1880	32
1855	8	1868	36	1881	75
1856	2	1869	23	1882	53
1857	6	1870	20	1883	90

Whole number...745

N. B.—The members will please scrutinize the above list of names *carefully*, and if any errors are noticed, or if any are known to be deceased and not marked as such, please notify the Secretary, so that a complete and correct record may be kept of the membership.

Also, if your address is not correctly given, or if any member knows the address of those marked unknown, please notify the Secretary, Wm. E. Krewson, No. 145 N. Tenth St , Philadelphia.

JUNIOR EXAMINATION.

The following were the Questions given to the Junior Class at their Examination, held Thursday, February 15th, 1883.

The Practical Examination took place in the forenoon, as follows :—

1. Make granulated Citrate of Potassium, using one fluid ounce of water and the weighed ingredients before you; put the product in the bottle which contained the Citric Acid.
2. Percolate four troy ounces of Ground Glycyrrhiza, with a menstruum made by mixing half a fluid ounce of Water of Ammonia with twelve fluid ounces of water.
   Label the bottle containing the Citrate of Potassium, and the funnel containing the Glycyrrhiza. Put your name and examination number on the label.

RULES TO BE OBSERVED.

The answers to each branch must be written *on separate pieces of paper*, the branch specified thereon, and handed in when completed

Commence the answer of each sub-division of the queries with a new line, and with its corresponding number.

Each paper must be headed by the name of the student, and the number of his desk.

Time allowed for writing the answers to the queries—from 3 until 8 o'clock, P. M.

Books or written memoranda are not allowed; nor is any intercourse whatever between the candidates permitted.

Time allowed for examining specimens—fifteen minutes.

The use of chemical reagents is not allowed.

The officinal names of the specimens should be given.

Questions must be asked and will be answered aloud, in the hearing of the entire class.

The Written Examination took place in the afternoon, and the Questions were as follows :—

PHARMACY.
PROF. JOSEPH P. REMINGTON.

A.

1. How many *grains* are there in a *kilogramme*, *decigramme* and *cubic centimetre* of water at 4° C?
2. Define *Percolation* and *Repercolation*, and illustrate the practical application of the latter in making twelve pints of a fluid extract.
3. What are *Fluid Extracts*?
   How do they differ in strength from those formerly officinal?
   What is an *Extract*?
   What is an *Abstract*?
4. Define a *Pharmaceutical Syrup*.
   Describe three methods of making *Syrups*, and give an example of each method, showing why you would prefer to use the particular method in the example that you have chosen.
5. What is the process of *Crystallization*?
   Describe three methods of producing crystals.
   Define *Dialysis*.

BOTANY AND MATERIA MEDICA.
PROF. JOHN M. MAISCH.
B.

1. Describe in a general way, the cells composing *fibro-vascular bundles,* and the arrangement of these bundles in the stems of *Dicotyledons* and *Monocotyledons.*
2. Define the terms *Tree, Shrub,* and *Annual, Biennial,* and *Perennial Herb.*
   Give an example of each.
3. What is the fruit of the *Graminaceæ* called, and which of its tissues contains starch?
4. Give the botanical name and habitat of *Boneset.*
   Describe the drug and give its medicinal properties.
5. Give the botanical characters of *Ranunculaceæ,* and name three drugs derived from this natural order.

CHEMISTRY.
PROF. SAMUEL P. SADTLER.
C.

1. How do we explain the fact that heat is necessary to change ice at 0° C. into water at 0° C., or water at 100° C. into steam at 100° C. ?
   Give an example of another liquid that produces cold by evaporation.
   Mention some practical applications of this principle.
   How is the same principle made use of in freezing mixtures?
2. What is a *Simple Magnet?*
   What is an *Electro-magnet?*
   What difference is there in their action?
   Of what different materials are they composed?
3. What is the proper chemical name of *Calx chlorata?*
   How is it made?
   What are its uses in pharmacy and in the arts?
4. Describe the commercial manufacture of *Sulphuric Acid,* and give the chemical reactions which take place in the course of the manufacture.
5. Describe the several varieties of *Phosphorus,* and mention the points of difference between them.

COMMITTEE.
D.

1. What is the source of *Sulphur?*
   In what forms does it occur in commerce?
   Give the officinal process for the preparation of *Precipitated Sulphur.*
   What impurity may the commercial article contain?
   What is this impurity, and how may it be detected?
2. What is understood by the *Specific Gravity* of a body?
   How would you take the *Specific Gravity* of a liquid?
   Of a solid heavier than water?
   Of a solid lighter than water?
3. Describe the appearance of *Iodine.*
   Give the source from which it is usually obtained.
   What are its compounds with other elements called?
   Name a test for *free Iodine* in solution, and state the effect produced.
   When *Iodine* is united with *Oxygen* or *Hydrogen,* what acid is formed in each case?
4. What is the officinal name and natural order of *Chamomile?*
   What part of the plant is officinal?
   Describe the appearance of the drug; also
   Give the officinal name and natural order of *German Chamomile.*
   State what part is officinal, and describe the appearance of the drug.
   What is the color of the volatile oils of these two chamomiles?
5. What is the object of the process of *Comminution?*
   State the five degrees of fineness of powder as directed by the United States Pharmacopœia of 1880, and give their corresponding numbers.
   What do these numbers indicate?

The specimens set for recognition were as follows :—

Rosa Gallica,	Extractum Ergotæ Fluidum,
Lavandula,	Syrupus Zingiberis.
Cetraria,	Tinctura Gentianæ Composita,
Mentha Piperita,	Acidum Boricum,
	Potassii Nitras,
	Acidum Hydrochloricum,
	Dilutum.

SENIOR CLASS, 1882–'83.

The Examination of the Students of the Senior Class commenced Tuesday afternoon, February 27th, 1883, and closed on Saturday noon, March 3d, with the Practical Examination in Pharmacy.

RULES TO BE OBSERVED.

Each paper must be headed by the name of the student, and the number of his desk.

Answer the questions in regular order, and mark them distinctly.

Commence the answer to each sub-division of the queries with a new line, and with its corresponding number.

Time allowed for writing the answers to the queries—from 3 until 8 o'clock, P. M.

Books or written memoranda are not allowed; nor is any intercourse whatever between the candidates permitted.

The use of chemical reagents is not allowed.

Time allowed for examining specimens—fifteen minutes.

The officinal names of the specimens should be given.

Questions must be asked, and will be answered aloud, in the hearing of the entire class.

The Questions in the different branches are as follows :—

QUESTIONS IN MATERIA MEDICA AND BOTANY.

Tuesday, February 27, 1883.

PROF. MAISCH.

A—*Burdock Root.*—Give (1) the botanical name; (2) natural order, and (3) habitat of the plant; (4) describe the root, and (5) its structural characteristics; (6) give its constituents; (7) its medicinal properties; (8) its dose; (9) briefly mention the distinguishing structural characters of the other officinal roots obtained from the same natural order.

B—*Black Snake Root.*—(1) What part of the plant is it? (2) From what plant; (3) natural order, and (4) country is it obtained? (5) Describe the drug, and (6) its structural characters; (7) give its constituents; (8) medicinal properties; (9) Dose.

C—(1) What is *Savine?* (2) Name the plant; (3) its natural order; (4) habitat; (5) describe the drug; (6) give its constituents; (7) medicinal properties; (8) dose; (9) how may it be distinguished from red cedar and arbor vitæ?

D—(1) Characterize the four principal *Cinchona alkaloids* (yielding crystallizable salts) according to their composition, behavior to solvents and to tests; (2) how is the officinal amorphos cinchona alkaloid tested for the absence of resin and alkaloidal and inorganic salts?

E—*Jaborandi Eucalyptus, Coca, and Boldo Leaves* —Give for each: (1) The botanical name; (2) natural order; (3) habitat of the plant; (4) the important distinguishing characters; (5) the principal constituents.

F—*Fig.*—Name: (1) The plant; (2) its natural order; (3) habitat; (4) the part used; (5) describe the drug; (6) give its medicinal properties; (7) enumerate its principal constituents; (8) state what changes in the constituents take place during the ripening of the fig.

G—Name: (1) The plants; (2) their natural order; (3) habitat; (4) describe the physical properties; (5) the structure of two officinal *mustard seeds;* (6) name the important principles; (7) state the influence of water upon them; (8) what effect has iodine upon the decoction after cooling?

H—(1) What percentage of *morphine* is required to be contained in *opium ?* (2) In *opii pulvis?* (3) In *opium dena>cotisatum ?* (4) Give some color reaction of morphine; (5) state its chemical relations to *codeine;* (6) to *apomorphine;* (7) what are the medicinal properties of the three alkaloids named? (8) Give the outline of the process for morphiometric assay of opium.

I—*Balsam of Peru* and *Balsam of Tolu.*—Give for each: (1) The botanical name; (2) natural order; (3) habitat of the plant; (4) in a brief manner the mode of production; (5) the characteristic properties; (6) principal constituents; (7) tests for purity.

K—Characterize the officinal *umbelliferous fruits:* (1) From the appearance of the commissure; (2) according to the number and location of oil vessels. (3) Name the officinal *umbelliferous gum-resins;* (4) give of each approximately the percentage of volatile oil, gum, and resin; (5) state which contain sulphuretted compounds; (6) from which country is each gum-resin obtained.

Specimens selected for recognition were as follows:—

Serpentaria.	Althœa.
Hæmatoxylon.	Gossypii Radicis Coxtex
Chondrus.	Galla.
Benzoinum.	Nux Vomica.
Illicium.	Salix.

QUESTIONS IN PHARMACY.

Wednesday, Feb. 28, 1883.

PROF. REMINGTON.

A—Write the answers to the following in the blanks provided for the purpose, showing the method of obtaining the results: 1. How many *c. c.* are there in a *pint* of distilled water at 4° C? 2. How many milligrammes in 1-64th of a grain? 3. How many *grains* in a *litre* of officinal Lactic acid? 4. How many *grammes* in a *kilo* of sugar? 5. How many *grains* in a *fluid ounce* of glycerin?

B—Give the unabbreviated officinal names, ingredients, outlines of process, and state briefly what improvement over the United States Pharmacopœia of 1870 process was made in the following United States Pharmacopœia of 1880 preparations: 1. *Fluid Extract of Ergot.* 2. *Tincture of Nux Vomica.* 3. *Solution of Chloride of Iron.* 4. *Syrup of Senega.* 5. *Cerate of Subacetate of Lead.*

C—Give the English names, medical uses, and the ingredients used in the preparation of: 1. *Aqua Chlori.* 2. *Glyceritum Vitelli.* 3. *Liquor Iodi Compositus.* 4. *Liquor Sodæ Chloratæ.* 5. *Pulvis Glycyrrhizæ Compositus.* 6. *Pulvis Morphineæ Compositus.* 7. *Syrupus Pruni Virginianæ.* 8. *Tinctura Arnicæ Florum.* 9. *Oleoresina Aspidii.* 10. *Vinum Ergotæ.*

D—Give the officinal name, quantities, and ingredients for a troy ounce of the following United States Pharmacopœia of 1880 preparations: 1. Dover's Powder. 2. Ointment. 3. Oleate of Veratrine.

E—1. Give the United States Pharmacopœia of 1880 name and formula for the wine which is directed as a menstrum for the officinal medicated wines. 2. State and explain the objects of the officinal alcoholo-metrical test for white wine.

F—Give the tests for recognizing: 1. Quinine. 2. Meconic Acid. 3. Strychnine.

G—1. How is Spirit of Nitrous Ether made? 2. How does the officinal formula differ from that of United States Pharmacopœia of 1870?

H—1. Give the officinal formula, with the quantities of the liquid preparations of opium. 2. In what respect does the officinal definition of powdered opium differ from that of the United States Pharmacopœia of 1870? 3 What were the strengths of the liquid preparations of opium of the United States Pharmacopœia of 1870?

I—1. Give the unabbreviated officinal names of four preparations of Glycyrrhiza of the United States Pharmacopœia of 1880. 2. What alkaline solution is used as an addition to the menstrua in three of the preparations? 3. Why is it used? 4. What compound is believed to be formed?

K—1. Describe three methods of making suppositories. 2. What are the advantages and disadvantages of each method?

Specimens:—

Extractum Sennæ Fluidum.	Aqua Fœniculi.
Massa Ferri Carbonatis.	Pulvis Rhei Compositus.
Aqua Destillata.	Syrupus Picis Liquidæ.
Ceratum.	Extractum Glycyrrhiza Purum.
Mistura Ferri et Ammonii Acetatis.	Syrupus Krameriæ.

QUESTIONS IN CHEMISTRY.
Thursday, March 1, 1883.
PROF. SADTLER.

A—1. What are the chief sources at present of potassium salts? 2. What is the chemical composition of *Potashes?* 3. What of *Argols?* 4. What of *Saltpetre?* 5. Give a description of these three salts when purified.

B—1. What is the chemical formula of the officinal *Sodii Phosphas?* 2. What of *Calcii Phosphas Præcipitatus?* 3. What of *Sodii Pyrophosphas?* 4. What of *Sodii Hypophosphis?* 5. What of *Calcii Hypophosphis?*

C—1. What is the difference between *Magnesia* and *Magnesia ponderosa?* 2. From what materials are they made respectively?

D—1. Describe the metal *copper* 2. Mention some of the more important alloys into which it enters. 3. What is the result of the action of sulphuric acid upon copper? 4. What of the action of nitric acid upon copper? 5. What of the action of aqua ammoniæ upon copper?

E—1. Give the exact chemical names and formulas of *Hydrargyrum chloridum corrosivum* and *Hydrargyrum chloridum mite.* 2. State the points of difference between them. 3. State the tests by which they may be distinguished. 4. And how they may be separated when found together.

F—Give the chemical formula of *Plumbi Carbonas.* 2. State how it is made ordinarily. 3. And what are its uses in pharmacy and the arts? 4. Give the chemical formula of *Plumbi Acetas.* 5. And of the salt present in Goulard's extract.

G—1. What is a *compound ether?* 2. Give one or more officinal compounds belonging to this class. 3. For what purpose are the compound ethers mostly used?

H—1. Mention the several groups of *Carbohydrates*, giving their formulas. 2. What simple relation exists between the formulas of these groups? 3. Which of these groups is capable of fermentation? 4. Show by reaction how the sugar formula is changed in this process. 5. By what means are the compounds of the third group changed successively into the second group and the first group?

I—1. What is *Phenol?* 2. From what simpler compound is it derived chemically? 3. Give the formulas of those phenols which are officinal.

K—1. How would you define an *alkaloid?* 2. What are some of the reagents specially used in their detection and separation? 3. Mention points of difference between an *alkaloid* and a *glucoside.* 4. In what respect does the formula of the sulphate of an alkaloid differ from that of a metallic sulphate? 5. Can you mention any alkaloids that have been made artificially?

Specimens:—

Acidum Salicylicum.	Potassii Bi-carbonas.
Acidum Gallicum.	Æther Aceticus.
Magnesii Sulphas.	Acidum Boricum.
Sodii Hyposulphis.	Alumen.
Sodii Acetas.	Alcohol

QUESTIONS BY COMMITTEE.
Friday, March 2d, 1883.

A—1. Describe briefly the chemical changes which occur in the preparation of the officinal hard soap.
2. How may soap be separated from the residual liquid?
3. What is soap chemically?
4. Name an officinal example of a chemically analogous compound, with an earthy or metallic base.

5. How may the quantity of fatty acids in soap be ascertained?
6. How may adulterations with earthy substances be detected?
7. How may the presence of animal fats in soap be proved.
8. To what class of poisons is soap an antidote?
9. Name three officinal preparations containing hard soap.
10. What is the object of soap as an ingredient in pills.

B—Give the botanical name, natural order and habitat of any five monocotyledonous plants which yield officinal drugs. Name the officinal portion and the important constituents of each.

C—1. What is the chemical composition of tartar emetic?
2. How is it prepared?
3. Name two officinal preparations into which it enters.
4. What quantity of tartar emetic is contained in each?
5. How would you distinguish tartar emetic from bi-tartrate of potassium?
6. What is the dose of tartar emetic as an emetic?.

D—1. What are the principal products of the destructive distillation of wood?
2. What is the specific gravity of acidum aceticum U. S. P.?
3. How much H C2H3O2 does it contain in one hundred parts by weight?
4. State how potassii acetas is prepared.
5. And show by an equation the chemical reaction that takes place.

E—Give the full officinal title of the following preparations. State their doses, name the part of the plant from which they are made, and give a general formula for their preparation: Abstracts of Aconite, Conium, Digitalis, Hyoscyamus, Ignatia, Jalap, Nux Vomica, Podophyllum, Senega, Valerian.

F—1. What is the officinal name of Calabar Bean?
2. What plant furnishes Calabar Bean?
3. To what natural order does this plant belong?
4. Where is this plant indigenous?
5. What two names have been given to the active principle?
6. What menstruum is used in making the extract, and what is the dose of this preparation?
7. What proportion of the drug is represented in the tincture, and what is its dose?
8. What salt of the active principle is officinal?
9. What is the therapeutic effect of Calabar Bean?
10. Describe briefly the appearance of the bean, and draw an outline of its shape.

G—Give the officinal name and definition of the following drugs. State the botanical name, natural order, and habitat of the plants which furnish them, and name and officinal preparation into which each one enters.
1. Gum Arabic.
2. Tragacanth.
3. Myrrh.
4. Kino.
5. Benzoin.
6. Mastic.

H—1. Give the botanical name, natural order, and habitat of the plant which yields asafœtida.
2. Describe the characteristics of the natural order to which this plant belongs.
3. What is the process employed in obtaining the drug?
4. Describe its appearance as found in commerce.
5. What are its chief constituents, and to which one is its odor due?
6. Why does it form an emulsion when rubbed with water?
7. Name three officinal preparations into which asafœtida enters.

I—1. Give a process for making Acidum Tannicum, and explain the process.
2. Show the chemical relation of Acidum Tannicum to Acidum Gallicum, and in what manner they differ in physical appearance.
3. Into how many groups may Tannins be divided? Give the distinguishing tests for the same, and name an officinal drug in each group.
4. State to which group Acidum Tannicum belongs, and name the botanical origin of the drug yielding it, and how the drug is produced.
5. Name two officinal preparations into which Acidum Tannicum enters. What is its chief medical property?

K—1. ℞

| Tincturæ Myrrhæ, | fℨij |
| Aquæ Rosæ, | fℨiv |

. . . .

Fiat Mistura.
Signa.—To be used as a gargle.

Write on the blank line the full officinal name, and proper quantity of the substance necessary to form a permanent mixture.

2. ℞

Physostigminæ Salicylatis,	gr. xx
Extracti Colocynth Comp.,	Ɖi
Cinchoninæ Sulphatis,	Ɛi
M. ft. Pil. x.	

Signa.—One to be taken every two hours.

Criticise this prescription. Would you dispense it?

3. Write a formula in unabbreviated Latin for 8⅓ Troy ounces of Basham's mixture, and give the officinal title.

℞

Tincture of Chloride of Iron,	2 parts
Diluted Acetic Acid,	3 parts
Solution of Acetate of Ammonium,	20 parts
Elixir of Orange,	10 parts
Syrup,	15 parts
Water,	50 parts

Mix.

4. Write a formula in unabbreviated Latin for 8⅓ ounces Troy of Dewees' Mixture, and give the officinal title.

℞

Carbonate of Magnesium,	5 parts
Tincture of Asafœtida,	7 parts
Tincture of Opium,	1 part
Sugar,	10 parts
Distilled Water—a sufficient quantity to make 100 parts	

Mix.

Specimens :—

Mistura Ferri et Ammonii Acetas.	Ferri Sulphas Exsiccatus.
Lycopodium.	Spiritus Ætheris Nitrosi.
Uva Ursi.	Ceratum Resinæ.
Pulvis Rhei Compositus.	Tinctura Myrrhæ.
Carum.	Acetum Scillæ.

Saturday, March 3d, 1883.

PRACTICAL EXAMINATION.

POWDERS.

℞

Pulv. Glycyrrhizæ Comp. ℥ss.*

Make into eight powders, wrap in paper and make a proper package.

2. ### PILLS.

Phosphori,	gr. ss.*
Pulv. Althææ,	gr. xl.
Pulv. Acaciæ,	gr. x.
Glycerini,	gtt. xv.
Aquæ,	gtt. x.
Chloroformi Pur.	f℥ss.

Dissolve the phosphorus in the chloroform, by the aid of a gentle heat, then make twenty-four pills according to the U. S. P. 1880 process.

3. ### OINTMENT.

Hydrargyri,	gr. xlvj.*
Acidi Nitrici,	∫ f℥ss.
	∫ f℥ss.
Ol. Adipis,	f℥j. f℥ij.

Make ointment of nitrate of mercury by the U. S. P. 1880 process.

4. ### PLASTER.

Spread a Warming Plaster, 6x4, on paper.

5. ### SOLUTION.

℞

Ferri Sulph.,	gr. mcxx.*
Acidi Nitrici,	f℥j.
Acidi Sulphurci,	f℥ij.
Aquæ,	f℥xiv.

Make Solution of tersulphate of iron by the U. S. P. process, adding sufficient water to the above ingredients, after the reaction has been completed, *to measure four fluid ounces.*

Label each preparation with your name and examination number.

---

* Ingredients marked thus (*) have been weighed out for you.

12

QUIZZES.

The Quizzes, under the auspices of the Alumni Association, will be held during the course of 1883–'84, on every Thursday afternoon, in the Alumni room. The Quiz for the Senior Students from 3 to 5, and for the Junior 2 to 3 P. M. The price of the Senior tickets, for the two hours' Quiz are $10.00, and, upon graduation, the certificate of membership will be presented, thereby making the member of the Senior Quiz Class, when he graduates, an Active member of the Association without further cost.

The attention of students is earnestly called to the above as conducted by the Alumni Association. There may be some who do not appreciate the objects and advantages of them, and to such a few words will not be misdirected in this place. They are in no wise antagonistic to those conducted by the College itself. The Alumni Association is composed almost exclusively, not merely of graduates, but of practical pharmacists and chemists, whose lives are spent in the pursuit of these branches of knowledge as a means of gaining their livelihood. It inevitably follows, therefore, that they are *practical*, eminently so. Herein lies their great advantage—the Quiz Masters bring out prominently those parts which their every-day experience teaches them are of most practical value. The student's life as such does not close with the receipt of his diploma; *then* he is only just fitted to study properly, to profit by experience, to correctly observe and discriminate between facts; and the more study and experience he gets, the better for him as a practical pharmacist.

It must not be understood, from the above remarks, that these Quizzes are not directed toward preparing students for their examinations. On the contrary, the preceding lectures as delivered by the Professors are reviewed and the salient points brought out, and the student, in addition, receives something more to take with him and serve as a guide with which to direct future effort. It is hoped that students will avail themselves of this opportunity of receiving thorough quizzing, and thereby also aid the Association to still further carry on its work to their advantage and the benefit of the student.

Those who have been members of the Alumni Quizzes during the past three years, can testify to their advantage to the student.

The hours of holding the Quizzes are subject to change to suit the convenience of the majority of the class.

For further particulars, address Wm. E. Krewson, Secretary, at the College, No. 145 N. Tenth street.

MICROSCOPY.

In the past year the Association has started a class for the microscopical examination of drugs. The application of the microscope to practical use in pharmaceutical study is becoming more and more general, and is recognized by the highest authorities as one of the essentials. The externals of drugs are no longer sufficient for their identification and correct study. With the large number of new ones constantly being brought forward, and the general sophistication of all in use, so many of which are externally very similar, the miscroscope is the pharmacist's friend in need. It is intended to teach the most approved methods of microscopical manipulations and investigations; also the preparing and mounting of different classes of objects.

The Class in Microscopy will meet on Fridays during the Course of Lectures, from 2 to 4 P. M., and will be under the care of Mr. A. P. Brown, Ph. G., a practical microscopist.

The course will consist of twelve or fifteen practical lessons, as follows :— '

Microscopical Manipulations, Drawing with Camera Lucida, Urinary Analysis, Quantitative and Qualitative, Section Cutting, Double Staining, Dry and Wet Mounts, Photo-Micrography, Detection of Adulterations, Finishing Slides, etc.

Price of tickets, $10.00 for the course.

For further information, address the Secretary, at College, No. 145 N. Tenth street.

ALUMNI PRIZES.

The GOLD MEDAL to the best student of the Graduating Class.

Certificates for excellence in the studies of Chemistry, Pharmacy, Materia Medica and Pharmaceutical Manipulation and General Pharmacy.

Also, a Testimonial to the best student of the Junior Examination.

A prize for Botany will be given at the Social Meeting, in January, for the best collection of plants correctly analyzed and gathered during the coming spring and summer months.

IMPORTANT NOTICE.

Any one wishing to purchase back numbers of the Alumni Reports for the purpose of completing the full set, can do so by applying to the Secretary, Wm. E. Krewson, N. E. cor. Eighth and Montgomery Ave. Also, extra copies of this Report. Price, 15 cents each. Those sending by mail should enclose *stamps* for postage. The money thus received is to be used for reprinting any of the Reports that may become exhausted.

ALUMNI CALENDAR FOR 1883-'84.

Thursday, May 3, 1883, First Meeting of the Executive Board.
Thursday, Aug. 2, 1883, Second Meeting of the Executive Board.
Tuesday, October 9, 1883, First Social Meeting.
Thursday, Nov. 1, 1883, Third Meeting of the Executive Board.
Tuesday, Nov. 13, 1883, Second Social Meeting.
Tuesday, December 11, 1883, Third Social Meeting.
Tuesday, January 8, 1884, Fourth Social Meeting.
Thursday, February 1, 1884, Fourth Meeting of the·Executive Board.
Tuesday, February 12, 1884, Fifth and last Social Meeting.
Wednesday, March 12, 1884, Twentieth Annual Meeting of the Association, and Annual Reception to Graduating Class.
Senior and Junior Quizzes every Thursday Afternoon, commencing October 4, 1883, and ending February 21, 1884.
Course in Microscopy begins Friday, October 5, 1883.
Spring Course in Microscopy about April 1, 1884.

NOTICE.

It is the desire of the officers of the Alumni Association that each member receives a copy of the Annual Reports from year to year. It is therefore hoped that each member will inform the Secretary by postal when he receives this number.